"*Angels in America* has proved to be a watershed drama, the most lyrical and ambitious augury of an era since Tennessee Williams's *The Glass Menagerie*."

—JOHN LAHR, *New Yorker*

"Glorious. A monumental, subversive, altogether remarkable masterwork . . . Details of specific catastrophes may have changed since this Reagan-era AIDS epic won the Pulitzer and the Tony, but the real cosmic and human obsessions—power, religion, sex, responsibility, the future of the world—are as perilous, yet as falling-down funny, as ever."

—LINDA WINER, *Newsday*

"The most influential American play of the last two decades."

—PATRICK HEALY, *New York Times*

"Daring and dazzling! The most ambitious American play of our time: an epic that ranges from earth to heaven; focuses on politics, sex and religion; transports us to Washington, the Kremlin, the South Bronx, Salt Lake City and Antarctica; deals with Jews, Mormons, WASPs, blacks; switches between realism and fantasy, from the tragedy of AIDS to the camp comedy of drag queens to the death or at least absconding of God."

—JACK KROLL, *Newsweek*

"Few plays have captured the spirit of an age more powerfully than *Angels in America* . . . and the passage of time has not clipped *Angels'* wings."

—PAUL TAYLOR, *Independant* (London)

D0038244

"Something rare, dangerous and harrowing . . . a roman candle hurled into a drawing room."

—NICHOLAS DE JONGH, *London Evening Standard*

"Angels breaks all the rules to achieve the astonishing integrity of its vision . . . It is a play that has remained utterly of-the-moment."

—JEREMY GERARD, *Bloomberg*

"That *Angels* came so close to the burning heart of the Zeitgeist left Kushner fearing he would never get there again. But in fact he has been there so often that he seems to have passed right through it . . . *Angels*, so much a cry in the dark about AIDS when it was written, seems now to be as much about the Earth's potentially fatal illness as gay men's."

—JESSE GREEN, *New York*

"The greatest American play of the waning years of the twentieth century."

—CHRIS JONES, *Chicago Tribune*

"An enormously impressive work of the imagination and intellect, a towering example of what theater stretched to its full potential can achieve."

—CLIFFORD A. RIDLEY, *Philadelphia Inquirer*

ANGELS in AMERICA

A Gay Fantasia on National Themes

Part One: MILLENNIUM APPROACHES

Part Two: PERESTROIKA

Tony Kushner

2013 Revised Edition

Theatre Communications Group
New York
2013

Angels in America: A Gay Fantasia on National Themes is published by
Theatre Communications Group, Inc., 520 8th Avenue, New York, NY 10018-4156

The publication of *Angels in America: A Gay Fantasia on National Themes*, by Tony
Kushner, is made possible in part by the New York State Council on the Arts with the
support of Governor Andrew Cuomo and the New York State Legislature.

TCG books are exclusively distributed to the book trade by Consortium Book Sales and
Distribution.

LIBRARY OF CONGRESS CATALOGING-IN-PUBLICATION DATA
Kushner, Tony.
Angels in America : a gay fantasia on national themes / Tony Kushner.
Revised and Complete edition.
pages cm
Includes bibliographical references.
ISBN 978-1-55936-384-6 (trade paper)—ISBN 978-1-55936-395-2 (trade cloth)
1. National characteristics, American—Drama. 2. AIDS (Disease)—Patients—Drama.
3. Sexual orientation—Drama. 4. Gay men—Drama. 5. Mormons—Drama.
6. Angels—Drama. [1. Cohn, Roy M.—Drama.] I. Title.
PS3561.U778A85   2013
812'.54—dc23   2013001994

Book design by Lisa Govan
Cover art by Milton Glaser
Cover design by Molly Watman

First Revised Combined Edition, November 2013
Fifth Printing, September 2017

Contents

Introduction

Should plays have introductions?

I started writing in the early 1980s, at a moment in American theater when introductions and other presumably helpful apparatuses—incredibly detailed historical timelines, research documentation and theoretical notation—announced the unapologetic embrace by narrative theater-makers of an intellectual and political seriousness that had previously been at home in European theaters and among American experimental theater artists. Dramaturgs arrived for the first time on the staffs of not-for-profit regional theaters; with the advent of production dramaturgy in America came a new deluge of prefatory and introductory information, served up from enormous black ring binders to the casts of plays as they sat around a table in the first days of rehearsal, and then offered to audiences in their theater programs. Formerly these programs were slim pamphlets containing lists of the production's personnel and short biographies, place and time settings, and restaurant ads. Staff dramaturgs were now instructed to jam-pack programs with poetry, imagery, critical theory and facts, messages from the playwright, director and artistic director. Before they'd opened their programs, audiences most likely would have passed through lobby displays revealing the historical truths behind the fiction to which they were about to be exposed. I was enamored of this extra-theatrical informational bombardment. As a young playwright, I loved reading Shaw's prefaces, and I looked forward to having plays of my own to preface. I felt only slightly guilty observing theatergoers diligently, frantically trying to absorb this embarrassment of supplementary illumination before the house lights dimmed and the play began.

I've changed, and in recent years I've grown averse to anything that intrudes itself upon an innocent audience and the play it's about to watch, or an innocent reader about to read a play for the first time. If the playwright has done his or her job, if the production team and cast are doing theirs, the text of the play and the experience of watching or reading it should be sufficient unto itself.

The moment a play begins, or a reader takes in the words of the script on the first page, is as exciting and scary as any plunge into the ocean ought to be. Disappointment, bewilderment, outrage, great terror, pity and joy may follow, but these are only to be encountered once the plunge is made. Introductory material is for reluctant dawdlers and lag-behinds. A dusty grammar school usher and a sub-sub-librarian take many pages to tell you everything known about whales before each steps aside (well, before each dies, actually) to permit you to hazard the extremely perilous, mind-, heart- and molecule-altering voyage that is *Moby-Dick*, in the course of which voyage you realize that neither the usher nor the sub-sub, nor you, nor for that matter the crew of the Pequod nor their lunatic captain knows Thing One about what a whale is. When it's a damp, drizzly November in your soul, Ishmael tells us, plunge in without preparation! The sea awaits!

If you're still reading this and haven't skipped ahead to the first scene, it could be because you strenuously disagree with me about introductions, or you're unconvinced or simply agnostic on the subject. You may be asking yourself why I'm continuing to write this introduction deploring introducing—a reasonable question. I suppose it's because a good deal of time has passed since I wrote *Angels*, and, while I have no desire to introduce the two plays of which it's comprised, I feel I ought to make mention of what's changed. Maybe I haven't changed as much as I hoped, or as much as I ought.

I began writing these plays—I thought at the time that I was writing a single play—in 1987, when I was thirty-one years old. The AIDS epidemic was in its sixth year, the Reagan administration in its seventh. It was a terrifying and galvanizing time. I finished the first draft of *Millennium Approaches* in 1988, and the first draft of *Perestroika* in 1990. So *Angels in America* is approximately twenty-two years old, and I'm precisely fifty-six.

This edition incorporates changes I've made to *Angels* over the past several years. Most of these changes are to be found in *Part Two, Perestroika*, which is now closer to complete than it's ever been. I can't quite bring myself to write that it's complete. Since the day I finished the first draft of *Perestroika*, I've always known that it's one of those plays that refuses to be entirely in harmony with itself. Some plays want to sprawl, some plays contain expansiveness, roughness, wildness and incompleteness in their DNA. These plays may, if they're not misunderstood and dismissed as failed attempts at tidiness, speak more powerfully about what's expansive, rough, wild and incomplete in human life than plays with tauter, more efficient, more cleanly constructed narratives.

Millennium Approaches has a taut, efficient narrative, and I've never seen any need to change it. In this edition it's substantially the same play that was first published nearly twenty years ago, although as a result of the work on both parts of Angels for the Signature Theatre's 2010 revival, a few minor alterations were made to it.

Significant changes have been made to Perestroika. I discovered what I believed to be a missing thread in its narrative, the substructural space for which, I realized, I'd laid in long before I knew what use to make of it. In this version, with a little help from my friends and a very long preview period, that thread has been woven in. I won't specify to which moments I'm referring, because calling attention to them would undermine the effort made to integrate the new material. Of course there are two other published versions of Perestroika, and anyone with sufficient time and interest can make comparisons, but most people have better things to do with their time. Life, after all, is always shorter than we think.

I think a lot more about mortality at fifty-six than I did at thirty-one. At fifty-six, I'm more certain of my own mortality, as it presses nearer, and much more uncertain about the future existence of my species than I was when I started writing Angels. Time has vindicated some of the plays' conflictedly optimistic spirit; progress has been made. Angels is not teleological, its apocalyptic forebodings notwithstanding. As the dead old rabbi says in Perestroika (in a scene relegated in this edition to the back of the book), hope, when it can't be discovered in certainty, can almost always be located in indeterminacy, and Angels is a hopeful work.

Unfortunately, the passing years have been equally if not more confirming of the plays' aforementioned apocalyptic forebodings, which loom darker and resound more ominously for contemporary audiences and readers.

Angels in America, more than twenty years old, survives, as do I. I'm utterly and happily in the dark about the longevity of my work, but I hope *Angels* outlasts me, I hope it will continue to be entertaining and of interest and use to people for years to come. I hope there'll be people for years to come.

I'm writing this introduction the day before America goes to the polls to vote for Mitt Romney or Barack Obama for president. This is the place from which it seems to me I've always written, perched on the knife's edge of terror and hope. It's familiar enough, though today the edge is sharper than it's ever been, and the two worlds it divides, one of light, one of darkness, seem respectively more brilliant and more abysmal, more extremely opposed than ever before.

Whatever tomorrow brings,* the future—I'm reasonably certain of this—remains indeterminate.

Tony Kushner
November 5, 2012

---

* It turned out OK. (TK, November 2013)

Part One:

MILLENNIUM
APPROACHES

THE CHARACTERS
IN *MILLENNIUM APPROACHES*

ROY M. COHN,* a successful New York lawyer and unofficial power broker.

JOSEPH PORTER PITT, chief clerk for Justice Theodore Wilson of the Federal Court of Appeals, Second Circuit.

HARPER AMATY PITT, Joe's wife, an agoraphobic with a mild Valium addiction.

LOUIS IRONSON, a word processor working for the Second Circuit Court of Appeals.

PRIOR WALTER, Louis's boyfriend. Occasionally works as a club designer or caterer, otherwise lives very modestly but with great style off a small trust fund.

HANNAH PORTER PITT, Joe's mother, currently residing in Salt Lake City, living off her deceased husband's army pension.

BELIZE, a registered nurse and former drag queen whose name was originally Norman Arriaga; Belize is a drag name that stuck.

THE ANGEL, four divine emanations, Fluor, Phosphor, Lumen and Candle; manifest in One: the Continental Principality of America. She has magnificent steel-gray wings.

Other Characters in Millennium Approaches

RABBI ISIDOR CHEMELWITZ, an orthodox Jewish rabbi, played by the actor playing Hannah.

MR. LIES, Harper's imaginary friend, a travel agent, played by the actor playing Belize. In style of dress and speech he suggests a jazz musician; he always wears a large lapel badge emblazoned "IOTA" (International Order of Travel Agents).

THE MAN IN THE PARK, played by the actor playing Prior.

THE VOICE, the voice of the Angel.

HENRY, Roy's doctor, played by the actor playing Hannah.

EMILY, a nurse, played by the actor playing the Angel.

MARTIN HELLER, a Reagan Administration Justice Department flackman, played by the actor playing Harper.

SISTER ELLA CHAPTER, a Salt Lake City real-estate saleswoman, played by the actor playing the Angel.

PRIOR 1, the ghost of a dead Prior Walter from the thirteenth century, played by the actor playing Joe. A blunt, grim, dutiful, medieval farmer, he speaks abruptly and rather loudly with a guttural Yorkshire accent.

PRIOR 2, the ghost of a dead Prior Walter from the seventeenth century, played by the actor playing Roy. A Londoner, a Restoration-era sophisticate and bon vivant; he speaks with an elegant Received English accent.

THE ESKIMO, played by the actor playing Joe.

A HOMELESS WOMAN, an unmedicated psychotic who lives on the streets of the South Bronx; played by the actor playing the Angel.

ETHEL ROSENBERG, played by the actor playing Hannah.

---

* The character Roy M. Cohn is based on the late Roy M. Cohn (1927–1986), who was all too real; for the most part the acts attributed to the character Roy, such as his illegal conferences with Judge Kaufmann during the trial of Ethel Rosenberg, are to be found in the historical record. But this Roy is a work of dramatic fiction; his words are my invention, and liberties have been taken.

Millennium Approaches *is dedicated to*
Mark Bronnenberg

In a murderous time
the heart breaks and breaks
and lives by breaking.

—Stanley Kunitz, "The Testing-Tree"

ACT ONE:

Bad News

October–November 1985

Scene 1

The end of October. Rabbi Isidor Chemelwitz alone onstage with a small coffin. It is a rough pine box with two wooden pegs, one at the foot and one at the head, holding the lid in place. A prayer shawl embroidered with a Star of David is draped over the lid, and at the head of the coffin, a yahrzeit candle is burning.

The Rabbi speaks sonorously, with a heavy Eastern European accent, unapologetically consulting a sheet of notes for the family names.

RABBI ISIDOR CHEMELWITZ: Hello and good morning. I am Rabbi Isidor Chemelwitz of the Bronx Home for Aged Hebrews. We are here this morning to pay respects at the passing of Sarah Ironson, devoted wife of Benjamin Ironson, also deceased, loving and caring mother of her sons Morris, Abraham, and Samuel, and her daughters

9

Esther and Rachel; beloved grandmother of Max, Mark, Louis, Lisa, Maria . . . uh . . . Lesley, Angela, Doris, Luke and Eric. *(Looks closer at paper)* Eric? This is a Jewish name? *(Shrugs)* Eric. A large and loving family. We assemble that we may mourn collectively this good and righteous woman.

(He looks at the coffin)

This woman. I did not know this woman. I cannot accurately describe her attributes, nor do justice to her dimensions. She was . . . Well, in the Bronx Home for Aged Hebrews are many like this, the old, and to many I speak but not to be frank with this one. She preferred silence. So I do not know her and yet I know her. She was . . . *(He touches the coffin)* . . . not a person but a whole kind of person, the ones who crossed the ocean, who brought with us to America the villages of Russia and Lithuania—and how we struggled, and how we fought, for the family, for the Jewish home, so that you would not grow up *here*, in this strange place, in the melting pot where nothing melted. Descendants of this immigrant woman, you do not grow up in America, you and your children and their children with the goyische names, you do not live in America, no such place exists. Your clay is the clay of some Litvak shtetl, your air the air of the steppes. Because she carried the old world on her back across the ocean, in a boat, and she put it down on Grand Concourse Avenue, or in Flatbush, and she worked that earth into your bones, and you pass it to your children, this ancient, ancient culture and home.

(Little pause)

You can never make that crossing that she made, for such Great Voyages in this world do not any more exist. But every day of your lives the miles that voyage between that place and this one you cross. Every day. You understand me? In you that journey is.

So . . .

She was the last of the Mohicans, this one was. Pretty soon . . . all the old will be dead.

Scene 2

Same day. Roy and Joe in Roy's office. Roy at an impressive desk, bare except for a very elaborate phone system, rows and rows of flashing buttons that bleep and beep and whistle incessantly, making chaotic music underneath Roy's conversations. Joe is sitting, waiting. Roy conducts business with great energy, impatience and sensual abandon: gesticulating, shouting, cajoling, crooning, playing the phone's receiver, its hold button and the buttons for its numerous lines with virtuosity and love.

ROY *(Hitting the hold button)*: Hold. *(To Joe)* I wish I was an octopus, a fucking octopus. Eight loving arms and all those suckers. Know what I mean?

JOE: No, I—

ROY *(Gesturing to a deli platter of little sandwiches on his desk)*: You want lunch?

JOE: No, that's OK really I just—

ROY *(Hitting a button)*: Ailene? Roy Cohn. Now what kind of a greeting is—I thought we were friends, Ai— Look Mrs. Soffer you don't have to get— You're upset. You're yelling. You'll aggravate your condition, you shouldn't yell, you'll pop little blood vessels in your face if you yell— No that was a joke, Mrs. Soffer, I was joking—I already apologized sixteen times for that, Mrs. Soffer, you . . . *(While she's fulminating, Roy covers the mouthpiece with his hand and talks to Joe)* This'll take a minute, *eat* already, what is this tasty sandwich here it's— *(He takes a bite of a sandwich)* Mmmmm, liver or some— Here. *(He pitches the sandwich to Joe, who catches it and returns it to the platter. Back to Mrs. Soffer)* Uh-huh, uh-huh . . . No, I already told you it wasn't a vacation it was business, Mrs. Soffer, I have clients in Haiti, Mrs. Soffer, I— Listen, Ailene, YOU THINK I'M THE ONLY GODDAMN LAWYER IN HISTORY EVER MISSED A COURT DATE?! Don't make such a big fucking— Hold. *(He hits the hold button)* You HAG!

JOE: If this is a bad time—

ROY: *Bad* time? This is a *good* time! *(Button)* Baby doll, get me— Oh fuck, wait. *(Button)* Hello? Yah. Sorry to keep you holding, Judge Hollins, I— Oh *Mrs.* Hollins, sorry dear, deep voice you got. Enjoying your visit? *(Hand over mouthpiece again; to Joe)* She sounds like a truck driver and he sounds like Kate Smith, very confusing. Nixon appointed him, all the geeks are Nixon appointees. *(To Mrs. Hollins)* Yeah, yeah right good so how many tickets dear? *Seven?* For what, *Cats, 42nd Street*, what? No you wouldn't like *La Cage*, trust me, I know. Oh for godsake. Hold. *(Hold button, button)* Baby doll, seven for *Cats* or something, anything hard to get, I don't give a fuck what and neither will they. *(Button; to Joe)* You see *La Cage*?

JOE: No, I—

ROY: Fabulous. Best thing on Broadway. Maybe ever. *(Button)* Who? Aw, Jesus H. Christ, Harry, *no*, Harry, Judge John Francis Grimes, Manhattan Family Court. Do I have to do every goddamn thing myself? *Touch* the bastard, Harry, and don't call me on this line again, I told you not to.

JOE *(Starting to get up)*: Roy, uh, should I wait outside or—

ROY *(To Joe)*: Oh sit. *(To Harry)* You hold. I pay you to hold fuck you Harry you jerk. Half-wit dick-brain. *(Hold button, then he looks at Joe. A beat, then:)*

I see the universe, Joe, as a kind of sandstorm in outer space with winds of mega-hurricane velocity, but instead of grains of sand it's shards and splinters of glass. You ever feel that way? Ever have one of those days?

JOE: I'm not sure I—

ROY: So how's life in Appeals? How's the judge?

JOE: He sends his best.

ROY: He's a good man. Loyal. Not the brightest man on the bench, but he has manners. And a nice head of silver hair.

JOE: He gives me a lot of responsibility.

ROY: Yeah, like writing his decisions and signing his name.

JOE: Well . . .

ROY: He's a nice guy. And you cover admirably.

JOE: Well, thanks, Roy, I—

ROY *(Button)*: Yah? Who is *this*? Well who the fuck are *you*? Hold. *(Hold button)* Harry? Eighty-seven grand, something like that. Fuck him. Eat me. New Jersey, chain of porno film stores in, uh, Weehawken. That's—Harry, that's the beauty of the law. *(Hold button, button)* So, baby doll, what? *Cats?* Ugh. *(Button) Cats!* It's about cats. Singing cats, you'll love it. Eight o'clock, the theater's always at eight. *(Button)* Fucking tourists. *(He puts his finger on the button for the line on which Harry is holding; before pushing it, to Joe)* Oh live a little, Joe, *eat* something for Christ sake.

JOE: Um, Roy, could you—

ROY: What? *(Pushing the button; to Harry)* Hold a minute. *(Hold button, button)* Mrs. Soffer? Mrs.— *(Button, to Baby Doll)* God-fucking-damnit to hell, where is— *(Continue below:)*

JOE: Roy, I'd really appreciate it if—

ROY *(Continuous from above)*: Well she was here a minute ago, baby doll, see if—

(The phone starts making three different beeping sounds, all at once.)

ROY *(Smashing buttons)*: Jesus fuck this goddamn thing! *(Continue below:)*

JOE: I really wish you wouldn't—

ROY *(Continuous from above)*: Baby doll? Ring the *Post* get me Suzy see if—

(The phone starts whistling loudly.)

ROY: CHRIST!

JOE: *Roy.*

ROY *(Into receiver)*: Hold. *(Hold button; to Joe)* What?

JOE: Could you please not take the Lord's name in vain?

(Pause.)

JOE: I'm sorry. But please. At least while I'm . . .

ROY *(Laughs, then)*: Right. Sorry. Fuck.

Only in America. *(Punches a button)* Baby doll, tell 'em all to fuck off. Tell 'em I died. You handle Mrs. Soffer. Tell her it's on the way. Tell her I'm schtupping the judge. I'll call her back. I *will* call her. I *know* how much I borrowed. She's got four hundred times that stuffed up her— Yeah, tell her I said that.

(Button. The phone is silent)

So Joe.

JOE: I'm sorry Roy, I just—

ROY: No no no no, principles count, I respect principles, I'm not religious but I like God and God likes me. Baptist, Catholic?

JOE: Mormon.

ROY: Mormon. Delectable. Absolutely. Only in America. So, Joe. Whattya think?

JOE: It's . . . well . . .

ROY: Crazy life.

JOE: Chaotic.

ROY: Well but God bless chaos. Right?

JOE: Ummm . . .

ROY: Huh. Mormons. I knew Mormons, in, um, Nevada.

JOE: Utah, mostly.

ROY: No, these Mormons were in Vegas.

So. So, how'd you like to go to Washington and work for the Justice Department?

JOE: Sorry?

ROY: How'd you like to go to Washington and work for the Justice Department? All I gotta do is pick up the phone, talk to Ed, and you're in.

JOE: In . . . what, exactly?

ROY: Associate Assistant Something Big. Internal Affairs, heart of the woods, something nice with clout.

JOE: Ed . . . ?

ROY: Meese. The Attorney General.

JOE: Oh.

ROY: I just have to pick up the phone . . .

JOE: I have to think.

ROY: Of course.

(Pause)

It's a great time to be in Washington, Joe.

JOE: Roy, it's incredibly exciting.

ROY: And it would mean something to me. You understand?

(Little pause.)

JOE: I . . . can't say how much I appreciate this Roy, I'm sort of . . . well, stunned, I mean . . . Thanks, Roy. But I have to give it some thought. I have to ask my wife.
ROY: Your wife. Of course.
JOE: But I really appreciate—
ROY: Of course. Talk to your wife.

Scene 3

Same day. Harper at home, alone, as she often is, listening to the radio. She speaks to the audience:

HARPER: People who are lonely, people left alone, sit talking nonsense to the air, imagining . . . beautiful systems dying, old fixed orders spiraling apart.

When you look at the ozone layer, from outside, from a spaceship, it looks like a pale blue halo, a gentle, shimmering aureole encircling the atmosphere encircling the earth. Thirty miles above our heads, a thin layer of three-atom oxygen molecules, product of photosynthesis, which explains the fussy vegetable preference for visible light, its rejection of darker rays and emanations. Danger from without. It's a kind of gift, from God, the crowning touch to the creation of the world: guardian angels, hands linked, make a spherical net, a blue-green nesting orb, a shell of safety for life itself. But everywhere, things are collapsing, lies surfacing, systems of defense giving way.

This is why, Joe, this is why I shouldn't be left alone.
(Little pause)

I'd like to go traveling. Leave you behind to worry. I'll send postcards with strange stamps and tantalizing messages on the back: "Later maybe." "Nevermore . . ."

(Mr. Lies, a travel agent, appears, carrying a briefcase.)

HARPER: Oh! You startled me!

MR. LIES: Cash, check or credit card?

HARPER: I remember you. You're from Salt Lake. You sold us the plane tickets when we flew here. What are you doing in Brooklyn?

MR. LIES: You said you wanted to travel . . .

HARPER: And here you are. How thoughtful.

MR. LIES: Mr. Lies. Of the International Order of Travel Agents. We mobilize the globe, we set people adrift, we stir the populace and send nomads eddying across the planet. We are adepts of motion, acolytes of the flux. Cash, check or credit card. Name your destination.

HARPER: Antarctica, maybe. I want to see the hole in the ozone. I heard on the radio—

(He opens his briefcase. Inside it, there is a computer terminal.)

MR. LIES *(His hands poised over the keyboard)*: I can arrange a guided tour. Now?

HARPER: Soon. Maybe soon. I'm not safe here you see. Things aren't right with me. Weird stuff happens.

MR. LIES: Like?

HARPER: Well, like you, for instance. Just appearing. Or last week . . . well never mind.

People are like planets, you need a thick skin. Things get to me, Joe stays away and now . . . Well look. My dreams are talking back to me.

MR. LIES: It's the price of rootlessness. Motion sickness. The only cure: to keep moving.

HARPER: I'm undecided. I feel . . . that something's going to give. It's 1985. Fifteen years till the third millennium. Maybe Christ will come again. Maybe seeds will be planted, maybe there'll be harvests then, maybe early figs to eat, maybe new life, maybe fresh blood, maybe companionship and love and protection, safety from what's outside, maybe the door will hold, or maybe . . . Maybe the troubles will come, and the end will come, and the sky will collapse and there will be terrible rains and showers of poison light, or maybe my life is really fine, maybe Joe loves me and I'm only crazy thinking otherwise, or maybe not, maybe it's even worse than I know, maybe . . . I want to know, maybe I don't. The suspense, Mr. Lies, it's killing me.

MR. LIES: I suggest a vacation.

HARPER *(Hearing something)*: That was the elevator. Oh God, I should fix myself up, I— You have to go, you shouldn't be here, you aren't even real.

MR. LIES: Call me when you decide.

HARPER: Go!

(Mr. Lies vanishes as Joe enters.)

JOE: Buddy?
    Buddy? Sorry I'm late. I was just . . . out. Walking. Are you mad?

HARPER: I got a little anxious.

JOE: Buddy kiss.

(They kiss.)

JOE: Nothing to get anxious about.
    So. So how'd you like to move to Washington?

Scene 4

Same day. Louis and Prior sitting outside on a bench near an Upper West Side funeral home, both dressed in funereal finery; Prior is elegant, Louis is rumpled/negligent. The funeral service for Sarah Ironson has just concluded and Louis is about to leave for the cemetery.

LOUIS: My grandmother actually saw Emma Goldman speak. In Yiddish. But all Grandma could remember was that she spoke well and wore a hat.

What a weird service. That rabbi.

PRIOR: A definite find. Get his number when you go to the graveyard. I want him to bury me.

LOUIS: Better head out there. Everyone gets to put dirt on the coffin once it's lowered in.

PRIOR: Oooh. Cemetery fun. Don't want to miss that.

LOUIS: It's an old Jewish custom to express love. Here, Grandma, have a shovelful. Latecomers run the risk of finding the grave completely filled.

She was pretty crazy. She was up there in that home for ten years, talking to herself. I never visited. She looked too much like my mother.

PRIOR *(Hugs him)*: Poor Louis. I'm sorry your grandma is dead.

LOUIS: Tiny little coffin, huh?

Sorry I didn't introduce you to— I always get so closety at these family things.

PRIOR: Butch. You get butch. *(Imitating)* "Hi, Cousin Doris, you don't remember me I'm Lou, Rachel's boy." Lou, not Louis, because if you say Louis they'll hear the sibilant S.

LOUIS: I don't have a—

PRIOR: I don't blame you, hiding. Bloodlines. Jewish curses are the worst. I personally would dissolve if anyone ever looked me in the eye and said "Feh." Fortunately WASPs don't say "Feh." Oh and by the way, darling, Cousin Doris is a dyke.

LOUIS: No.

Really?

PRIOR: You don't notice anything. If I hadn't spent the last four years fellating you I'd swear you were straight.

LOUIS: You're in a pissy mood. Cat still missing?

(Little pause.)

PRIOR: Not a furball in sight. It's your fault.

LOUIS: It is?

PRIOR: I warned you, Louis. Names are important. Call an animal Little Sheba and you can't expect it to stick around. Besides, it's a dog's name.

LOUIS: I wanted a dog in the first place, not a cat. He sprayed my books.

PRIOR: He was a female cat.

LOUIS: Cats are stupid, high-strung predators. Babylonians sealed them up in bricks. Dogs have brains.

PRIOR: Cats have intuition.

LOUIS: A sharp dog is as smart as a really dull two-year-old child.

PRIOR: Cats know when something's wrong.

LOUIS: Only if you stop feeding them.

PRIOR: They know. That's why Sheba left, because she knew.

LOUIS: Knew what?

(Pause.)

PRIOR: I did my best Shirley Booth this morning, floppy slippers, housecoat, curlers, can of Little Friskies: "Come back, Little Sheba, come back . . ." To no avail. Le chat, elle ne reviendra jamais, jamais . . .

(He removes his jacket, rolls up his sleeve, shows Louis a dark purple spot on the underside of his arm near the shoulder.)

PRIOR: See.

LOUIS: That's just a burst blood vessel.

PRIOR: Not according to the best medical authorities.

LOUIS: What?
(Pause)
Tell me.

PRIOR: K.S., baby. Lesion number one. Lookit. The winedark kiss of the angel of death.

LOUIS *(Very softly, holding Prior's arm)*: Oh please . . .

PRIOR: I'm a lesionnaire. The Foreign Lesion. The American Lesion. Lesionnaire's disease.

LOUIS: Stop.

PRIOR: My troubles are lesion.

LOUIS: Will you *stop*.

PRIOR: Don't you think I'm handling this well?
I'm going to die.

LOUIS: Bullshit.

PRIOR: Let go of my arm.

LOUIS: No.

PRIOR: Let go.

LOUIS *(Grabbing Prior, embracing him ferociously)*: No.

PRIOR: I can't find a way to spare you, baby. No wall like the wall of hard scientific fact. K.S. Wham. Bang your head on that.

LOUIS: Fuck you. *(Letting go)* Fuck you fuck you fuck you.

PRIOR: Now that's what I like to hear. A mature reaction.
Let's go see if the cat's come home.
Louis?
LOUIS: When did you find this?
PRIOR: I couldn't tell you.
LOUIS: Why?
PRIOR: I was scared, Lou.
LOUIS: Of what?
PRIOR: That you'll leave me.
LOUIS: Oh.

(*Little pause.*)

PRIOR: Bad timing, funeral and all, but I figured as long as
we're on the subject of death.
LOUIS: I have to go bury my grandma.
PRIOR: Lou?
(*Pause*)
Then you'll come home?
LOUIS: Then I'll come home.

Scene 5

*Same day. Split scene: Joe and Harper at home, as before; Louis at
the cemetery after his family has gone, lingering behind, staring
down at Sarah Ironson's coffin in her open grave.*

HARPER: Washington?
JOE: It's an incredible honor, buddy, and—
HARPER: I have to think.

JOE: Of course.

HARPER: Say no.

JOE: You said you were going to think about it.

HARPER: I don't want to move to Washington.

JOE: Well I do.

HARPER: It's a giant cemetery, huge white graves and mausoleums everywhere.

JOE: We could live in Maryland. Or Georgetown.

HARPER: We're happy here.

JOE: That's not really true, buddy, we—

HARPER: Well happy enough! Pretend-happy. That's better than nothing.

JOE: It's time to make some changes, Harper.

HARPER: No changes. Why?

JOE: I've been chief clerk for four years. I make twenty-nine-thousand dollars a year. That's ridiculous. I graduated fourth in my class and I make less than anyone I know. And I'm ... I'm tired of being a clerk, I want to go where something good is happening.

HARPER: Nothing good happens in Washington. We'll forget church teachings and buy furniture at, at, *Conran's* and become yuppies. I have too much to do here.

JOE: Like what?

HARPER: I *do* have things.

JOE: What things?

HARPER: I have to finish painting the bedroom.

JOE: You've been painting in there for over a year.

HARPER: I know, I— It just isn't done because I never get time to finish it.

JOE: Oh that's ... That doesn't make sense. You have all the time in the world. You could finish it when I'm at work.

HARPER: I'm afraid to go in there alone.

JOE: Afraid of what?

HARPER: I heard someone in there. Metal scraping on the wall. A man with a knife, maybe.

JOE: There's no one in the bedroom, Harper.

HARPER: Not now.

JOE: Not this morning either.

HARPER: How do you know? You were at work this morning.

There's something creepy about this place. Remember *Rosemary's Baby?*

JOE: *Rosemary's Baby?*

HARPER: Our apartment looks like that one. Wasn't that apartment in Brooklyn?

JOE: No, it was—

HARPER: Well, it looked like this. It did.

JOE: Then let's move.

HARPER: Georgetown's worse. *The Exorcist* was in Georgetown.

JOE: The devil, everywhere you turn, huh, buddy.

HARPER: Yeah. Everywhere.

JOE: How many pills today, buddy?

HARPER: None. One. Three. Only three.

(At the cemetery: Rabbi Isidor Chemelwitz, heading home, walks past Louis, who is still staring into the grave. Louis stops the Rabbi with a question.)

LOUIS: Why are there just two little wooden pegs holding the lid down?

RABBI ISIDOR CHEMELWITZ: So she can get out easier if she wants to.

LOUIS: I hope she stays put.

I pretended for years that she was already dead. When they called to say she had died it was a surprise. I abandoned her.

RABBI ISIDOR CHEMELWITZ: "Sharfer vi di tson fun a shlang iz an umdankbar kind!"

LOUIS: I don't speak Yiddish.

RABBI ISIDOR CHEMELWITZ: "Sharper than the serpent's tooth is the ingratitude of children." Shakespeare. *Kenig Lear.*

LOUIS: Rabbi, what does the Holy Writ say about someone who abandons someone he loves at a time of great need?

RABBI ISIDOR CHEMELWITZ: Why would a person do such a thing?

LOUIS: Because he has to.

Maybe because this person's sense of the world, that it will change for the better with struggle, maybe a person who has this neo-Hegelian positivist sense of constant historical progress towards happiness or perfection or something, who feels very powerful because he feels connected to these forces, moving uphill all the time . . . Maybe that person can't, um, incorporate sickness into his sense of how things are supposed to go. Maybe vomit . . . and sores and disease . . . really frighten him, maybe . . . he isn't so good with death.

RABBI ISIDOR CHEMELWITZ: The Holy Scriptures have nothing to say about such a person.

LOUIS: Rabbi, I'm afraid of the crimes I may commit.

RABBI ISIDOR CHEMELWITZ: Please, mister. I'm a sick old rabbi facing a long drive home to the Bronx. You want to confess, better you should find a priest.

LOUIS: But I'm not a Catholic, I'm a Jew.

RABBI ISIDOR CHEMELWITZ: Worse luck for you, bubbulah. Catholics believe in Forgiveness. Jews believe in Guilt.

(The Rabbi turns to leave.)

LOUIS: You just make sure those pegs are in good and tight.

(The Rabbi stops, looks down into the grave, then at Louis:)

RABBI ISIDOR CHEMELWITZ: Don't worry, mister. The life she had, she'll stay put. She's better off.

(The Rabbi exits. Louis looks into the grave, one last, quick glance, then follows.)

JOE: Look, I know this is scary for you. But try to understand what it means to me. Will you try?

HARPER: Yes.

JOE: Good. Really try.

I think things are starting to change in the world.

HARPER: But I don't want—

JOE: Wait. For the good. Change for the good. America has rediscovered itself. Its sacred position among nations. And people aren't ashamed of that like they used to be. This is a great thing. The truth restored. Law restored. That's what President Reagan's done, Harper. He says: "Truth exists and can be spoken proudly." And the country responds to him. We become better. More good. I need to be a part of that, I need something big to lift me up. I mean, six years ago the world seemed in decline, horrible, hopeless, full of unsolvable problems and crime and confusion and hunger and—

HARPER: But it still seems that way. More now than before. They say the ozone layer is—

JOE: Harper . . .

HARPER: And today out the window on Atlantic Avenue there was a schizophrenic traffic cop who was making these—

JOE: Stop it! I'm trying to make a point.

HARPER: So am I.

JOE: You aren't even making sense, you—

HARPER: My point is the world seems just as—

JOE: It only seems that way to you because you never go out in the world, Harper, and you have emotional problems.

HARPER: I do so get out in the world.

JOE: You don't. You stay in all day, fretting about imaginary—

HARPER: I get out. I do. You don't know what I do.

JOE: You don't stay in all day.

HARPER: No.

JOE: Well . . . Yes you do.

HARPER: That's what you think.

JOE: Where do you go?

HARPER: Where do *you* go? When you walk.

(Pause, then very angry) And I DO NOT have emotional problems.

JOE: I'm sorry.

HARPER: And if I do have emotional problems it's from living with you. Or—

JOE: I'm sorry, buddy, I didn't mean to—

HARPER: Or if you do think I do then you should never have married me. You have all these secrets and lies.

JOE: I want to be married to you, Harper.

HARPER: You shouldn't. You never should.

(Pause)

Hey, buddy. Hey, buddy.

JOE: Buddy kiss.

(They kiss.)

HARPER: I heard on the radio how to give a blowjob.

JOE: What?

HARPER: You want to try?

JOE: You really shouldn't listen to stuff like that.

HARPER: Mormons can give blowjobs.

JOE: *Harper.*

HARPER *(Imitating his tone)*: *Joe.*

>It was a little Jewish lady with a German accent. This is a good time. For me to make a baby.

(Little pause. Joe turns away from her, then leaves the living room.)

HARPER: Then they went on to a program about holes in the ozone layer. Over Antarctica. Skin burns, birds go blind, icebergs melt. The world's coming to an end.

Scene 6

First week of November. In the men's room of the offices of the Brooklyn Federal Court of Appeals. Louis is crying over the sink; Joe enters.

JOE: Oh, um . . . Morning.

LOUIS: Good morning, Counselor.

JOE *(He watches Louis cry)*: Sorry, I . . . I don't know your name.

LOUIS: Don't bother. Word processor. The lowest of the low.

JOE *(Holding out his hand)*: Joe Pitt. I'm with Justice Wilson.

LOUIS: Oh, I know that. Counselor Pitt. Chief Clerk.

JOE: Were you . . . Are you OK?

LOUIS: Oh, yeah. Thanks. What a nice man.

JOE: Not so nice.

LOUIS: What?

JOE: Not so nice. Nothing. You sure you're—

LOUIS: Life sucks shit. Life . . . just sucks shit.

JOE: What's wrong?

LOUIS: Run in my nylons.

JOE: Sorry . . . ?

LOUIS: Forget it. Look, thanks for asking.

JOE: Well . . .

LOUIS: I mean it really is nice of you.

   (He starts crying again)

   Sorry, sorry. Sick friend . . .

JOE: Oh, I'm sorry.

LOUIS: Yeah, yeah, well, that's sweet.

   Three of your colleagues have preceded you to this baleful sight and you're the first one to ask. The others just opened the door, saw me, and fled. I hope they had to pee real bad.

JOE *(Handing him a wad of toilet paper)*: They just didn't want to intrude.

LOUIS: Hah. Reaganite heartless macho asshole lawyers.

JOE: Oh, that's unfair.

LOUIS: What is? Heartless? Macho? Reaganite? Lawyer?

JOE: I voted for Reagan.

LOUIS: You did?

JOE: Twice.

LOUIS: Twice? Well, oh boy. A Gay Republican.

JOE: Excuse me?

LOUIS: Nothing.

JOE: I'm not—

   Forget it.

LOUIS: Republican? Not Republican? Or . . .

JOE: What?

LOUIS: What?

JOE: Not gay. I'm not gay.

LOUIS: Oh. Sorry.

   (Blows his nose loudly) It's just—

JOE: Yes?

LOUIS: Well, sometimes you can tell from the way a person sounds, that— I mean you *sound* like a—

JOE: No I don't.

Like what?

LOUIS: Like a Republican.

(Little pause. Joe knows he's being teased; Louis knows he knows. Joe decides to be a little brave.)

JOE: Do I? Sound like a . . . ?

LOUIS: What? Like a . . . ? Republican, or . . . ?

Do I?

JOE: Do you what?

LOUIS: Sound like a . . . ?

JOE: Like a . . . ?

I'm . . . confused.

LOUIS: Yes.

My name is Louis. But all my friends call me Louise. I work in Word Processing. Thanks for the toilet paper.

(Louis offers Joe his hand. Joe reaches, Louis feints and pecks Joe on the cheek, then exits.)

Scene 7

A week later. Mutual dream scene. Prior is dreaming that he's at a fantastic makeup table, applying his face. Harper is having a pill-induced hallucination. She has these from time to time. For some reason, Prior has appeared in this one. Or Harper has appeared in Prior's dream. It is bewildering.

PRIOR *(His makeup complete, he examines its perfection in the mirror; then he turns to the audience)*: I'm ready for my closeup, Mr. DeMille.

One wants to move through life with elegance and grace, blossoming infrequently but with exquisite taste, and perfect timing, like a rare bloom, a zebra orchid . . . One wants . . .

But one so seldom gets what one wants, does one?

No. One does not. *(Sorrow and anger well up, overwhelming the grand manner)* One gets fucked. Over. One . . . dies at thirty, robbed of . . . decades of majesty . . .

(Angry) Fuck this shit. Fuck this shit.

(He consults the mirror, attempting to resume the pose)

I look like a corpse. A . . . corpsette!

(It doesn't work. Commiserating with his reflection)

Oh my queen; you know you've hit rock-bottom when even drag is a drag.

(Harper appears. Prior is surprised!)

HARPER: Are you . . . Who are you?

PRIOR: Who are you?

HARPER: What are you doing in my hallucination?

PRIOR: I'm not in your hallucination. You're in my dream.

HARPER: You're wearing makeup.

PRIOR: So are you.

HARPER: But you're a man.

PRIOR *(He looks in his mirror, SCREAMS!, mimes slashing his throat with his lipstick and dies, fabulously tragic. Then)*: The hands and feet give it away.

HARPER: There must be some mistake here. I don't recognize you. You're not— Are you my . . . some sort of imaginary friend?

PRIOR: No. Aren't you too old to have imaginary friends?

HARPER: I have emotional problems. I took too many pills. Why are you wearing makeup?

PRIOR: I was in the process of applying the face, trying to make myself feel better—I swiped the new fall colors at the Clinique counter at Macy's.

(He shows her.)

HARPER: You stole these?

PRIOR: I was out of cash; it was an emotional emergency!

HARPER: Joe will be so angry. I promised him. No more pills.

PRIOR: These pills you keep alluding to?

HARPER: Valium. I take Valium. Lots of Valium.

PRIOR: And you're dancing as fast as you can.

HARPER: I'm not *addicted*. I don't believe in addiction, and I never— Well, I *never* drink. And I *never* take drugs.

PRIOR: Well, smell *you*, Nancy Drew.

HARPER: Except Valium.

PRIOR: Except Valium; in wee fistfuls.

HARPER: It's terrible. Mormons are not supposed to be addicted to anything. I'm a Mormon.

PRIOR: I'm a homosexual.

HARPER: Oh! In my church we don't believe in homosexuals.

PRIOR: In my church we don't believe in Mormons.

HARPER: What church do . . . Oh! *(She laughs)* I get it.

I don't understand this. If I didn't ever see you before and I don't think I did, then I don't think you should be here, in this hallucination, because in my experience the mind, which is where hallucinations come from, shouldn't be able to make up anything that wasn't there to start with, that didn't enter it from experience, from the real world. Imagination can't create anything new, can it? It only recycles bits and pieces from the world and reassembles them into visions . . . Am I making sense right now?

PRIOR: Given the circumstances, yes.

HARPER: So when we think we've escaped the unbearable ordinariness and, well, untruthfulness of our lives, it's really only the same old ordinariness and falseness rearranged into the appearance of novelty and truth. Nothing unknown is knowable. Don't you think it's depressing?

PRIOR: The limitations of the imagination?

HARPER: Yes.

PRIOR: It's something you learn after your second theme party: It's All Been Done Before.

HARPER: The world. Finite. Terribly, terribly . . . Well . . .
This is the most depressing hallucination I've ever had.

PRIOR: Apologies. I do try to be amusing.

HARPER: Oh, well, don't apologize, you . . . I can't expect someone who's really sick to entertain me.

PRIOR: How on earth did you know . . . ?

HARPER: Oh that happens. This is the very threshold of revelation sometimes. You can see things . . . how sick you are.
Do you see anything about me?

PRIOR: Yes.

HARPER: What?

PRIOR: You are amazingly unhappy.

HARPER: Oh big deal. You meet a Valium addict and you figure out she's unhappy. That doesn't count. Of course I . . . Something else. Something surprising.

PRIOR: Something surprising.

HARPER: Yes.

PRIOR: Your husband's a homo.

(Pause.)

HARPER: Oh, ridiculous.

> *(Pause, then very quietly:)*
> Really?

PRIOR *(Shrugs)*: Threshold of revelation.

HARPER: Well I don't like your revelations. I don't think you intuit well at all. Joe's a very normal man, he . . .

> Oh God. Oh God. He . . . Do homos take, like, lots of long walks?

PRIOR *(A beat, then)*: Yes. We do. In stretch pants with lavender coifs. I just looked at you, and there was . . .

HARPER: A sort of blue streak of recognition.

PRIOR: Yes.

HARPER: Like you knew me incredibly well.

PRIOR: Yes.

HARPER: Yes.

> I have to go now, get back, something just . . . fell apart.
> Oh God, I feel so sad . . .

PRIOR: I . . . I'm sorry. I usually say, "Fuck the truth," but mostly, the truth fucks you.

HARPER: I see something else about you.

PRIOR: Oh?

HARPER: Deep inside you, there's a part of you, the most inner part, entirely free of disease. I can see that.

PRIOR: Is that— That isn't true.

HARPER: Threshold of revelation.

> Home . . .

(She vanishes. Prior's startled. Then he feels very alone.)

PRIOR: People come and go so quickly here . . .

> I don't think there's any uninfected part of me. My heart is pumping polluted blood. I feel dirty.

(He starts to wipe off his makeup; suddenly, he smears it furiously around.
A large gray feather falls from above. Prior stops smearing the makeup and looks at the feather. He goes to it and picks it up.)

A VOICE *(It is an incredibly beautiful voice)*: Look up!
PRIOR *(Looking up, not seeing anyone)*: Hello?
A VOICE: Look up!
PRIOR: Who is that?
A VOICE: Prepare the way!
PRIOR: I don't see any—

(There is a dramatic change in lighting, from above.)

A VOICE: Look up, look up,
        prepare the way
        the infinite descent
        A breath in air
        floating down
        Glory to . . .

(Silence.)

PRIOR: Hello? Is that it? Helloooo!
        (Very frightened) What the fuck? . . . *(He holds himself)*
        Poor me. Poor poor me. Why me? Why poor poor me?
        Oh I don't feel good right now. I really don't.

Scene 8

That night. Split scene: Prior and Louis in their bed. Louis reading, Prior cuddled next to him. Harper in Brooklyn, alone. Joe enters.

HARPER: Where were you?

JOE: Out.

HARPER: Where?

JOE: Just out. Thinking.

HARPER: It's late.

JOE: I had a lot to think about.

HARPER: I burned dinner.

JOE: Sorry.

HARPER: Not my dinner. My dinner was fine. Your dinner. I put it back in the oven and turned everything up as high as it could go and I watched till it burned black. It's still hot. Very hot. Want it?

JOE: You didn't have to do that.

HARPER: I know. It just seemed like the kind of thing a mentally deranged sex-starved pill-popping housewife would do.

JOE: Uh-huh.

HARPER: So I did it. Who knows anymore what I have to do?

JOE: How many pills?

HARPER: A bunch. Don't change the subject.

JOE: I won't talk to you when you—

HARPER: No. No. Don't do that! I'm . . . I'm fine, pills are not the problem, not our problem. I WANT TO KNOW WHERE YOU'VE BEEN! I WANT TO KNOW WHAT'S GOING ON!

JOE: Going on with what? The job?

HARPER: Not the job.

JOE: I said I need more time.

HARPER: Not the job!

JOE: Mr. Cohn, I talked to him on the phone, he said I had to hurry—

HARPER: Not the—

JOE: But I can't get you to talk sensibly about anything so—

HARPER: SHUT UP!

JOE: Then what?

HARPER: Stick to the subject.

JOE: I don't know what that is. You have something you want to ask me? Ask me. Go.

HARPER: I . . . can't. I'm scared of you.

JOE: I'm tired, I'm going to bed.

HARPER: Tell me without making me ask. Please.

JOE: This is crazy, I'm not—

HARPER: When you come through the door at night your face is never exactly the way I remembered it. I get surprised by something . . . mean and hard about the way you look. Even the weight of you in the bed at night, the way you breathe in your sleep seems unfamiliar.

You terrify me.

JOE: I know who you are.

HARPER: Yes. I'm the enemy. That's easy. That doesn't change.

You think you're the only one who hates sex; I do; I hate it with you; I do. I dream that you batter away at me till all my joints come apart, like wax, and I fall into pieces. It's like a punishment. It was wrong of me to marry you. I knew you—

(She stops herself)

It's a sin, and it's killing us both.

JOE: I can always tell when you've taken pills because it makes you red-faced and sweaty and frankly that's very often why I don't want to . . .

HARPER: Because . . .

JOE: Well you aren't pretty. Not like this.

HARPER: I have something to ask you.

JOE: Then ASK! ASK! What in hell are you—

HARPER: *Are you a homo?*

> *(Pause)*

> Are you?

> If you try to walk out right now I'll put your dinner back in the oven and turn it up so high the whole building will fill with smoke and everyone in it will asphyxiate. So help me God I will.

> Now answer the question.

[handwritten: Try to leave]

JOE: What if I . . .

(Small pause.)

HARPER: Then tell me, please. And we'll see.

JOE: No. I'm not.

> I don't see what difference it makes.

(Louis and Prior are lying on the bed, Prior's head resting on Louis's chest.)

LOUIS: Jews don't have any clear textual guide to the afterlife; even that it exists. I don't think much about it. I see it as a perpetual rainy Thursday afternoon in March. Dead leaves.

PRIOR: Eeeugh. Very Greco-Roman.

LOUIS: Well for us it's not the verdict that counts, it's the act of judgment. That's why I could never be a lawyer. In court all that matters is the verdict.

PRIOR: You could never be a lawyer because you are oversexed. You're too distracted.

LOUIS: Not distracted; *ab*stracted. I'm trying to make a point:

PRIOR: Namely:

LOUIS: It's the judge in his or her chambers, weighing, books open, pondering the evidence, ranging freely over categories: good, evil, innocent, guilty; the judge in the chamber of circumspection, not the judge on the bench with the gavel. The shaping of the law, not its execution.

PRIOR: The point, dear, the point . . .

LOUIS: That it should be the questions and shape of a life, its total complexity gathered, arranged and considered, which matters in the end, not some stamp of salvation or damnation which disperses all the complexity in some unsatisfying little decision—the balancing of the scales . . .

PRIOR: I like this; very zen; it's . . . reassuringly incomprehensible and useless. We who are about to die thank you.

LOUIS: You are not about to die.

PRIOR: It's not going well, really . . . Two new lesions. My leg hurts. There's protein in my urine, the doctor says, but who knows what the fuck that portends. Anyway it shouldn't be there, the protein. My butt is chapped from diarrhea and yesterday I shat blood.

LOUIS: I really hate this. You don't tell me—

PRIOR: You get too upset, I wind up comforting you. It's easier—

LOUIS: Oh thanks.

PRIOR: If it's bad I'll tell you.

LOUIS: Shitting blood sounds bad to me.

PRIOR: And I'm telling you.

LOUIS: And I'm handling it.

PRIOR: Tell me some more about justice.

LOUIS: I *am* handling it.

PRIOR: Well Louis you win Trooper of the Month.

(Louis starts to cry.)

39

PRIOR: I take it back. You aren't Trooper of the Month.
This isn't working.
Tell me some more about justice.

LOUIS: You are not about to die.

PRIOR: Justice . . .

LOUIS: . . . is an immensity, a . . . confusing vastness.
Justice is God.
(Little pause)
Prior?

PRIOR: Hmmm?

LOUIS: You love me.

PRIOR: Yes.

LOUIS: What if I walked out on this?
Would you hate me forever?

(Prior kisses Louis on the forehead.)

PRIOR: Yes.

(Prior sits at the foot of the bed, facing out, away from Louis.)

JOE: I think we ought to pray. Ask God for help. Ask him
together.

HARPER: God won't talk to me. I have to make up people to
talk to me.

JOE: You have to keep asking.

HARPER: I forgot the question.
Oh yeah. God, is my husband a—

JOE *(Scary)*: Stop it. Stop it. I'm warning you.
Does it make any difference? That I might be one thing
deep within, no matter how wrong or ugly that thing is,
so long as I have fought, with everything I have, to kill it.
What do you want from me? What do you want from me,

Harper? More than that? For God's sake, there's nothing
left, I'm a shell. There's nothing left to kill.

As long as my behavior is what I know it has to be.
Decent. Correct. That alone in the eyes of God.

HARPER: No, no, not that, that's Utah talk, Mormon talk,
I hate it, Joe, tell me, say it.

JOE: All I will say is that I am a very good man who has worked
very hard to become good and you want to destroy that.
You want to destroy me, but I am not going to let you
do that.

(Little pause.)

HARPER: I'm going to have a baby.

JOE: Liar.

HARPER: You liar.

A baby born addicted to pills. A baby who does not
dream but who hallucinates, who stares up at us with big
mirror eyes and who does not know who we are.

(Pause.)

JOE: Are you really . . . ?

HARPER: No.

(He turns to go.)

HARPER: Yes.

(He stops. He believes her.)

HARPER: No.
Yes.

(He tries to approach her.)

HARPER: Get away from me.
Now we both have a secret.

(Joe leaves the room.)

PRIOR *(Speaking to Louis but not looking at him)*: One of my
ancestors was a ship's captain who made money bringing
whale oil to Europe and returning with immigrants—
Irish mostly, packed in tight, so many dollars per head.
The last ship he captained foundered off the coast of
Nova Scotia in a winter tempest and sank to the bottom.
He went down with the ship—*La Grande Geste*—but
his crew took seventy women and kids in the ship's only
longboat, this big, open rowboat, and when the weather got too rough, and they thought the boat was over-
crowded, the crew started lifting people up and hurling
them into the sea. Until they got the ballast right. They
walked up and down the longboat, eyes to the waterline,
and when the boat rode low in the water they'd grab the
nearest passenger and throw them into the sea. The boat
was leaky, see; seventy people; they arrived in Halifax
with nine people on board.

LOUIS: Jesus.

PRIOR: I think about that story a lot now. People in a boat,
waiting, terrified, while implacable, unsmiling men, irre-
sistibly strong, seize . . . maybe the person next to you,
maybe you, and with no warning at all, with time only
for a quick intake of air you are pitched into freezing,
turbulent water and salt and darkness to drown.

I like your cosmology, baby. While time is running
out I find myself drawn to anything that's suspended,

that lacks an ending. But it seems to me that it lets you off scot-free.

LOUIS: What do you mean?

PRIOR: No judgment, no guilt or responsibility.

LOUIS: For me.

PRIOR: For anyone. It was an editorial "you."

LOUIS: Please get better. Please.

Please don't get any sicker.

Scene 9

A week later. Roy and Henry, his doctor, in Henry's office.

HENRY: Nobody knows what causes it. And nobody knows how to cure it. The best theory is that we blame a retrovirus, the Human Immunodeficiency Virus. Its presence is made known to us by the useless antibodies which appear in reaction to its entrance into the bloodstream through a cut, or an orifice. The antibodies are powerless to protect the body against it. Why, we don't know. The body's immune system ceases to function. Sometimes the body even attacks itself. At any rate it's left open to a whole horror house of infections from microbes which it usually defends against.

Like Kaposi's sarcomas. These lesions. Or your throat problem. Or the glands.

We think it may also be able to slip past the blood-brain barrier into the brain. Which is of course very bad news.

And it's fatal in we don't know what percent of people with suppressed immune responses.

(Pause. Roy sits, brooding. Henry waits. Then:)

ROY: This is very interesting, Mr. Wizard, but why the fuck are you telling me this?

HENRY *(Hesitating, confused, then)*: Well, I have just removed one of three lesions which biopsy results will probably tell us is a Kaposi's sarcoma lesion. And you have a pronounced swelling of glands in your neck, groin, and armpits—lymphadenopathy is another sign. And you have oral candidiasis and maybe a little more fungus under the fingernails of two digits on your right hand. So that's why—

ROY: This disease.

HENRY: Syndrome.

ROY: *Whatever.* It afflicts mostly homosexuals and drug addicts.

HENRY: Mostly. Hemophiliacs are also at risk.

ROY: Homosexuals and drug addicts. So why are you implying that I . . .

(Roy stares hard at Henry, who begins to feel nervous.)

ROY: What are you implying, Henry?

HENRY: I don't . . .

ROY: I'm not a drug addict.

HENRY: Oh come on Roy.

ROY: What, what, come on Roy what? Do you think I'm a junkie, Henry, do you see tracks?

HENRY: This is absurd.

ROY: Say it.

HENRY: Say what?

ROY: Say: "Roy Cohn, you are a . . ."

HENRY: Roy? I don't—

ROY: "You are a . . ." Go on. Not "Roy Cohn you are a drug
fiend." "Roy Marcus Cohn, you are a . . ."
Go on, Henry. It starts with an "H."
HENRY: Oh I'm not going to—
ROY: *With an "H,"* Henry, and it isn't "hemophiliac." Come
on . . .
HENRY: What are you doing, Roy?
ROY: No, say it. I mean it. Say: "Roy Cohn, you are a homo-
sexual."
(With deadly seriousness)
And I will proceed, systematically, to destroy your rep-
utation and your practice and your career in New York
State, Henry. Which you know I can do.

(Pause. Henry summons his courage.)

HENRY: Roy, you have been seeing me since 1958. Apart
from the facelifts I have treated you for everything from
syphilis—
ROY: From a whore in Dallas.
HENRY: From syphilis to venereal warts. In your rectum.
Which you may have gotten from a whore in Dallas, but
it wasn't a female whore.

(A standoff. Then:)

ROY: So say it.
HENRY: Roy Cohn, you are . . .
(Roy's too scary. He tries a different approach)
You have had sex with men, many many times, Roy,
and one of them, or any number of them, has made you
very sick. You have AIDS.

45

ROY *(A beat, then)*: AIDS.

Your problem, Henry, is that you are hung up on words, on labels, that you believe they mean what they seem to mean. AIDS. Homosexual. Gay. Lesbian. You think these are names that tell you who someone sleeps with, but they don't tell you that.

HENRY: No?

ROY: No. Like all labels they tell you one thing and one thing only: where does an individual so identified fit in the food chain, in the pecking order? Not ideology, or sexual taste, but something much simpler: clout. Not who I fuck or who fucks me, but who will pick up the phone when I call, who owes me favors. This is what a label refers to. Now to someone who does not understand this, homosexual is what I am because I have sex with men. But really this is wrong. Homosexuals are not men who sleep with other men. Homosexuals are men who in fifteen years of trying cannot pass a pissant antidiscrimination bill through City Council. Homosexuals are men who know nobody and who nobody knows. Who have zero clout. Does this sound like me, Henry?

HENRY: No.

ROY: No. I have clout. A lot. I can pick up this phone, punch fifteen numbers, and you know who will be on the other end in under five minutes, Henry?

HENRY: The president.

ROY: Even better, Henry. His wife.

HENRY: I'm impressed.

ROY: I don't want you to be impressed. I want you to understand. This is not sophistry. And this is not hypocrisy. This is reality. I have sex with men. But unlike nearly every other man of whom this is true, I bring the guy I'm screwing to the White House and President Reagan smiles at us and shakes his hand. Because *what* I am is defined entirely by *who* I am. Roy Cohn is not a homosexual. Roy Cohn is a heterosexual man, Henry, who fucks around with guys.

HENRY: OK, Roy.

ROY: And what is my diagnosis, Henry?

IIENRY: You have AIDS, Roy.

ROY: *No*, Henry, *no*. AIDS is what homosexuals have. I have liver cancer.

(Little pause.)

HENRY: Well, whatever the fuck you have, Roy, it's very serious, and I haven't got a damn thing for you. The NIH in Bethesda has a new drug called AZT with a two-year waiting list that not even I can get you onto. So get on the phone, Roy, and dial the fifteen numbers, and tell the First Lady you need in on an experimental treatment for liver cancer, because you can call it any damn thing you want, Roy, but what it boils down to is very bad news.

ACT TWO:

In Vitro

December 1985

Scene 1

The first week in December. Night. Prior in his underwear alone on the floor in the hallway outside his bedroom; he is much worse.

PRIOR: Louis, Louis, please wake up, oh God.

(Louis runs in.)

PRIOR: I think something horrible is wrong with me I can't
    breathe . . .
LOUIS *(Starting to exit)*: I'm calling the ambulance.
PRIOR: No, wait, I—
LOUIS: *Wait?* Are you fucking crazy? Oh God you're on fire,
    your head is on fire.
PRIOR: It hurts, it hurts . . .
LOUIS: I'm calling the ambulance.

PRIOR: I don't want to go to the hospital, I don't want to go to the hospital please let me lie here, just—

LOUIS: No, no, God, Prior, stand up—

PRIOR: DON'T TOUCH MY LEG!

LOUIS: We have to . . . Oh God this is so crazy.

PRIOR: I'll be OK if I just lie here Lou, really, if I can only sleep a little . . .

(Louis exits.)

PRIOR: Louis?

NO! NO! Don't call, you'll send me there and I won't come back, please, please Louis I'm begging, baby, please.

(Screams) LOUIS!!

LOUIS *(From off; hysterical)*: WILL YOU SHUT THE FUCK UP!

PRIOR *(Trying to stand)*: Aaaah. I have . . . to go to the bathroom. Wait. Wait, just— Oh. Oh God. *(He shits himself)*

LOUIS *(Entering)*: Prior? They'll be here in—

Oh my God.

PRIOR: I'm sorry, I'm sorry.

LOUIS: What did . . . ? What?

PRIOR: I had an accident.

(Louis goes to him.)

LOUIS: This is blood.

PRIOR: Maybe you shouldn't touch it . . . me . . . I . . . *(He faints)*

LOUIS *(Quietly)*: Oh help. Oh help. Oh God oh God oh God help me I can't I can't I can't.

Scene 2

Night. Harper at home, sitting on the floor, all alone, with no lights on. We can barely see her. Joe enters, but he doesn't turn on the lights.

JOE: Why are you sitting in the dark? Turn on the light.

HARPER: *No.* I heard the sounds in the bedroom again. I know someone was in there.

JOE: No one was.

HARPER: Maybe actually in the bed, under the covers with a knife.

Oh, boy. Joe. I, um, I'm thinking of going away. By which I mean: I think I'm going off again. You . . . you know what I mean?

JOE: Please don't. Stay. We can fix it. I pray for that. This is my fault, but I can correct it. You have to try, too.

(Joe walks to a floor lamp and switches on the light, then sits next to her on the floor. As soon as he sits, Harper stands, goes to the lamp, turns off the light, and then returns to sit beside him. They sit quietly, close together, in the dark. Then:)

HARPER: When you pray, what do you pray for?

JOE: I pray for God to crush me, break me up into little pieces and start all over again.

HARPER: Oh. Please. Don't pray for that.

JOE: I had a book of Bible stories when I was a kid. There was a picture I'd look at twenty times every day: Jacob wrestles with the angel. I don't really remember the story, or why the wrestling—just the picture. Jacob is young and very strong. The angel is . . . a beautiful man, with golden hair and wings, of course. I still dream about it. Many nights. I'm . . . It's me. In that struggle. Fierce, and unfair. The angel is not human, and it holds nothing back, so how could anyone human win, what kind of a fight is that? It's not just. Losing means your soul thrown down in the dust, your heart torn out from God's. But you can't not lose.

HARPER: In the whole entire world, you are the only person, the only person I love or have ever loved. And I love you terribly. Terribly. That's what's so awfully, irreducibly real. I can make up anything but I can't dream that away.

JOE: Are you . . . Are you really going to have a baby?

HARPER: It's my time, and there's no blood. I don't really know. I suppose it wouldn't be a great thing. Maybe I'm just not bleeding because I take too many pills. Maybe I'll give birth to a pill.

(He laughs a little.)

HARPER: That would give a new meaning to pill-popping, huh?

(They both laugh.)

HARPER: I think you should go to Washington. Alone. Change, like you said.

JOE: I'm not going to leave you, Harper.

HARPER *(A beat, then)*: Well maybe not. But I'm going to leave you.

Scene 3

One A.M., the next morning. A hospital room. Prior is in a bed, oxygen mask on his face, IV tubes draining bags of fluids into his veins. Emily, a nurse, finishes checking the tubes, the machines. Louis watches Emily; he avoids looking at Prior.

EMILY: He'll be all right now.

LOUIS: No he won't.

EMILY: No. I guess not. I gave him something that makes him sleep.

LOUIS: Deep asleep?

EMILY: Orbiting the moons of Jupiter.

LOUIS: A good place to be.

EMILY: Anyplace better than here. You his . . . uh . . . ?

LOUIS: Yes. I'm his uh.

EMILY: This must be hell for you.

LOUIS: It is. Hell. The After Life. Which is not at all like a rainy afternoon in March, by the way, Prior. A lot more vivid than I'd expected. Dead leaves, but the crunchy kind. Sharp, dry air. The kind of long, luxurious dying feeling that breaks your heart.

EMILY *(Not following, exactly)*: Yeah, well. We all get to break our hearts on this one.

He seems like a nice guy. Cute.

LOUIS: Not like this.

Yes, he is. Was. Whatever.

EMILY: Weird name. Prior Walter. Like, "The Walter before this one."

LOUIS: Lots of Walters before this one. Prior is an old old family name in an old old family. The Walters go back to the Mayflower and beyond. Back to the Norman Conquests.

He says there's a Prior Walter stitched into the Bayeux tapestry.

EMILY: Is that impressive?

LOUIS: Well, it's old. Very old. Which in some circles equals impressive.

EMILY: Not in my circle. What's the name of the tapestry?

LOUIS: The Bayeux tapestry. Embroidered by La Reine Mathilde.

EMILY: I'll tell my mother. She embroiders. Drives me nuts.

LOUIS: Manual therapy for anxious hands.

EMILY: Maybe you should try it.

(Louis looks at her, then finally looks directly at Prior. Then he looks away.)

LOUIS: Mathilde stitched while William the Conqueror was off to war. She was capable of . . . more than loyalty. Devotion.

She waited for him, she stitched for years. And if he had come back broken and defeated from war, she would have loved him even more. And if he had returned mutilated, ugly, full of infection and horror, she would still have loved him; fed by pity, by a sharing of pain, she would love him even more, and even more, and she would never, never have prayed to God, please let him die if he can't return to me whole and healthy and able to live a normal life . . . If he had died, she would have buried her heart with him.

So what the fuck is the matter with me?

(Little pause)

Will he sleep through the night?

EMILY: At least.

LOUIS: I'm going.

EMILY: It's one A.M. Where do you have to go at—

LOUIS: I know what time it is. A walk. Night air, good for the . . . *(Quickly brushing his hand across his heart; then)* The park.

EMILY: Be careful.

LOUIS: Yeah. Danger.

Tell him, if he wakes up and you're still on, tell him good-bye, tell him I had to go.

Scene 4

Same night. Split scene: Joe and Roy sitting at the bar in an elegant restaurant; Louis and a Man, dressed in leather, in the Ramble in Central Park. Roy's in a tuxedo, bowtie loosened. He's been drinking heavily, a rye and soda before him. Joe's dressed casually, nursing a tumbler of club soda. Louis and the Man are eyeing each other, alternating interest and indifference.

JOE: The pills were something she started when she miscarried or . . . no, she took some before that. She had a really bad time at home, when she was a kid, her home was really bad. I think a lot of drinking and physical stuff. She doesn't talk about that, instead she talks about . . . the sky falling down, people with knives hiding under sofas. Monsters. Mormons. Everyone thinks Mormons don't come from homes like that, we aren't supposed to behave that way, but we do. It's not lying, or being two-faced. Everyone tries very hard to live up to God's strictures, which are very . . . um . . .

ROY: Strict.

JOE: I shouldn't be bothering you with this.

ROY: No, please. Heart to heart. Want another . . . What is that, seltzer?

JOE: The failure to measure up hits people very hard. From such a strong desire to be good they feel very far from goodness when they fail.

What scares me is that maybe what I really love in her is the part of her that's farthest from the light, from God's love; maybe I was drawn to that in the first place. And I'm keeping it alive because I need it.

ROY: Why would you need it?

JOE: There are things . . . I don't know how well we know ourselves. I mean, what if? I know I married her because she . . . because I loved it that she was always wrong, always doing something wrong, like one step out of step. In Salt Lake City that stands out. I never stood out, on the outside, but inside, it was hard for me. To pass.

ROY: Pass?

JOE: Yeah.

ROY: Pass as what?

JOE: Oh. Well . . . As someone cheerful and strong. Those who love God with an open heart unclouded by secrets and struggles are cheerful; God's easy simple love for them shows in how strong and happy they are. The saints.

ROY: But you had secrets? Secret struggles . . .

JOE: I wanted to be one of the elect, one of the Blessed. You feel you ought to be, that the blemishes are yours by choice, which of course they aren't. Harper's sorrow, that really deep sorrow, she didn't choose that. But it's there.

ROY: You didn't put it there.

JOE: No.

ROY: You sound like you think you did.

JOE: I am responsible for her.

ROY: Because she's your wife.

JOE: That. And I do love her.

ROY: Whatever. She's your wife. And so there are obligations.
To her. But also to yourself.

JOE: She'd fall apart in Washington.

ROY: Then let her stay here.

JOE: She'll fall apart if I leave her.

ROY: Then bring her to Washington.

JOE: I just can't, Roy. She needs me.

ROY: Listen, Joe. I'm the best divorce lawyer in the business.

(Little pause.)

JOE: Can't Washington wait?

ROY: You do what you need to do, Joe. What *you* need. *You.*
Let her life go where it wants to go. You'll both be better
for that. *Somebody* should get what they want.

MAN: What do you want?

LOUIS: I want you to fuck me, hurt me, make me bleed.

MAN: I want to.

LOUIS: Yeah?

MAN: I want to hurt you.

LOUIS: Fuck me.

MAN: Yeah?

LOUIS: Hard.

MAN: Yeah? You been a bad boy?

(Pause. Louis laughs, softly.)

LOUIS: Very bad. Very bad.

MAN: You need to be punished, boy?

LOUIS: Yes. I do.

MAN: Yes what?

(Little pause.)

ANGELS IN AMERICA

LOUIS: Um, I . . .

MAN: Yes *what*, boy?

LOUIS: Oh. Yes sir.

MAN: I want you to take me to your place, boy.

LOUIS: No, I can't do that.

MAN: No *what*?

LOUIS: No sir, I can't, I—
   I don't live alone, sir.

MAN: Your lover know you're out with a man tonight, boy?

LOUIS: No sir, he—
   My lover doesn't know.

MAN: Your lover know you—

LOUIS: Let's change the subject, OK? Can we go to your place?

MAN: I live with my parents.

LOUIS: Oh.

ROY: Everyone who makes it in this world makes it because
   somebody older and more powerful takes an interest.
   The most precious asset in life, I think, is the ability to
   be a good son. You have that, Joe. Somebody who can be
   a good son to a father who pushes them farther than they
   would otherwise go. I've had many fathers, I owe my life
   to them, powerful, powerful men. Walter Winchell,
   Edgar Hoover. Joe McCarthy most of all. He valued me
   because I am a good lawyer, but he loved me because
   I was and am a good son. He was a very difficult man,
   very guarded and cagey; I brought out something tender
   in him. He would have died for me. And me for him.
   Does this embarrass you?

JOE: I had a hard time with my father.

ROY: Well sometimes that's the way. Then you have to find
   other fathers, substitutes, I don't know. The father-
   son relationship is central to life. Women are for birth,
   beginning, but the father is continuance. The son offers

the father his life as a vessel for carrying forth his father's dream. Your father's living?

JOE: Um, dead.

ROY: He was . . . what? A difficult man?

JOE: He was in the military. He could be very unfair. And cold.

ROY: But he loved you.

JOE: I don't know.

ROY: No, no, Joe, he did, I know this. Sometimes a father's love has to be very, very hard, unfair even, cold to make his son grow strong in a world like this. This isn't a good world.

MAN: Here, then.

LOUIS: I . . . Do you have a rubber?

MAN: I don't use rubbers.

LOUIS: You should. *(He takes one from his coat pocket)* Here.

MAN: I don't use them.

LOUIS: Forget it, then. *(He starts to leave)*

MAN: No, wait.

Put it on me. Boy.

LOUIS: Forget it, I have to get back. Home. I must be going crazy.

MAN: Oh come on please he won't find out.

LOUIS: It's cold. Too cold.

MAN: It's never too cold, let me warm you up. Please?

(Louis puts the condom on the Man's cock, and they begin to fuck.)

MAN: Relax.

LOUIS *(A grim, small laugh)*: Not a chance.

(More fucking. It gets rough. Louis falls on his hands and knees. Then the Man stops.)

MAN: It . . .

LOUIS: What?

MAN: I think it must've . . . It broke, or slipped off, you didn't
put it on right, or— You want me to keep going?
Pull out? Should I—

LOUIS: Keep going.
Infect me.
I don't care. I don't care.

(The Man pulls out.)

MAN: I . . . um, look, I'm sorry, but I think I want to go.

LOUIS: Yeah.
Give my best to Mom and Dad.

(The Man slaps him.)

LOUIS: Ow!

(They stare at each other.)

LOUIS: It was a joke.

(The Man leaves.)

ROY: How long have we known each other?

JOE: Since 1980.

ROY: Right. A long time. I feel close to you, Joe. Do I advise
you well?

JOE: You've been an incredible friend, Roy, I'm—

ROY: I want to be family. *Famiglia*, as my Italian friends call it.
La Famiglia. A lovely word. It's important for me to help
you, like I was helped.

JOE: I owe practically everything to you, Roy.

ROY: I'm dying, Joe. Cancer.

JOE: Oh my God.

ROY: Please. Let me finish.

Few people know this and I'm telling you this only because . . . I'm not afraid of death. What can death bring that I haven't faced? I've lived; life is the worst. *(Gently mocking himself)* Listen to me, I'm a philosopher.

Joe. You must do this. You must must must. Love; that's a trap. Responsibility; that's a trap, too. Like a father to a son I tell you this: Life is full of horror; nobody escapes, nobody; save yourself. Whatever pulls on you, whatever needs from you, threatens you. Don't be afraid; people are so afraid; don't be afraid to live in the raw wind, naked, alone . . . Learn at least this: What you are capable of. Let nothing stand in your way.

Scene 5

Several days later. Prior and Belize in Prior's hospital room. Prior is very sick but improving. Belize has just arrived, stopping on his way to work to check up on Prior, with little time to spare.

PRIOR: Miss Thing.

BELIZE: Ma cherie bichette.

PRIOR: Stella.

BELIZE: Stella for star. Let me see. *(Scrutinizing Prior)* You look like shit, why yes indeed you do, comme la merde!

PRIOR: Merci.

BELIZE: Not to despair, Belle Reeve. Lookie!
(Taking a little plastic bottle from his bag)
Magic goop!

(Belize hands the bottle to Prior, who opens it and sniffs it suspiciously, as Belize looks over the IV bags feeding meds to Prior.)

PRIOR *(Reacting to the smell from the bottle with alarm)*: Pooh! What kinda crap is that?

BELIZE: Beats me. Let's rub it on your poor blistered body and see what it does.

PRIOR: This is not Western medicine, this bottle . . .

BELIZE: Voodoo cream. From the botanica 'round the block.

PRIOR: And you a registered nurse.

(Belize takes the bottle back and sniffs it.)

BELIZE: Beeswax and cheap perfume. Cut with Jergen's lotion. Full of good vibes and love from some little black Cubana witch in Miami.

(He pours some in his hands, ready to give Prior a backrub.)

PRIOR *(Frightened)*: Get that trash away from me, I am immune-suppressed.

BELIZE *(Firm, slightly offended)*: I *am* a health professional. I *know* what I'm doing.

(Prior hesitates, then reluctantly offers his back to be rubbed. Belize gets on the bed and rubs, gently.)

PRIOR: It stinks.
    Any word from Louis?

(Little pause; Belize rubs Prior's back.)

PRIOR: Gone.

BELIZE: He'll be back. I know the type. Likes to keep a girl on edge.

PRIOR: It's been . . .

(Pause.)

BELIZE *(Trying to jog Prior's memory)*: How long?

PRIOR: I don't remember.

BELIZE: How long have you been here?

PRIOR *(Suddenly upset)*: I don't remember, I don't give a fuck. I want Louis. I want my fucking boyfriend, where the fuck is he? I'm dying, I'm dying, where's Louis?

(Prior is crying, hard. Belize cradles him.)

BELIZE: Ssssh, sssh . . .

PRIOR: This is a very strange drug, this drug. Emotional lability, for starters.

BELIZE: Save a tab or two for me.

PRIOR: Oh no, not this drug, ce n'est pas pour la joyeux noël et la bonne année, this drug she is serious poisonous chemistry, ma pauvre bichette.

And not just disorienting. I hear things.

Voices.

BELIZE *(Covering, but alarmed)*: Voices.

PRIOR: A voice.

BELIZE: Saying what?

(Pause.)

PRIOR: I'm not supposed to tell.

BELIZE *(Earnest)*: You better tell the doctor. Or I will.

PRIOR: No no don't. Please. I want the voice; it's wonderful. It's all that's keeping me alive. I don't want to talk to some intern about it.

You know what happens? When I hear it, I get hard.

BELIZE: Oh my.

PRIOR: Comme ça. *(He uses his arm to demonstrate)* And you know I am slow to rise.

BELIZE: My jaw aches at the memory.

PRIOR *(Pleading)*: And would you deny me this little solace? Betray my concupiscence to Florence Nightingale's storm troopers?

BELIZE: Perish the thought, ma bébé.

PRIOR: They'd change the drug just to spoil the fun.

BELIZE: You and your boner can depend on me.

PRIOR: Je t'adore, ma belle nègre.

BELIZE *(With an edge)*: All this girl-talk shit is politically incorrect, you know. We should have dropped it back when we gave up drag.

PRIOR *(Indignant)*: I'm sick, I get to be politically incorrect if it makes me feel better. You sound like Lou.

(Little pause)

Well, at least I have the satisfaction of knowing he's in anguish somewhere. I loved his anguish. Watching him stick his head up his asshole and eat his guts out over some relatively minor moral conundrum—it was the best show in town. But Mother warned me: if they get overwhelmed by the little things—

BELIZE: —they'll be belly-up bustville when something big comes along.

PRIOR: Mother warned me.

BELIZE: And they do come along.

PRIOR: But I didn't listen.

BELIZE: No. *(Doing Katharine Hepburn)* Men are beasts.

PRIOR *(Also Hepburn)*: The absolute lowest.

BELIZE: I have to go. If I want to spend my whole lonely life looking after white people I can get underpaid to do it.

PRIOR: You're just a Christian martyr.

BELIZE: Whatever happens, baby, I will be here for you.

PRIOR: Je t'aime.

BELIZE: Je t'aime. Don't go crazy on me, girlfriend, I already got enough crazy queens for one lifetime. For two. I can't be bothering with dementia.

PRIOR: I promise.

BELIZE *(Touching him with his forefinger; softly, doing E.T.)*: Ouch.

PRIOR: Ouch. Indeed.

BELIZE: Why'd they have to pick on you?

And eat more, girlfriend, you really do look like shit.

(He leaves.)

PRIOR *(A beat, then)*: He's gone.

Are you still—

A VOICE: I can't stay. I will return.

PRIOR: Are you one of those "Follow me to the other side" voices?

A VOICE: No. I am no nightbird. I am a messenger . . .

PRIOR: You have a beautiful voice, it sounds . . . like a viola, like a perfectly tuned, tight string, balanced, the truth . . . Stay with me.

A VOICE: Not now. Soon I will return, I will reveal myself to you; I am glorious, glorious; my heart, my countenance and my message. You must prepare.

PRIOR *(Afraid again)*: For what? I don't want to—

A VOICE: No death, no:

A marvelous work and a wonder we undertake, an edifice awry we sink plumb and straighten, a great Lie we abolish, a great error correct, with the rule, sword and broom of Truth!

PRIOR: What are you talking about, I—

A VOICE: I am on my way; when I am manifest, our Work begins:
>Prepare for the parting of the air,
>The breath, the ascent,
>Glory to . . .

Scene 6

Several days later. Martin, a relentlessly upbeat official in the Reagan Administration's Justice Department, is at a table with Roy and Joe in a fancy Manhattan restaurant.

MARTIN: It's a revolution in Washington, Joe. We have a new agenda and finally a real leader. They got back the Senate but we have the courts. By the nineties the Supreme Court will be block-solid Republican appointees, and the federal bench—Republican judges like land mines, everywhere, everywhere they turn. Affirmative action? Take it to court. Boom! Land mine. And we'll get our way on just about everything: abortion, defense, Central America, family values, a live investment climate. We have the White House locked till the year 2000. And beyond. A permanent fix on the Oval Office? It's possible. By '92 we'll get the Senate back, and in ten years the South is going to give us the House. It's really the end of Liberalism. The end of New Deal Socialism. The end of ipso facto secular humanism. The dawning of a genuinely American political personality. Modeled on Ronald Wilson Reagan.

JOE: It sounds great, Mr. Heller.

MARTIN: Martin. And Justice is the hub. Especially since Ed Meese took over. He doesn't specialize in Fine Points of the Law. He's a flatfoot, a cop. He reminds me of Teddy Roosevelt.

JOE: I can't wait to meet him.

MARTIN: Too bad, Joe, he's been dead for sixty years!

(There is a little awkwardness. Joe doesn't respond.)

MARTIN: Teddy Roosevelt. You said you wanted to . . . Little joke. It reminds me of the story about the—

ROY *(Smiling, but nasty)*: Aw shut the fuck up, Martin.

> *(To Joe)* You see that? Mr. Heller here is one of the mighty, Joseph, in D.C., he sitteth on the right hand of the man who sitteth on the right hand of The Man. And yet I can say "shut the fuck up" and he will take no offense. Loyalty.

MARTIN: This man, Joe, is a Saint of the Right.

JOE: I know, Mr. Heller, I—

ROY: And you see what I mean, Martin? He's special, right?

MARTIN: Don't embarrass him, Roy.

ROY: Gravity, decency, smarts! His strength is as the strength of ten because his heart is pure! *And* he's a Royboy, one hundred percent.

MARTIN: We're on the move, Joe. On the move.

JOE: Mr. Heller, I—

MARTIN: We can't wait any longer for an answer.

(Little pause.)

JOE: Oh. Um, I—

ROY: Joe's a married man, Martin.

MARTIN: Aha.

ROY: With a wife. She doesn't care to go to D.C., and so Joe cannot go. And keeps us dangling. We've seen that kind of thing before, haven't we? These men and their wives.

MARTIN: Oh yes. Beware.

JOE: I really can't discuss this under—

MARTIN: Then *don't* discuss. Say yes, Joe.

ROY: Now.

MARTIN: Say yes I will.

ROY: Now.

Now. I'll hold my breath till you do, I'm turning blue waiting . . .

(Too loud) Now, goddamnit!

MARTIN *(Looking around)*: Roy, calm down, it's not—

ROY: Aw, fuck it.

(Roy takes a letter from his jacket pocket, hands it to Joe.)

ROY: Read. Came today.

(Joe removes the letter from its envelope and reads. Then he looks up at Roy.)

JOE: Roy. This is . . . Roy, this is terrible.

ROY: You're telling me.

A letter from the New York State Bar Association, Martin.

They're gonna try and disbar me.

MARTIN: Oh my.

JOE: Why?

ROY: Why, Martin?

MARTIN: Revenge.

ROY: The whole Establishment. Their little rules. Because I know no rules. Because I don't see the Law as a dead and arbitrary collection of antiquated dictums, thou shall, thou shalt not, because, because I know the Law's a pliable, breathing, sweating . . . *organ*, because, because—

MARTIN: Because he borrowed half a million from one of his clients.

ROY: Yeah, well, there's that.

MARTIN: *And* he forgot to *return* it.

JOE: Roy, that's . . . You borrowed money from a client?

ROY: I'm deeply ashamed.

(Little pause.)

JOE: Roy, you know how much I admire you. Well I mean I know you have unorthodox ways, but I'm sure you only did what you thought at the time you needed to do. And I have faith that—

ROY: Not so damp, please. I'll deny it was a loan. She's got no paperwork. Can't prove a fucking thing.

(Little pause. Martin studies the menu.
Joe puts the letter back in its envelope and hands it to Roy.)

JOE *(A little stiff, formal)*: Roy I really appreciate your telling me this, and I'll do whatever I can to help.

ROY *(Holding up a hand, then, carefully)*: I'll tell you what you can do.

I'm about to be tried, Joe, by a jury that is not a jury of my peers. The disbarment committee: genteel gentlemen Brahmin lawyers, country-club men. I offend them, to these men I'm what, Martin? Some sort of filthy little Jewish troll?

MARTIN *(With an embarrassed laugh)*: Oh well, I wouldn't go so far as—

ROY *(Imitating the laugh)*: Oh well I would.

Very fancy lawyers, these disbarment committee lawyers, fancy lawyers with fancy corporate clients and complicated cases. Antitrust suits. Deregulation. Environmental control. Complex cases like these need Justice Department cooperation like flowers need the sun. Wouldn't you say that's an accurate assessment, Martin?

MARTIN: I'm not here, Roy. I'm not hearing any of this.

ROY: No. Of course not.

Without the light of the sun, Joe, these cases, and the fancy lawyers who represent them, will wither and die.

A well-placed friend, someone in the Justice Department, say, can turn off the sun. Cast a deep shadow on my behalf. Make them shiver in the cold. If they overstep. They would fear that.

(Pause.)

JOE: Roy. I don't understand.

ROY: You do.

(Pause.)

JOE: You're not asking me to—

ROY: Sssshhhh. Careful.

JOE *(A beat, then)*: Even if I said yes to the job, it would be illegal to interfere. With the hearings. It's unethical. No. I can't.

ROY: Un-ethical.

Would you excuse us, Martin?

MARTIN: Excuse you?

ROY: Take a walk, Martin. For real.

(Martin hesitates, then stands. He shoots Joe a quick "you just stepped in it" look, then leaves.)

ROY: Un-ethical. Are you trying to embarrass me in front of my friend?

JOE: Well it is unethical, I can't—

ROY: Boy, you are really something, what the fuck do you think this is, Sunday school?

JOE: No, but Roy this is—

ROY: This is—this is gastric juices churning, this is enzymes and acids, this is intestinal is what this is, bowel movement and blood-red meat! This stinks, this is *politics*, Joe, the game of being alive. And you think you're . . . What? Above that? Above alive is what? Dead! In the clouds! You're on earth, goddamnit! Plant a foot, stay a while.

   I'm sick. They smell I'm weak. They want blood this time. I must have eyes in Justice. In Justice you will protect me.

JOE: Why can't Mr. Heller—

ROY: Grow up, Joe. The administration can't get involved.

JOE: But I'd be part of the administration. The same as him.

ROY: Not the same. Martin's Ed's man. And Ed's Reagan's man. So Martin's Reagan's man.

   And you're mine.

   (Little pause. He holds up the letter)

   This will never be. Understand me?

   (He tears up the letter)

   I'm gonna be a lawyer, Joe, I'm gonna be a lawyer, Joe, I'm gonna be a goddamn motherfucking legally licensed member of the bar lawyer, just like my daddy was, till my last bitter day on earth, Joseph, until the day I die.

(Martin returns.)

ROY: Ah, Martin's back.
MARTIN: So are we agreed?
ROY: Joe?

(Little pause.)

JOE: I will think about it.
　　　(To Roy) I will.
ROY *(A beat, then, contemplatively)*: Huh.
MARTIN: It's the fear of what comes after the doing that makes
　　　the doing hard to do.
ROY: Amen.
MARTIN: But you can almost always live with the consequences.

Scene 7

That afternoon. On the granite steps outside the Hall of Justice, Brooklyn. It is cold and sunny. A Sabrett wagon is selling hot dogs. Louis, in a shabby overcoat, is sitting on the steps contemplatively eating one. Joe enters with three hot dogs and a can of Coke.

JOE: Can I . . . ?
LOUIS: Oh sure. Sure. Crazy cold sun.
JOE *(Sitting)*: Have to make the best of it.
　　　How's your friend?
LOUIS: My . . . ? Oh. He's worse. My friend is worse.
JOE: I'm sorry.
LOUIS: Yeah, well. Thanks for asking. It's nice. You're nice.
　　　I can't believe you voted for Reagan.

JOE: I hope he gets better.

LOUIS: Reagan?

JOE: Your friend.

LOUIS: He won't. Neither will Reagan.

JOE: Let's not talk politics, OK?

LOUIS *(Pointing to Joe's lunch)*: You're eating *three* of those?

JOE: Well . . . I'm . . . hungry.

LOUIS: They're really terrible for you. Full of rat poo and beetle legs and wood shavings 'n' shit.

JOE: Huh.

LOUIS: And . . . um . . . irridium, I think. Something toxic.

JOE: You're eating one.

LOUIS: Yeah, well, the shape, I can't help myself, plus I'm *trying* to commit suicide, what's your excuse?

JOE: I don't have an excuse. I just have Pepto-Bismol.

(Joe takes a bottle of Pepto-Bismol and chugs it. Louis shudders audibly.)

JOE: Yeah I know but then I wash it down with Coke.

(He does this. Louis mimes barfing in Joe's lap. Joe pushes Louis's head away.)

JOE: Are you *always* like this?

LOUIS: I've been worrying a lot about his kids.

JOE: Whose?

LOUIS: Reagan's. Maureen and Mike and little orphan Patti and Miss Ron Reagan, Jr., the you-should-pardon-the-expression heterosexual.

JOE: Ron Reagan, Jr. is *not*— You shouldn't just make these assumptions about people. How do you know? About him? What he is? You don't know.

LOUIS *(Doing Tallulah Bankhead)*: Well darling he never sucked *my* cock but—

JOE: Look, if you're going to get vulgar—

LOUIS: No no *really*, I mean, what's it like to be the child of the Zeitgeist? To have the American Animus as your dad? It's not really a *family*, the Reagans, I read *People*, there aren't any connections there, no love, they don't ever even speak to each other except through their agents. So what's it like to be Reagan's kid? Enquiring minds want to know.

JOE: You can't believe everything you—

LOUIS: But . . .

I think we all know what that's like. Nowadays. No connections. No responsibilities. All of us . . . falling through the cracks that separate what we owe to our selves and . . . and what we owe to love.

JOE *(A beat, then)*: You just . . . Whatever you feel like saying or doing, you don't care, you just . . . do it.

LOUIS *(Catching at something in Joe's tone)*: Do what?

JOE: It. Whatever. Whatever it is you want to do.

LOUIS *(A beat; then, quietly challenging)*: Are you trying to tell me something?

(Little pause, sexual. They look at each other, then Joe looks away.)

JOE: No, I'm just observing that you—

LOUIS *(Nodding, letting him off the hook)*: Impulsive.

JOE: Yes, I mean it must be scary, you—

LOUIS: Land of the free, home of the brave, call me irresponsible.

JOE: It's kind of terrifying.

LOUIS *(Shrugging)*: Yeah, well, freedom is. Heartless, too.

JOE: Oh you're not heartless.

(Little pause. Louis stops smiling.)

LOUIS: You don't know.

> Finish your weenie.

(Louis pats Joe on the knee, stands and starts to leave.)

JOE: Um . . .

(Louis turns, looks at him. Joe searches for something to say; then, mostly avoiding looking at Louis:)

JOE: Yesterday was Sunday but I've been a little unfocused recently and I thought it was Monday. So I came here like I was going to work. And the whole place was empty. And at first I couldn't figure out why, and I had this moment of incredible . . . fear and also . . . It just flashed through my mind: the whole Hall of Justice, it's empty, it's deserted, it's gone out of business. Forever. The people that make it run have up and abandoned it.

LOUIS *(Looking at the building)*: Creepy.

JOE: Well yes but. I felt that I was going to scream. Not because it was creepy, but because the emptiness felt so *fast*.

> And . . . well, good. A . . . happy scream.

> I just wondered what a thing it would be . . . if overnight everything you owe anything to, justice, or love, had really gone away. Free.

> It would be . . . heartless terror. Yes. Terrible, and . . .

> Very great. To shed your skin, every old skin, one by one and then walk away, unencumbered, into the morning.

> *(Pause. He looks at the building, then down)*

> I can't go in there today.

LOUIS: Then don't.

JOE: I can't go in, I need . . .

> *(He looks for what he needs. He takes a swig of Pepto-Bismol)*

I can't *be* this anymore. I need . . . a change, I should just . . .

LOUIS: Want some company? For whatever?

(A possibility of sex still hangs in the air.)

LOUIS: Sometimes, even if it scares you to death, you have to be willing to break the law. Know what I mean?

(Little pause.)

JOE: Yes.

LOUIS *(A beat, then)*: I moved out. I moved out on my . . .

(Little pause; Louis looks down. The sexual possibility disappears.)

LOUIS: I haven't been sleeping well.

JOE: Me neither.

(Louis licks his napkin and goes up to Joe. He dabs at Joe's upper lip.)

LOUIS: Antacid moustache.

(Louis starts to walk away, then stops and stares at the courthouse. Not looking at Joe:)

LOUIS: Maybe the court won't convene. Ever again. Maybe we are free. To do whatever.

Children of the new morning, criminal minds. Selfish and greedy and loveless and blind. Reagan's children.
(Looking at Joe) You're scared. So am I. Everybody is in the land of the free.

(Louis turns and leaves. As he's exiting:)

LOUIS: God help us all.

Scene 8

Late that night. Joe at a payphone calling Hannah at home in Salt Lake City. Joe's a little drunk.

JOE: Mom?

HANNAH: Joe?

JOE: Hi.

HANNAH: You're calling from the street. It's . . . it must be four in the morning. What's happened?

JOE: Nothing, nothing, I—

HANNAH: It's Harper. Is Harper—
     Joe?
     Joe?

JOE: Yeah, hi. No, Harper's fine. Well, no, she's . . . *(He finds this slightly funny)* not fine.
     (With a grin) How are you, Mom?

HANNAH: What's happened?

JOE: I just wanted to talk to you. I, uh, wanted to try something out on you.

HANNAH: Joe, you haven't— Have you been drinking, Joe?

JOE *(A bigger grin)*: Yes, ma'am. I'm drunk.

HANNAH: That isn't like you.

JOE: No. I mean— *(Again, finding this a little funny)* Who's to say?

HANNAH: Why are you out on the street at four A.M.? In that crazy city. It's dangerous.

JOE: Actually, Mom, I'm not on the street. I'm near the boathouse in the park.

HANNAH: What park?

JOE: Central Park.

HANNAH: CENTRAL PARK! Oh my Lord. What on earth are you doing in Central Park at this time of night? Are you—

(Very stern) Joe, I think you ought to go home right now. Call me from home.

(Little pause.)

HANNAH: Joe?

JOE: I come here to watch, Mom. Sometimes. Just to watch.

HANNAH: Watch what? What's there to watch at four in the—

JOE: Mom, did Dad love me?

HANNAH: What?

JOE: Did he?

HANNAH: You ought to go home and call from there.

JOE: Answer.

HANNAH: Oh now really. This is maudlin. I don't like this conversation.

JOE: Yeah, well, it gets worse from here on.

(Pause.)

HANNAH: Joe?

JOE: Mom. Momma. I'm a homosexual, Momma.
  (He lowers the receiver and laughs quietly to himself)
  Boy, did that come out awkward.
  (He lifts the receiver to his ear)
  Hello? Hello?
  I'm a homosexual.
  (Pause)
  Please, Momma. Say something.

HANNAH: You're old enough to understand that your father didn't love you without being ridiculous about it.

JOE: What?

HANNAH: You're ridiculous. You're being ridiculous.

JOE: I'm— *What?*

HANNAH: You really ought to go home now to your wife. I need to go to bed. This phone call— We will just forget this phone call.

JOE: Mom.

HANNAH: No more talk. Tonight. This . . .
  (Suddenly very angry) Drinking is a sin! A sin! I raised you better than that. *(She hangs up)*

Scene 9

The following morning, early. Split scene: Harper and Joe at home; Louis and Prior in Prior's hospital room. Joe and Louis have each just entered. This should be fast. No freezing; even when one of the couples isn't talking, they remain furiously alive.

HARPER: Oh God. Home. The moment of truth has arrived.

JOE: Harper.

LOUIS: I'm going to move out.

PRIOR: The fuck you are.

JOE: Harper. Please listen. I still love you very much. You're still my best buddy; I'm not going to leave you.

HARPER: No, I don't like the sound of this. I'm leaving.

LOUIS: I'm leaving.

> I already have.

JOE: Please listen. Stay. This is really hard. We have to talk.

HARPER: We are talking. Aren't we. Now please shut up. OK?

PRIOR: Bastard. Sneaking off while I'm flat out here, that's low. If I could get up now I'd beat the holy shit out of you.

JOE: Did you take pills? How many?

HARPER: No pills. Bad for the . . . *(Pats stomach)*

JOE: You aren't pregnant. I called your gynecologist.

HARPER: I'm seeing a new gynecologist.

PRIOR: You have no right to do this.

LOUIS: Oh, that's ridiculous.

PRIOR: No right. It's criminal.

JOE: Forget about that. Just listen. You want the truth. This is the truth.

> I knew this when I married you. I've known this I guess for as long as I've known anything, but . . . I don't know, I thought maybe that with enough effort and will I could change myself . . . but I can't . . .

PRIOR: Criminal.

LOUIS: There oughta be a law.

PRIOR: There is a law. You'll see.

JOE: I'm losing ground here, I go walking, you want to know where I walk, I . . . go to the park, or up and down 53rd Street, or places where . . . And I keep swearing I won't go walking again, but I just can't.

LOUIS: I need some privacy.

PRIOR: That's new.

LOUIS: Everything's new, Prior.

JOE: I try to tighten my heart into a knot, a snarl, I try to learn to live dead, just numb, but then I see someone I want, and it's like a nail, like a hot spike right through my chest, and I know I'm losing.

PRIOR: Apartment too small for three? Louis and Prior comfy but not Louis and Prior and Prior's disease?

LOUIS: Something like that.

　　I won't be judged by you. This isn't a crime, just—the inevitable consequence of people who run out of—whose limitations—

PRIOR: Bang bang bang. The court will come to order.

LOUIS: I mean let's talk practicalities, schedules; I'll come over if you want, spend nights with you when I can, I can—

PRIOR: Has the jury reached a verdict?

LOUIS: I'm doing the best I can.

PRIOR: Pathetic. Who cares?

JOE: My whole life has conspired to bring me to this place, and I can't despise my whole life. I think I believed when I met you I could save you, you at least if not myself, but . . .

　　I don't have any sexual feelings for you, Harper. And I don't think I ever did.

(Little pause.)

HARPER: I think you should go.

JOE: Where?

HARPER: Washington. Doesn't matter.

JOE: What are you talking about?

HARPER: Without me.

　　Without me, Joe. Isn't that what you want to hear?

(Little pause.)

JOE: Yes.

LOUIS: You can love someone and fail them. You can love someone and not be able to—

PRIOR: You *can*, theoretically, yes. A person can, maybe an editorial "you" can love, Louis, but not *you*, specifically you. I don't know, I think you are excluded from that general category.

HARPER: You were going to save me, but the whole time you were spinning a lie. I just don't understand that.

PRIOR: A person could theoretically love and maybe many do but we both know now you can't.

LOUIS: I do.

PRIOR: You can't even say it.

LOUIS: I love you, Prior.

PRIOR: I repeat. Who cares?

HARPER: This is so scary, I want this to stop, to go back.

PRIOR: We have reached a verdict, Your Honor. This man's heart is deficient. He loves, but his love is worth nothing.

JOE: Harper . . .

HARPER: Mr. Lies, I want to get away from here. Far away. Right now. Before he starts talking again. Please, please—

JOE: As long as I've known you Harper you've been afraid of . . . of men hiding under the bed, men hiding under the sofa, men with knives.

PRIOR *(Shattered; almost pleading; trying to reach him)*: I'm dying! You stupid fuck! Do you know what that is! Love! Do you know what love means? We lived together four and a half years, you animal, you idiot.

LOUIS: I have to find some way to save myself.

JOE: Who are these men? I never understood it. Now I know.

HARPER: What?

JOE: It's me.

HARPER: It is?

PRIOR: Get out of my room.

JOE: I'm the man with the knives.

HARPER: You are?

PRIOR: If I could get up now I'd kill you. I would. Go away. Go away or I'll scream.

HARPER: Oh God . . .

JOE: I'm sorry.

HARPER: It is you.

LOUIS: Please don't scream.

PRIOR: Go.

HARPER: I recognize you now.

LOUIS: Please . . .

JOE: Oh. Wait, I . . . Oh!

(He covers his mouth with his hand, gags, and removes his hand, red with blood)

I'm bleeding.

(Prior closes his eyes and screams.)

HARPER: Mr. Lies.

MR. LIES *(Appearing, dressed in Antarctic explorer's apparel)*: Right here.

HARPER: I want to go away. I can't see him anymore.

MR. LIES: Where?

HARPER: Anywhere. Far away.

MR. LIES: Absolutamento.

(Harper and Mr. Lies vanish. Joe looks up, sees that she's gone.)

PRIOR: When I open my eyes you'll be gone.

(Louis leaves.)

JOE: Harper?
PRIOR *(Opening his eyes)*: Huh. It worked.
JOE *(Calling)*: *Harper?*
PRIOR: I hurt all over. I wish I was dead.

Scene 10

The same day, sunset, in front of Hannah's house in Salt Lake City. Hannah and Sister Ella Chapter, a real-estate saleswoman and Hannah Pitt's closest friend—although Hannah is never friendly and Ella is severely intimidated by her.

SISTER ELLA CHAPTER: Look at that view! A view of Heaven. Like the living city of Heaven, isn't it, it just fairly glimmers in the sun.
HANNAH: Glimmers.
SISTER ELLA CHAPTER: Even the stone and brick it just glimmers and glitters like Heaven in the sunshine. Such a nice view you get, perched up on a canyon rim. Some kind of beautiful place.
HANNAH: It's just Salt Lake, and you're selling the house *for* me, not *to* me.
SISTER ELLA CHAPTER: I like to work up an enthusiasm for my properties.
HANNAH: Just get me a good price.
SISTER ELLA CHAPTER: Well, the market's off.
HANNAH: At least fifty.
SISTER ELLA CHAPTER: Forty'd be more like it.
HANNAH: Fifty.

SISTER ELLA CHAPTER: Wish you'd wait a bit.

HANNAH: Well I can't.

SISTER ELLA CHAPTER: Wish you would. You're about the only friend I got.

HANNAH: Oh well now.

SISTER ELLA CHAPTER: Know why I decided to like you? I decided to like you 'cause you're the only unfriendly Mormon I ever met.

HANNAH: Your wig is crooked.

SISTER ELLA CHAPTER: Fix it.

(Hannah straightens Ella's wig.)

SISTER ELLA CHAPTER: New York City. All they got there is tiny rooms.

I always thought: People ought to stay put. That's why I got my license to sell real estate. It's a way of saying: Have a house! Stay put! It's a way of saying traveling's no good. Plus I needed the cash.

(She takes out a pack of cigarettes from her purse, lights one, offers the pack to Hannah.)

HANNAH: Not out here, anyone could come by.

(Ella smokes. Hannah looks out over the ledge.)

HANNAH: There's been days I've stood at this ledge and thought about stepping over.

(This is news to Ella.)

HANNAH: It's a hard place, Salt Lake: baked dry. Abundant energy; not much intelligence. That's a combination that

85

can wear a body out. No harm looking someplace else. I don't need much room.

My sister-in-law Libby thinks there's radon gas in the basement.

SISTER ELLA CHAPTER *(Immediately alarmed)*: Is there gas in the—

HANNAH: Of course not. Libby's a fool.

SISTER ELLA CHAPTER *(Still alarmed)*: 'Cause I'd have to include that in the description.

HANNAH *(Ending it)*: *There's no gas, Ella.*
(*Little pause, then*) Give a puff.

(*Hannah takes a furtive drag of Ella's cigarette. Then she hands the cigarette back to Ella.*)

HANNAH: Put it away now.

(*Ella carefully knocks the ash off the cigarette, extinguishes it and returns it to the pack. Desolate, she looks at Hannah.*)

SISTER ELLA CHAPTER: So I guess it's good-bye.

HANNAH *(Uncomfortable)*: You'll be all right, Ella, I wasn't ever much of a friend.

SISTER ELLA CHAPTER: I'll say something but don't laugh, OK?
(*Tentative, careful*) This is the home of saints, the godliest place on earth, they say, and I think they're right. That mean there's no evil here? No. Evil's everywhere. Sin's everywhere. But this . . . is the spring of sweet water in the desert, the desert flower. Every step a Believer takes away from here is a step fraught with peril. I fear for you, Hannah Pitt, because you are my friend. Stay put. This is the right home of saints.

HANNAH: Latter-day saints.

SISTER ELLA CHAPTER: Only kind left.

HANNAH: But still. Late in the day . . . for saints and everyone. That's all. That's all.

Fifty thousand dollars for the house, Sister Ella Chapter; don't undersell. It's an impressive view.

ACT THREE:

Not-Yet-Conscious, Forward Dawning

December 1985

Scene 1

Late night, several days after the end of Act Two. Prior's bedroom, completely dark. Prior is in bed, having a nightmare. He wakes up, sits up in bed, and switches on a lamp. He looks at his clock. Seated by the table near the bed is a man, fierce and gloomy, dressed in the clothing of a thirteenth-century British farmer/squire, carrying a scythe. Prior is terrified.

PRIOR: Who are you?!
PRIOR 1: My name is Prior Walter.

(Little pause.)

PRIOR: My name is Prior Walter.

PRIOR 1: I know that.

PRIOR: Explain.

PRIOR 1: You're alive. I'm not. We have the same name. What do you want me to explain?

PRIOR: A ghost?

PRIOR 1: An ancestor.

PRIOR: Not *the* Prior Walter? The Bayeux tapestry Prior Walter?

PRIOR 1: His great-great-grandson. The fifth of the name.

PRIOR: I'm the thirty-fourth, I think.

PRIOR 1: Actually the thirty-second.

PRIOR: Not according to Mother.

PRIOR 1 *(Angry!)*: She's including the two bastards, then; I say leave them out. I say no room for bastards! The little things you swallow . . .

(The ghost snatches up a plastic pill bottle from Prior's nightstand.)

PRIOR: Pills.

PRIOR 1: Pills. For the pestilence. *(He struggles to open the bottle but can't get past the safety cap)* I too— *(He throws the bottle aside)*

PRIOR: Pestilence . . . You too what?

PRIOR 1: The pestilence in my time was much worse than now. Whole villages of empty houses. You could look outdoors and see Death walking in the morning, dew dampening the ragged hem of his black robe. Plain as I see you now.

PRIOR: You died of the plague.

PRIOR 1: The spotty monster. Like you, alone.

PRIOR: I'm not alone.

PRIOR 1: You have no wife, no children.

PRIOR: I'm gay.

PRIOR 1: So? Be gay, dance in your altogether for all I care, what's that to do with not having children?

PRIOR: Gay homosexual, not bonny, blithe and—never mind.

PRIOR 1: I had twelve. When I died.

(A second ghost appears, this one dressed in the clothing of an elegant seventeenth-century Londoner.)

PRIOR 1 *(Pointing to the new ghost)*: And I was three years younger than him.

(Prior sees the new ghost and screams!)

PRIOR: Oh God another one.

PRIOR 2: Prior Walter. Prior to you by some seventeen others.

PRIOR 1: He's counting the bastards.

PRIOR: Are we having a convention?

PRIOR 2: We've been sent to declare Her fabulous incipience. They love a well-paved entrance with lots of heralds, and—

PRIOR 1: The messenger come. Prepare the way. The infinite descent, a breath in air—

PRIOR 2: They chose us, I suspect, because of the mortal affinities. In a family as long-descended as the Walters there are bound to be a few carried off by plague.

PRIOR 1: The spotty monster.

PRIOR 2: Black Jack. Came from a water pump, half the city of London, can you imagine? His came from fleas. Yours, I understand, is the lamentable consequence of venery—

PRIOR 1: Fleas on rats, but who knew that?

PRIOR: Am I going to die?

PRIOR 2: We aren't allowed to discuss—

PRIOR 1: When you do, you don't get ancestors to help you through it. You may be surrounded by children but you die alone.

PRIOR: I'm afraid.

PRIOR 1 *(Grim)*: You should be. There aren't even torches, and the path's rocky, dark and steep.

PRIOR 2: Don't alarm him. There's good news before there's bad.

  We two come to strew rose petal and palm leaf before the triumphal procession. Prophet. Seer. Revelator. It's a great honor for the family.

PRIOR 1: He hasn't got a family.

PRIOR 2: I meant for the Walters, for the family in the larger sense.

PRIOR *(Singing)*:

  All I want is a room somewhere,
  Far away from the cold night air—

PRIOR 2 *(Putting a hand on Prior's forehead)*: Calm, calm, this is no brain fever . . .

(Prior keeps his eyes closed. The lights begin to change. Distant Glorious Music.)

PRIOR 1 *(Low chant)*: Adonai, Adonai,
  Olam ha-yichud,
  Zefirot, Zazahot,
  Ha-adam, ha-gadol
  Daughter of Light,
  Daughter of Splendors,
  Fluor! Phosphor!
  Lumen! Candle!

PRIOR 2 (*Simultaneously, louder than Prior 1*): Even now,
    From the mirror-bright halls of Heaven,
    Across the cold and lifeless infinity of space,
    The Messenger comes
    Trailing orbs of light,
    Fabulous, incipient,
    Oh Prophet,
    To you!
PRIOR 1 AND PRIOR 2: Prepare, prepare,
    The Infinite Descent,
    A breath, a feather,
    Glory to—

(They vanish.)

Scene 2

The next day. Split scene: Prior in an exam room in an outpatient clinic at the hospital; he's seated on a stool, hooked up to a pent-amidine IV drip. Louis and Belize facing one another at a table in a coffee shop. Louis, responding to something Belize has said, is pursuing an idea as he always does, by thinking aloud.

LOUIS: Why has democracy succeeded in America? Of course by succeeded I mean comparatively, not literally, not in the present, but what makes for the prospect of some sort of radical democracy spreading outward and growing up? Why does the power that was once so carefully preserved at the top of the pyramid by the original framers of the Constitution seem drawn inexorably downward and outward in spite of the best effort of the Right to stop this? I mean it's the really hard thing about being Left in this country, the American Left can't help but trip over all these petrified little fetishes: freedom, that's the worst; you know, *Jeane Kirkpatrick* for God's sake will go on and on about freedom and so what does that mean, the word "freedom," when she talks about it, or human rights; you have Bush talking about human rights, and so what are these people talking about, they might as well be talking about the mating habits of Venusians, these people don't begin to know what, ontologically, freedom is or human rights, like they see these bourgeois property-based Rights-of-Man-type rights but that's not enfranchisement, not democracy, not what's implicit, what's potential within the idea, not the idea with blood in it. That's just liberalism, the worst kind of liberalism, really, bourgeois tolerance, and what I think is that what AIDS shows us is the limits of tolerance, that it's not enough to be tolerated, because when the shit hits the fan you find out how much tolerance is worth. Nothing. And underneath all the tolerance is intense, passionate hatred.

BELIZE: Uh-huh.

LOUIS: Well don't you think that's true?

BELIZE: Uh-huh. It is.

LOUIS: *Power* is the object, not being tolerated. Fuck assimilation. But I mean in spite of all this the thing about America, I think, is that ultimately we're different from every other nation on earth, in that, with people here of every race, we can't— Ultimately what defines us isn't race, but politics. Not like any European country where there's an insurmountable fact of a kind of racial, or ethnic, monopoly, or monolith, like all Dutchmen, I mean Dutch people, are well, Dutch, and the Jews of Europe were never Europeans, just a small problem. Facing the monolith. But here there are so many small problems, it's really just a collection of small problems, the monolith is missing. Oh, I mean, of course I suppose there's the monolith of White America. White Straight Male America.

BELIZE: Which is not unimpressive, even among monoliths.

LOUIS: Well, no, but when the race thing gets taken care of— and I don't mean to minimalize how major it is, I mean I know it is, this is a really, really incredibly racist country but it's like, well, the British. I mean, all these blue-eyed pink people. And it's just weird, you know, I mean I'm not all that Jewish-looking, or . . . well, maybe I am but, you know, in New York, everyone is . . . well, not everyone, but so many are but so but in England, in London I walk into bars and I feel like Sid the Yid, you know I mean like Woody Allen in *Annie Hall*, with the payess and the gabardine coat, like never, never anywhere so much—I mean, not actively despised, not like they're Germans, who I think are still terribly anti-Semitic, and racist too, I mean black-racist, they pretend otherwise but, anyway, in London, there's just— And at one point I met this black gay guy from Jamaica who talked with a lilt but he said his family'd been living in London since before the Civil War—the American one—and how the English never let him forget for a minute that he wasn't blue-eyed and pink and I said yeah, me too, these people are anti-Semites and he said yeah but the British Jews have the clothing business all sewed up and blacks there can't get a foothold. And it was an incredibly awkward moment of just . . . I mean here we were, in this bar that was gay but it was a *pub*, you know, the beams and the plaster and those horrible little, like, two-day-old fish-

and-egg sandwiches—and just so British, so *old*, and I felt, well, there's no way out of this because both of us are, right now, too much immersed in this history, hope is dissolved in the sheer age of this place, where race is what counts and there's no real hope of change. It's the racial destiny of the Brits that matters to them, not their political destiny, whereas in America—

BELIZE: Here in America race doesn't count.

LOUIS: No, no, that's not—I mean you *can't* be hearing that.

BELIZE: I—

LOUIS: It's— Look, race, yes, but ultimately race here is a political question, right? Racists just try to use race here as a tool in a political struggle. It's not really about race. Like the spiritualists try to use that stuff, are you enlightened, are you centered, channeled, whatever, this reaching out for a spiritual past in a country where no indigenous spirits exist—only the Indians, I mean Native American spirits and we killed them off so now, there are no gods here, no ghosts and spirits in America, there are no angels in America, no spiritual past, no racial past, there's only the political, and the decoys and the ploys to maneuver around the inescapable battle of politics, the shifting downwards and outwards of political power to the people—

BELIZE: POWER to the People! AMEN! *(Looking at his watch) OH MY GOODNESS!* Will you look at the time, I gotta—

LOUIS: Do you— You think this is, what, racist or naive or something?

BELIZE: Well it's certainly *something*. Look, I just remembered I have an appointment—

LOUIS: What? I mean I really don't want to, like, speak from some position of privilege and—

BELIZE: I'm sitting here, thinking, eventually he's *got* to run out of steam, so I let you rattle on and on saying about maybe seven or eight things I find really offensive—

LOUIS: What?

BELIZE: But I know you, Louis, and I know the guilt fueling this peculiar tirade is obviously already swollen bigger than your hemorrhoids—

LOUIS: I don't have hemorrhoids.

BELIZE: I hear different. May I finish?

LOUIS: Yes, but I don't have hemorrhoids.

BELIZE: So finally, when I—

LOUIS: Prior told you— He's an asshole, he shouldn't have—

BELIZE: You promised, Louis. Prior is not a subject.

LOUIS: You brought him up.

BELIZE: I brought up hemorrhoids.

LOUIS: So it's indirect. Passive-aggressive.

BELIZE: Unlike, I suppose, banging me over the head with your theory that America doesn't have a race problem.

LOUIS: Oh be fair I never said that.

BELIZE: Not exactly, but—

LOUIS: I said—

BELIZE: —but it was close enough, because if it'd been that blunt I'd've just walked out and—

LOUIS: You deliberately misinterpreted! I—

BELIZE: Stop interrupting! I haven't been able to—

LOUIS: Just let me—

BELIZE: NO! What, talk? You've been running your mouth nonstop since I got here, yaddadda yaddadda blah blah blah, up the hill, down the hill, playing with your MONOLITH— *(Continue below:)*

LOUIS: Well, you could have joined in at any time instead of—

BELIZE *(Continuous from above)*: —and, girlfriend, it is truly an *awesome* spectacle but I got better things to do with my time than sit here listening to this racist bullshit just because I feel sorry for you that—

LOUIS: I am not a racist!

BELIZE: Oh come on!

LOUIS: So maybe I am a racist but—

BELIZE: Oh I really hate that! It's no fun picking on you Louis; you're so guilty, it's like throwing darts at a glob of jello, there's no satisfying hits, just quivering, the darts just blop in and vanish.

LOUIS: I just think when you are discussing lines of oppression it gets very complicated and—

BELIZE: Oh is that a fact? You know, we black drag queens have a rather intimate knowledge of the complexity of the lines of—

LOUIS: *Ex*-black drag queen.

BELIZE: Actually ex-ex.

LOUIS: You're doing drag again?

BELIZE: I don't— Maybe. I don't have to tell you. *Maybe.*

LOUIS: I think it's sexist.

BELIZE: I didn't ask you.

LOUIS: Well it is. The gay community, I think, has to adopt the same attitude towards drag as black women have to take towards black women blues singers.

BELIZE: Oh my we *are* walking dangerous tonight . . .

LOUIS: Well, it's all internalized oppression, right, I mean the masochism, the stereotypes, the—

BELIZE: Louis, are you deliberately trying to make me hate you?

LOUIS: No, I—

BELIZE: I mean, are you deliberately transforming yourself into an arrogant, sexual-political Stalinist-slash-racist flag-waving thug for my benefit?

(Pause.)

LOUIS: You know what I think?

BELIZE: What?

LOUIS: You hate me because I'm a Jew.

BELIZE: I'm leaving.

LOUIS: It's true.

BELIZE: You have no basis except your—

Louis, it's good to know you haven't changed; you are still an honorary citizen of the *Twilight Zone*, and after your pale, pale white polemics on behalf of racial insensitivity you have a flaming *fuck* of a lot of nerve calling me an anti-Semite. Now I really gotta go.

LOUIS: You called me Lou the Jew.

BELIZE: That was a joke.

LOUIS: I didn't think it was funny. It was hostile.

BELIZE: It was three years ago.

LOUIS: So?

BELIZE: You just called yourself Sid the Yid.

LOUIS: That's not the same thing.

BELIZE: Sid the Yid is different from Lou the Jew.

LOUIS: Yes.

BELIZE: Some day you'll have to explain that to me, but right now—

You hate me because you hate black people.

LOUIS: I do not. But I do think most black people are anti-Semitic.

BELIZE: "Most black people." *That's* racist, Louis, and *I* think most Jews—

LOUIS: Louis Farrakhan.

BELIZE: Ed Koch.

LOUIS: Jesse Jackson.

BELIZE: Jackson. Oh really, Louis, this is—

LOUIS: Hymietown! Hymietown!

BELIZE: Louis, you voted for Jesse Jackson! You send checks to the Rainbow Coalition!

LOUIS: I'm ambivalent. The checks bounced.

BELIZE: All your checks bounce, Louis; you're ambivalent about everything.

LOUIS: What's that supposed to mean?

BELIZE: You may be dumber than shit but I refuse to believe you can't figure it out. Try.

LOUIS: I was never ambivalent about Prior. I love him. I do. I really do.

BELIZE: Nobody said different.

LOUIS: Love and ambivalence are . . . Real love isn't ambivalent.

BELIZE: "Real love isn't ambivalent." I'd swear that's a line from my favorite bestselling paperback novel, *In Love with the Night Mysterious*, except I don't think you ever read it.

(Little pause.)

LOUIS: I never read it, no.

BELIZE: You ought to. Instead of spending the rest of your life trying to get through *Democracy in America*. It's about this white woman whose daddy owns a plantation in the Deep South in the years before the Civil War—the American one—and her name is Margaret, and she's in love with her daddy's number-one slave, and his name is Thaddeus, and she's married but her white slave-owner husband has AIDS: Antebellum Insufficiently Developed Sexorgans. And there's a lot of hot stuff going down when Margaret and Thaddeus can catch a spare torrid ten under the cotton-picking moon, and then of course the Yankees come, and they set the slaves free, and the slaves string up old daddy, and so on. Historical fiction. Somewhere in there I recall Margaret and Thaddeus find the time to discuss the nature of love. Her face is reflecting the flames of the burning plantation—you know, the way white people do—and his black face is dark in the night; and she says to him, "Thaddeus, real love isn't ever ambivalent."

(In the outpatient clinic, Emily enters, wearing latex gloves. She turns off Prior's IV drip.)

BELIZE: Thaddeus looks at her; he's contemplating her thesis; and he isn't sure he agrees.

(Emily removes the drip needle from Prior's arm and bandages the puncture wound.)

EMILY: Treatment number . . . *(Consulting chart)* four.
PRIOR: Pharmaceutical miracle. Lazarus breathes again.
LOUIS: Is he . . . How bad is he?
BELIZE: You want the laundry list?
EMILY: Shirt off, let's check the . . .

(Prior takes off his shirt. Emily examines his lesions.)

BELIZE: There's the weight problem and the shit problem and the morale problem.
EMILY: Only six. That's good. Pants.

(Prior removes his pants and underwear. He's naked. She examines his crotch, then he turns around and she examines his butt, looking for new lesions.)

BELIZE: And. He thinks he's going crazy.

(Prior puts his underwear back on.)

EMILY: Looking good. What else?

PRIOR: Ankles sore and swollen, but the leg's better. The nausea's mostly gone with the little orange pills. BM's pure liquid but not bloody anymore, for now, my eye doctor says everything's OK, for now, my dentist says, "Yuck!" when he sees my fuzzy tongue, and now he wears little condoms on his thumb and forefinger. And a mask. So what? My dermatologist is in Hawaii and my mother . . . well leave my mother out of it. Which is usually where my mother is, out of it. My glands are like walnuts, my weight's holding steady for week two, and a friend died two days ago of bird tuberculosis; bird tuberculosis; that scared me and I didn't go to the funeral today because he was an Irish Catholic and it's probably open casket and I'm afraid of . . . something, the bird TB or seeing him or . . . So I guess I'm doing OK. Except for of course I'm going nuts.

EMILY: We ran the toxoplasmosis series and there's no indication—

PRIOR: I know, I know, but I feel like something terrifying is on its way, you know, like a missile from outer space, and it's plummeting down towards the earth, and I'm ground zero, and . . . I am generally known where I am known as one cool, collected queen. And I am ruffled.

EMILY: There's really nothing to worry about. I think that shochen bamromim hamtzeh menucho nechono al kanfey haschino.

PRIOR: What?

EMILY: Everything's fine. Bemaalos k'doshim ut'horim kezohar horokeea mazhirim.

PRIOR: Oh I don't understand what you're—

EMILY: Es nishmas Prior sheholoch leolomoh, baavur shenod-voo z'dokoh b'ad hazkoras nishmosoh—

PRIOR: WHY ARE YOU DOING THAT! Stop it! Stop it!

EMILY *(Shocked)*: Stop what?

PRIOR: You were just— Weren't you just speaking in Hebrew or something.

EMILY: *Hebrew? (Laughs)* I'm basically Italian-American. No. I didn't speak in Hebrew.

PRIOR: Oh no, oh God please I really think I—

EMILY: Look, I'm sorry, I have a waiting room full of—

(Prior starts dressing, frantic, terrified.)

EMILY: I think you're one of the lucky ones, you'll live for years, probably—you're pretty healthy for someone with no immune system. Are you seeing someone? Loneliness is a danger. A therapist?

PRIOR: No, I don't need to see anyone, I just—

EMILY: Well think about it. You aren't going crazy. You're just under a lot of stress. No wonder. *(She starts to write in his chart)*

(Suddenly there is an astonishing blaze of light and a menacing subterranean rumble; then, a huge chord is sounded by a gigantic choir, and a great book with steel pages mounted atop a molten-red pillar bursts through the floor! In rapid succession: The book flies open! Instantly a large Aleph, inscribed on the right-hand page, glows red and bursts into flames, whereupon the book immediately slams shut, and with the molten-red pillar it disappears in an eye blink under the floor, as the lights restore to reveal the floor perfectly unmarred, not a trace of its having been torn asunder. All of this occurs in

under thirty seconds! Emily, making notes in Prior's file, has noticed none of this. Prior is agog.)

EMILY *(Laughing, exiting)*: Hebrew . . .

(Prior is paralyzed with fear. Then, partly undressed, he flees.)

LOUIS: Help me.

BELIZE: I beg your pardon?

LOUIS: You're a nurse, give me something, I . . . don't know what to do anymore, I . . . Last week at work I screwed up the Xerox machine like permanently and so I . . . Then I tripped on the subway steps and my glasses broke and I cut my forehead, here, see? And now I can't see much and my forehead—it's like the Mark of Cain, stupid, right, but it won't heal and every morning I see it and I think, Mark of Cain, Biblical things, people who . . . in betraying what they love betray what's truest in themselves, I feel . . . nothing but cold for myself, just cold. And every night I miss him, I miss him so much but then . . . those sores, and the smell and . . . where I thought it was going. I could be . . . I could be sick, too, maybe I'm sick, too. I don't know.

Belize. Tell him I love him. Can you do that?

BELIZE *(Tough, cold)*: I've thought about it for a very long time, and I still don't understand what love is. Justice is simple. Democracy is simple. Those things are unambivalent. But love is very hard. And it goes bad for you if you violate the hard law of love.

LOUIS: I'm dying.

BELIZE: *He's* dying. You just wish you were.

Oh cheer up, Louis. Look at that heavy sky out there.

LOUIS: Purple.

BELIZE: *Purple?* Boy, what kind of a homosexual are you, anyway? That's not purple, Mary, that color up there is *(Very grand)* mauve.

    All day today it's felt like Thanksgiving. Soon, this . . . ruination will be blanketed white. You can smell it— can you smell it?

LOUIS: Smell what?

BELIZE: Softness, compliance, forgiveness, grace.

LOUIS: No . . .

BELIZE: I can't help you learn that. I can't help you, Louis. You're not my business. *(He exits)*

(Louis puts his head in his hands, inadvertently touching his cut forehead.)

LOUIS: Ow FUCK! *(He stands slowly, looks toward where Belize exited)* Smell what?

    (He looks both ways to be sure no one is watching, then inhales deeply, and is surprised) Huh. Snow.

Scene 3

Harper in a very white, cold place, with a brilliant blue sky above; a delicate snowfall. She is dressed in a beautiful snowsuit. The sound of the sea, faint.

HARPER: Snow! Ice! Mountains of ice! Where am I? I . . . I feel better, I do, I . . . feel better. There are ice crystals in my lungs, wonderful and sharp. And the snow smells like cold, crushed peaches. And there's something . . .

some current of blood in the wind, how strange, it has that iron taste.

(Mr. Lies appears, also in splendid snowgear; his is emblazoned on the back with the IOTA logo.)

MR. LIES: Ozone.

HARPER: Ozone! Wow! Where am I?

MR. LIES: The Kingdom of Ice, the bottommost part of the world.

HARPER *(Looking around, then realizing)*: Antarctica. This is Antarctica!

MR. LIES: Cold shelter for the shattered. No sorrow here, tears freeze.

HARPER: Antarctica, Antarctica, oh boy oh boy, LOOK at this, I— Wow, I must've really snapped the tether, huh?

MR. LIES: Apparently . . .

HARPER: That's great. I want to stay here forever. Set up camp. Build things. Build a city, an enormous city made up of frontier forts, dark wood and green roofs and high gates made of pointed logs and bonfires burning on every street corner. I should build by a river. Where are the forests?

MR. LIES: No timber here. Too cold. Ice, no trees.

HARPER: Oh details! I'm sick of details! I'll plant them and grow them. I'll live off caribou fat, I'll melt it over the bonfires and drink it from long, curved goat-horn cups. It'll be great. I want to make a new world here. So that I never have to go home again.

MR. LIES: As long as it lasts. Ice has a way of melting.

HARPER: No. Forever. I can have anything I want here— maybe even companionship, someone who has . . . desire for me.

You, maybe.

MR. LIES: It's against the by-laws of the International Order of Travel Agents to get involved with clients. Rules are rules. Anyway, I'm not the one you really want.

HARPER: There isn't anyone . . . Maybe an Eskimo. Who could ice-fish for food. And help me build a nest for when the baby comes.

MR. LIES: There are no Eskimo in Antarctica. And you're not really pregnant. You made that up.

HARPER: Well all of this is made up. So if the snow feels cold I'm pregnant. Right? Here, I can be pregnant. And I can have any kind of a baby I want.

MR. LIES: This is a retreat, a vacuum, its virtue is that it lacks everything; deep-freeze for feelings. You can be numb and safe here, that's what you came for. Respect the delicate ecology of your delusions.

HARPER: You mean like no Eskimo in Antarctica.

MR. LIES: Correcto. Ice and snow, no Eskimo. Even hallucinations have laws.

HARPER: Well then who's that?

(The Eskimo appears.)

MR. LIES: An Eskimo.

HARPER: An Antarctic Eskimo. A fisher of the polar deep.

MR. LIES: There's something wrong with this picture.

(The Eskimo beckons.)

HARPER: I'm going to like this place. It's my own *National Geographic* Special! Oh! Oh! *(She holds her stomach)* I think . . . I think I felt her kicking. Maybe I'll give birth to a baby covered with thick white fur, and that way she won't be cold. My breasts will be full of hot cocoa so she doesn't get chilly. And if it gets really cold, she'll have a pouch I can crawl into. Like a marsupial. We'll mend together. That's what we'll do; we'll mend.

Scene 4

Same day as Scene 2. Snowfall. An abandoned lot in the South Bronx. Trash around. A Homeless Woman is standing near an oil drum in which a fire is burning; she's sipping soup from a cloudy plastic container.

Hannah enters, frightened, angry and cold, dragging two heavy suitcases.

HANNAH: Excuse me? I said excuse me? Can you tell me where I am? Is this Brooklyn? Do you know a Pineapple Street? Is there some sort of bus or train or . . . ?

(The Homeless Woman looks at Hannah but doesn't respond. Hannah continues, trying to get through to her.)

HANNAH: I'm lost, I just arrived from Salt Lake. City. Utah?

(The Homeless Woman sips some soup. Hannah tries again.)

HANNAH: I took the bus that I was told to take and I got off—Well it was the very last stop, so I had to get off, and I *asked* the driver was this Brooklyn, and he nodded yes but he was from one of those foreign countries where they think it's good manners to nod at everything even if you have no idea what it is you're nodding at, and in truth I think he spoke no English at all, which I think would make him ineligible for employment on public transportation. The public being English-speaking, mostly. Do you speak English?

(The Homeless Woman nods. Hannah, realizing that the woman is crazy, looks around; seeing no one else in the desolate vicinity, she forges ahead.)

HANNAH: I was supposed to be met at the airport by my son. He didn't show and I don't wait more than three and three-quarters hours for *anyone*. I should have been patient, I guess, I . . . Is this—

HOMELESS WOMAN: Bronx.

HANNAH: Is that—The *Bronx*? Well how in the name of Heaven did I get to the Bronx when the bus driver said—

(The Homeless Woman turns to the empty air beside her and begins to berate it.)

HOMELESS WOMAN: Slurp slurp slurp will you STOP that disgusting slurping! YOU DISGUSTING SLURPING FEEDING ANIMAL! Feeding yourself, just feeding yourself, what would it matter, to you or to ANYONE, if you just stopped. Feeding. And DIED?

(Pause.)

HANNAH: Can you just tell me where I—

HOMELESS WOMAN *(To Hannah)*: Why was the Kosciuszko Bridge named after a Polack?

HANNAH: I don't know what you're—

HOMELESS WOMAN: That was a joke.

HANNAH: Well what's the punchline?

HOMELESS WOMAN: I don't know.

HANNAH (*Looking around desperately*): Oh for pete's sake, is there anyone else who—

(*The Homeless Woman turns again to the person she's hallucinating:*)

HOMELESS WOMAN: Stand further off you fat loathsome whore! You can't have any more of this soup, slurp slurp slurp you animal, and the—I know you'll just go pee it all away and where will you do that? Behind what bush? It's FUCKING COLD out here and I—

Oh that's right, because it was supposed to have been a tunnel!

That's not very funny.

Have you read the prophecies of Nostradamus?

HANNAH: Who?

HOMELESS WOMAN: Some guy I went out with once somewhere, Nostradamus. Prophet, outcast, eyes like— Scary shit, he—

HANNAH: *Shut up.* Please! (*Taking a step closer to the Homeless Woman*) Now I want you to stop jabbering for a minute and pull your wits together and tell me how to get to Brooklyn. Because you know! And you are going to tell me! Because there is no one else around to tell me and I am wet and cold and I am very angry! So I am sorry you're psychotic but just make the effort. (*Another step closer*) Take a deep breath. DO IT!

(*Hannah and the Homeless Woman breathe together.*)

HANNAH: That's good. Now exhale.

(*They do.*)

HANNAH: Good. Now how do I get to Brooklyn?

HOMELESS WOMAN: Don't know. Never been. Sorry. Want some soup?

HANNAH: Manhattan? Maybe you know . . . *(Giving up: hopelessly)* I don't suppose you know the location of the Mormon Visitors'—

HOMELESS WOMAN: 65th and Broadway.

HANNAH: How do you—

HOMELESS WOMAN: Go there all the time. Free movies. Boring, but you can stay all day.

HANNAH: Well . . . So how do I—

HOMELESS WOMAN: Take the D train. Next block make a right.

HANNAH: Thank you.

(Hannah hoists her suitcases and starts to leave.)

HOMELESS WOMAN: Oh yeah.
   In the new century I think we will all be insane.

Scene 5

Same day. Joe and Roy in the living room of Roy's brownstone. Joe has just come in and is still in his coat. Roy wears an elegant bathrobe.

JOE: I can't. The answer's no. I'm sorry.

ROY: Oh, well, apologies.
   I can't see that there's anyone asking for apologies.

(Pause.)

JOE: I'm sorry, Roy.

ROY: Oh, well, apologies.

JOE: My wife is missing, Roy. My mother's coming from Salt Lake to . . . to help look, I guess. I'm supposed to be at the airport now, picking her up but . . . I just spent two days in a hospital, Roy, with a bleeding ulcer, I was spitting up blood.

ROY: Blood, huh? Look, I'm very busy here and—

JOE: It's just a job.

ROY: A job? A *job*? *Washington!* Dumb Utah Mormon hick shit!

JOE: Roy—

ROY: *WASHINGTON!* When Washington called me I was younger than you, you think I said, "Aw fuck no I can't go I got two fingers up my asshole and a little moral nosebleed to boot!" When Washington calls you my pretty young punk friend you go or you can go fuck yourself sideways 'cause the train has pulled out of the station, and you are *out*, nowhere, out in the cold. Fuck you, Mary Jane, get outta here.

JOE: Just let me—

ROY: Explain? Ephemera. You broke my heart. Explain that. Explain that.

JOE: I love you. Roy.

There's so much that I want, to be . . . what you see in me, I want to be a participant in the world, in your world, Roy, I want to be capable of that, I've tried, really I have but . . . I can't do this. Not because I don't believe in you, but because I believe in you so much, in what you stand for, at heart, the order, the decency. I would give anything to protect you, but . . . There are laws I can't break. It's too ingrained. It's not me. There's enough damage I've already done.

Maybe you were right, maybe I'm dead.

ROY: You're not dead, boy, you're a sissy.

You love me; that's moving, I'm moved. It's nice to be loved. I warned you about her, didn't I, Joe? But you don't listen to me, why, because you say Roy is smart and Roy's a friend but Roy . . . well, he isn't nice, and you wanna be nice. Right? A nice, nice man!

(Little pause)

You know what my greatest accomplishment was, Joe, in my life, what I am able to look back on and be proudest of? And I have helped make presidents and unmake them and mayors and more goddamn judges than anyone in NYC ever—AND several million dollars, tax-free— and what do you think means the most to me?

You ever hear of Ethel Rosenberg? Huh, Joe, huh?

JOE: Well, yeah, I guess I . . . Yes.

ROY: Yes. Yes. You have heard of Ethel Rosenberg. Yes. Maybe you even read about her in the history books.

If it wasn't for me, Joe, Ethel Rosenberg would be alive today, writing some personal-advice column for *Ms.* magazine. She isn't. Because during the trial, Joe, I was on the phone every day, talking with the judge—

JOE: Roy—

ROY: Every day, doing what I do best, talking on the telephone, making sure that timid Yid nebbish on the bench did his duty to America, to history. That sweet unprepossessing woman, two kids, boo-hoo-hoo, reminded us all of our little Jewish mamas—she came this close to getting life; I pleaded till I wept to put her in the chair. Me. I did that. I would have fucking pulled the switch if they'd have let me. Why? Because I fucking hate traitors. Because I fucking hate communists. Was it legal? Fuck legal. Am I a nice man? Fuck nice. They say terrible things about me in the *Nation.* Fuck the *Nation.* You want to be Nice, or you want to be Effective? Make the law, or subject to it. Choose. Your wife chose. A week from today, she'll be back. SHE knows how to get what SHE wants. Maybe I ought to send *her* to Washington.

JOE: I don't believe you.

ROY: Gospel.

JOE: You can't possibly mean what you're saying. Roy, you were the Assistant United States Attorney on the Rosenberg case, ex-parte communication with the judge during the trial would be . . . censurable, at least, probably conspiracy and . . . in a case that resulted in execution, it's . . .

ROY: What? *(Challenging)* Murder?

(Pause.)

JOE: You're not well is all.

ROY: What do you mean, not well? Who's not well?

(Pause.)

JOE: You said—

ROY: No I didn't. I said what?

JOE: Roy, you have cancer.

ROY: No I don't.

(Pause.)

JOE: You told me you were dying.

ROY: What the fuck are you talking about, Joe? I never said that. I'm in perfect health. There's not a goddamn thing wrong with me.
    (He smiles)
    Shake?

(Joe hesitates. He holds out his hand to Roy. Roy pulls Joe into a close, strong clench.)

ROY: It's OK that you hurt me because I love you, baby Joe. That's why I'm so rough on you.

(Roy releases Joe. Joe backs away a step or two.)

ROY: Prodigal son. The world will wipe its dirty hands all over you.

JOE: It already has, Roy.

ROY: Now go.

(Roy shoves Joe, hard. Joe turns to leave. Roy stops him, turns him around. He smooths the lapels on Joe's coat, tenderly.)

ROY: I'll always be here, waiting for you . . .

(Then with sudden violence, Roy grabs Joe's lapels and pulls him close, shaking him violently.)

ROY: What did you want from me?! What was all this?! What do you want, treacherous ungrateful little—

(Joe grabs Roy by the front of his robe, and propels him across the length of the room, slamming him against a bookcase. Joe holds Roy at arm's length, the other arm ready to hit.)

ROY *(Laughing softly, daring Joe)*: Transgress a little, Joseph.

(Joe releases Roy.)

ROY: There are so many laws; find one you can break.

(Joe hesitates, then turns and hurries out.
Roy doubles over in great pain, which he's been hiding
while Joe was in the room. As he sinks to the floor:)

ROY: Ah, Christ . . .
Andy! Andy! Get in here! Andy!

(The door opens, but it isn't Andy. A small Jewish woman
dressed modestly in a fifties hat and coat enters the room. The
room darkens.)

ROY: Who the fuck are you? The new nurse?

(The figure in the doorway says nothing. She stares at Roy.
A pause. Roy forces himself to stand, then he crosses to her.
He stares at her closely. Then he crosses back to a chair, and
sits heavily.)

ROY: Aw, fuck. Ethel.
ETHEL ROSENBERG *(Her manner is pleasant; her voice is ice-cold)*:
You don't look good, Roy.
ROY: Well, Ethel. I don't feel good.
ETHEL ROSENBERG: But you lost a lot of weight. That suits
you. You were heavy back then. Zaftig, mit hips.
ROY: I haven't been that heavy since 1960. We were all heavier
back then, before the body thing started. Now I look like
a skeleton. They stare.
ETHEL ROSENBERG: The shit's really hit the fan, huh, Roy?

(Roy nods.)

ETHEL ROSENBERG: Well the fun's just started.
ROY: What is this, Ethel, Halloween? You trying to scare me?

(Ethel says nothing.)

ROY: Well you're wasting your time! I'm scarier than you any day of the week! So beat it, Ethel! BOOO! BETTER DEAD THAN RED! Somebody trying to shake me up? HAH HAH! From the throne of God in Heaven to the belly of Hell, you can all fuck yourselves and then go jump in the lake because I'M NOT AFRAID OF YOU OR DEATH OR HELL OR ANYTHING!

ETHEL ROSENBERG: Be seeing you soon, Roy. Julius sends his regards.

ROY: Yeah, well send this to Julius!

(He flips the bird in her direction, stands and moves toward her, intending to slam the door in her face. Halfway across the room he collapses, in terrible abdominal pain.)

ETHEL ROSENBERG: You're a very sick man, Roy.

ROY: Oh God . . . ANDY!

ETHEL ROSENBERG: Hmmm. He doesn't hear you, I guess. We should call the ambulance.
  (She goes to the phone)
  Hah! Buttons! Such things they got now.
  What do I dial, Roy?

(Pause. Roy looks at her, then:)

ROY: 911.

ETHEL ROSENBERG *(Dials the phone)*: It sings!
  (Imitating dial tones) La la la . . .
  Huh.
  Yes, you should please send an ambulance to the home of Mr. Roy Cohn, the famous lawyer.
  Beats me. A pain in his gut. Bad. A bad pain.
  What's the address, Roy?

ROY *(A beat, then)*: 244 East 87th.

ETHEL ROSENBERG: 244 East 87th Street. No apartment number, he's got the whole building.

My name? *(A beat)* Ethel Greenglass Rosenberg.

(Small smile) Me? No I'm not related to Mr. Cohn. An old friend.

(She hangs up)

They said a minute.

ROY: I have all the time in the world.

ETHEL ROSENBERG: You're immortal.

ROY: I'm immortal. Ethel. *(He wills himself to his feet)*

I have *forced* my way into history. I ain't never gonna die.

ETHEL ROSENBERG: History is about to crack wide open. Millennium approaches.

Scene 6

That night, Prior's bedroom. Prior, in bed, even more frightened than before. Prior 1 stands before him, wearing a weird hat and robes ornamented with strange signs over his coarse farmer's tunic. He carries a long palm-leaf bundle.

PRIOR 1: Tonight's the night! Aren't you excited? Tonight She arrives! Right through the roof! Ha-adam, ha-gadol . . .

PRIOR 2 *(Appearing, similarly attired)*: Lumen! Phosphor! Fluor! Candle! An unending billowing of scarlet and—

(Prior flings off his covers. He's prepared.)

PRIOR: Look. Garlic. A mirror. Holy Water. *(He squirts water at Prior 1 from a small plastic squirt bottle)* A crucifix. FUCK OFF! Get the fuck out of my room! GO!

PRIOR 1 *(Leering a little; to Prior 2)*: Hard as a hickory knob, I'll bet.

PRIOR 2: We all tumesce when they approach. We wax full, like moons.

PRIOR 1 *(A barked command)*: Dance.

PRIOR: Dance?

PRIOR 1: Stand up, damnit, give us your hands, dance!

PRIOR 2: Listen . . .

(A lone oboe begins to play a little dance tune.)

PRIOR 2: Delightful sound. Care to dance?

PRIOR: Please leave me alone, please just let me sleep.

PRIOR 2: Ah, he wants someone familiar. A partner who knows his steps. *(To Prior)* Close your eyes. Imagine . . .

PRIOR: I don't—

PRIOR 2: Hush. Close your eyes.

(Prior does.)

PRIOR 2: Now open them.

(Prior does.
Louis appears. He looks gorgeous. The dance tune transitions into a lovely instrumental version of "Moon River.")

PRIOR: Lou.

LOUIS: Dance with me.

PRIOR: I can't, my leg, it hurts at night.
Are you . . . a ghost, Lou?

LOUIS: No. Just spectral. Lost to my self. Sitting all day on cold park benches. Wishing I could be with you. Dance with me, babe . . .

(Prior stands, gingerly putting weight on his bad leg. He's surprised there's no pain. He walks to Louis.
They begin to dance. The music is beautiful.)

PRIOR 1 *(To Prior 2)*: Hah. Now I see why he's got no children. He's a sodomite.

PRIOR 2: Oh be quiet, you medieval gnome, and let them dance.

PRIOR 1: I'm not interfering, I've done my bit. Hooray, hooray, the messenger's come, now I'm blowing off. I don't like it here.

(Prior 1 vanishes. Prior 2 watches Louis and Prior dance.)

PRIOR 2: The twentieth century. Oh dear, the world has gotten so terribly, terribly old.

(Prior 2 vanishes. Louis and Prior dance.
Louis vanishes.
Prior dances alone, his arms holding empty air, as if not realizing that Louis has gone.
The lights return to normal.
Then suddenly, the sound of the beating of enormous wings.
Prior opens his eyes. The pain in his leg returns.)

Scene 7

Same night, continuous with Scene 6. Split scene: Prior alone in his apartment; Louis alone in the park.
Again, the sound of beating wings.

PRIOR *(Looking up in terror at the ceiling)*: Oh don't come in here don't come in—

(Limping back to his bed. Scared, broken, he calls out)
Louis!
(Summoning defiance) No! My name is Prior Walter,
I am . . . the scion of an ancient line, I am . . . abandoned
I— NO. My name is . . . is . . . *Prior* and I live . . . *here and*
now, and—

(The lights in the room intensify slightly as, to Prior's horror,
an inhuman voice comes out of his mouth:)

PRIOR: —*in the dark, in the dark, the Recording Angel opens its*
hundred eyes and snaps the spine of the Book of Life and—

(Prior clamps his hand over his mouth; the lights return to
normal.)

PRIOR: Hush! Hush! I'm talking nonsense, I—
(Trying to calm himself) No more mad scene, hush,
hush . . .

(Louis is on a bench in Central Park. Joe approaches, stands
at a distance. They stare at each other. Louis stands.)

LOUIS: Do you know the story of Lazarus?
JOE: Lazarus?
LOUIS: Lazarus. I can't remember what happens, exactly.
JOE: I don't . . . Well, he was dead, Lazarus, and Jesus breathed
life into him. He brought him back from death.
LOUIS: Come here often?
JOE: No. Yes. Yes.
LOUIS: Back from the dead. You believe that really happened?
JOE: I don't know anymore what I believe.
LOUIS: This is quite a coincidence. Us meeting.

JOE: I followed you.
> From work. I . . . followed you here.

(Little pause.)

LOUIS: You followed me.
> You probably saw me that day in the washroom and thought: there's a sweet guy, sensitive, cries for friends in trouble.

JOE: Yes.

LOUIS: You thought maybe I'll cry for you.

JOE: Yes.

LOUIS: Well I fooled you. Crocodile tears. *(He touches his heart, shrugs, then harshly)* Nothing.

(Joe reaches tentatively to touch Louis's face. Louis pulls back.)

LOUIS: What are you doing? Don't do that.

(Joe withdraws his hand and takes several steps back, ready to run.)

JOE: Sorry. I'm sorry.

LOUIS: I'm . . . just not— *(Warning him away)* I think, if you touch me, your hand might fall off or something. Worse things have happened to people who have touched me.

JOE: Please.

(Joe walks up to Louis.)

JOE: Oh, boy . . .
> Can I . . .

I . . . want . . . to touch you. Can I please just touch you . . . um, here?

(He puts his hand on one side of Louis's face. He holds it there.)

JOE: I'm going to Hell for doing this.

LOUIS: Big deal. You think it could be any worse than New York City?

(Louis takes Joe's hand away from his face and holds it, then:)

LOUIS: Come on.

JOE: Where?

LOUIS: Home. With me.

JOE: This makes no sense. I mean I don't know you.

LOUIS: Likewise.

JOE: And what you do know about me you don't like.

LOUIS: The Republican stuff?

JOE: Yeah, well for starters.

LOUIS *(Meaning it)*: I don't not like that. I *hate* that.

JOE: So why on earth should we—

(Louis kisses Joe.)

LOUIS: Strange bedfellows. I don't know. I never made it with one of the damned before.

I would really rather not have to spend tonight alone.

JOE: I'm a pretty terrible person, Louis.

LOUIS: Lou.

(Joe steps back from Louis.)

JOE: No, I really really am. I don't think I deserve being loved.

LOUIS *(A nod)*: There? See? We already have a lot in common.

(Louis begins to walk away. He turns, looks back at Joe. Joe follows. They exit.
Prior listens. At first he hears nothing, then all at once, the sound of beating wings again, now frighteningly near. Prior stares up at the ceiling, terrified.)

PRIOR: That sound, that sound, it . . . *What is that*, like birds or something, like a really *big* bird, I'm frightened, I . . . No! No fear, find the anger, find the . . . anger! *(Standing on the bed, fierce, up at the ceiling)* My blood is clean, my brain is fine, I can handle pressure, I am a gay man and I am used to pressure, to trouble, I am tough and strong and . . . Oh. Oh my goodness. I . . . *(He is washed over by an intense sexual feeling)* Ooohhhh . . . I'm hot, I'm . . . so . . . *(He sinks to his knees)* Aw Jeez what is going on here I . . . must have a fever, I—

(The bedside lamp flickers wildly! Prior screams. Then the bed begins to lurch violently back and forth. The room is filled with a deep bass creaking and groaning, like the timbers of a ship under immense stress, coming from the ceiling. The bed stops moving as the creaking and groaning sounds intensify; the bedside lamp glows brighter and brighter as, from the ceiling, there's a fine rain of plaster dust.)

PRIOR: OH! PLEASE, OH PLEASE! Something's coming in here, I'm scared, I don't like this at all, something's approaching and I—

(There is a great blaze of triumphal music, heralding.)

PRIOR: OH!

(Four thunderous chords sound, and with each chord the bedroom is saturated with colored light: first, extraordinary, harsh, cold, pale blue; then, rich, brilliant, warm gold; then, hot, bilious green; and finally, spectacular royal purple. Then there's silence for several beats. Prior stares wildly around the purple-colored room.)

PRIOR *(An awestruck whisper)*: God almighty.
    Very Steven Spielberg.

(A sound, like a plummeting meteor, tears down from very, very far above the earth, hurtling at an incredible velocity toward the bedroom. The light seems to be sucked out of the room as the projectile approaches. Right before the light is completely extinguished, there's a terrifying CRASH as something immense strikes earth. The bedroom shudders and pieces of the ceiling's plaster, lathe and wiring rain down on and around Prior's bed; as the room is plunged into absolute darkness, we hear the whole ceiling give way.

A beat, and then, in a shower of unearthly white light, spreading great opalescent gray-silver wings, the Angel descends through the ceiling into the room and floats above the bed.)

ANGEL: Greetings, Prophet;
    The Great Work begins:
    The Messenger has arrived.

(Blackout.)

END OF PART ONE

Part Two:
PERESTROIKA

First draft completed at the Russian River
April 11, 1991

THE CHARACTERS
IN PERESTROIKA

ROY M. COHN,* a successful New York lawyer and unofficial power broker.

JOSEPH PORTER PITT, chief clerk for Justice Theodore Wilson of the Federal Court of Appeals, Second Circuit.

HARPER AMATY PITT, Joe's wife, an agoraphobic with a mild Valium addiction.

LOUIS IRONSON, a word processor working for the Second Circuit Court of Appeals.

PRIOR WALTER, Louis's boyfriend. Occasionally works as a club designer or caterer, otherwise lives very modestly but with great style off a small trust fund.

HANNAH PORTER PITT, Joe's mother, formerly of Salt Lake City, now in Brooklyn, staying in Harper and Joe's apartment.

BELIZE, a registered nurse and former drag queen whose name was originally Norman Arriaga; Belize is a drag name that stuck.

THE ANGEL, four divine emanations, Fluor, Phosphor, Lumen and Candle; manifest in One: the Continental Principality of America. She has magnificent steel-gray wings.

Other Characters in Perestroika

ALEKSII ANTEDILLUVIANOVICH PRELAPSARIANOV *(pronounced AntedilooviAHNuhvich PrelapsARianohv)*, the World's Oldest Bolshevik, is played by the actor playing Hannah. He should speak with a Russian accent, strong but comprehensible.

MR. LIES, Harper's imaginary friend, a travel agent, played by the actor playing Belize. In style of dress and speech he suggests a jazz musician; he always wears a large lapel badge emblazoned "IOTA" (International Order of Travel Agents).

HENRY, Roy's doctor, played by the actor playing Hannah.

ETHEL ROSENBERG, played by the actor playing Hannah.

The mannequins in the Diorama Room in the Mormon Visitors' Center in Act Three:

> THE FATHER, played by the actor playing Joe.
>
> THE RECORDED VOICE OF CALEB, his son, done by the actor playing Belize.
>
> THE RECORDED VOICE OF ORRIN, his other son, done by the actor playing the Angel.
>
> THE MOTHER, played by the actor playing the Angel.

EMILY, a nurse, played by the actor playing the Angel.

The Continental Principalities, inconceivably powerful Apparatchik/Bureaucrat Aggregate Angelic Entities of whom the Angel of America is a peer:

THE ANGEL EUROPA, played by the actor playing Joe.

THE ANGEL AFRICANII, played by the actor playing Harper.

THE ANGEL OCEANIA, played by the actor playing Belize.

THE ANGEL ASIATICA, played by the actor playing Hannah.

THE ANGEL AUSTRALIA, played by the actor playing Louis.

THE ANGEL ANTARCTICA, played by the actor playing Roy.

The voice at the top of Act One, Scene 1, announcing Prelapsarianov; the recorded greeting in the Mormon Visitors' Center in Act Three, Scene 3; the voice introducing the Council of Principalities in Act Five, Scene 5; and the voice of the BBC reporter in the same scene should be the voice of the actor playing the Angel.

---

* See the footnote in The Characters list of *Millennium Approaches*.

Perestroika *is dedicated to Kimberly T. Flynn*

Because the soul is progressive, it never quite repeats itself, but in every act attempts the production of a new and fairer whole.

—Ralph Waldo Emerson, "On Art"

ACT ONE:

Spooj

December 1985

Scene 1

In the darkness a Voice announces:

A VOICE: In the Hall of Deputies, the Kremlin. December 1985.
Aleksii Antedilluvianovich Prelapsarianov, the World's
Oldest Living Bolshevik.

(*Lights up on Prelapsarianov at a podium before a great red
flag. He is unimaginably old and totally blind.*)

ALEKSII ANTEDILLUVIANOVICH PRELAPSARIANOV: The Great
Question before us is: Are we doomed? The Great Question before us is: Will the Past release us? The Great
Question before us is: Can we Change? In Time? And
we all desire that Change will come.
     (*A little pause, then with sudden, violent passion:*)

And *Theory?* How are we to proceed without *Theory?* What System of Thought have these Reformers to present to this mad swirling planetary disorganization, to the Inevident Welter of fact, event, phenomenon, calamity? Do they have, as we did, a beautiful Theory, as bold, as Grand, as comprehensive a construct? You can't imagine, when we first read the Classic Texts, when in the dark vexed night of our ignorance and terror the seed-words sprouted and shoved incomprehension aside, when the incredible bloody vegetable struggle up and through into Red Blooming gave us Praxis, True Praxis, True Theory married to Actual Life . . . You who live in this Sour Little Age cannot imagine the grandeur of the prospect we gazed upon: like standing atop the highest peak in the mighty Caucasus, and viewing in one all-knowing glance the mountainous, granite order of creation. We were one with the Sidereal Pulse then, in the blood in our heads we heard the tick of the Infinite. You cannot imagine it. I weep for you.

And what have you to offer now, children of this Theory? What have you to offer in its place? *(Blistering contempt)* Market Incentives? American Cheeseburgers? Watered-down Bukharinite stopgap makeshift Capitalism! NEPmen! Pygmy children of a gigantic race!

Change? Yes, we must must change, only show me the Theory, and I will be at the barricades, show me the book of the next Beautiful Theory, and I promise you these blind eyes will see again, just to read it, to devour that text. Show me the words that will reorder the world, or else *keep silent.*

If the snake sheds his skin before a new skin is ready, naked he will be in the world, prey to the forces of chaos.

Without his skin he will be dismantled, lose coherence and die. Have you, my little serpents, a new skin? *(An immense, booming command)* Then we dare not, we *cannot*, we MUST NOT move ahead!

Scene 2

The same night as the end of Millennium Approaches. *Joe and Louis enter Louis's new apartment in the arctic wastes of Alphabetland; barren of furniture, unpainted, messy, grim.*
Tense little pause. Louis embarrassed takes in the room, and begins to gather up the books, newspapers and clothing strewn on the floor, tossing them behind the bed, talking all the while:

LOUIS: Alphabetland. This is where the Jews lived when they first arrived. And now, a hundred years later, the place to which their more seriously fucked-up grandchildren repair. *(Yiddish accent)* This is progress?
(Giving up the housecleaning) It's a terrible mess.
JOE: It's a little dirty.
LOUIS *(Defensive)*: *Messy*, not dirty. That's an important distinction. It's dust, not dirt, chemical-slash-mineral, not organic, not like microbes, more like—
(He walks toward Joe) Can I take your tie off?
JOE *(Stepping back)*: No, wait, I'm, um, um, uncomfortable, actually.
LOUIS: Me, too, actually. Being uncomfortable turns me on.
JOE: Your, uh, boyfriend. He's sick. And I . . .
LOUIS: Very. He's not my boyfriend, we—

We can cap everything that leaks in latex, we can smear our bodies with nonoxynol-9, safe, chemical sex. Messy, but not dirty.

(Little pause)

Look I want to but I don't want to beg.

JOE: No, I—

LOUIS: Oh come on. *Please.*

JOE: I should go.

LOUIS: Fine! Ohblahdee, ohblahdah, life goes on. Rah.

JOE: What?

LOUIS: Hurry home to the missus.

(Points to Joe's left-hand ring finger)

Married gentlemen before cruising the Ramble should first remove their bands of gold.

(Joe stares at his wedding ring.)

LOUIS: Go if you're going. Go.

(Joe starts to leave, hesitates, then turns back; he hesitates again, then goes to Louis and hugs him, awkwardly, collegially.)

JOE: I'm not staying.

LOUIS *(Sniffing)*: What kind of cologne is that?

JOE *(A beat, then)*: Fabergé.

LOUIS: OH! *Very* butch, very heterosexual high school. Fabergé.

(Louis gently breaks the hug, steps back a little.)

LOUIS: You smell nice.

JOE: So do you.

LOUIS: Smell is . . . an incredibly complex and underappreciated physical phenomenon. Inextricably bound up with sex.

JOE: I . . . didn't know that.

LOUIS: It is. The nose is really a sexual organ.
Smelling. Is desiring. We have five senses, but only two that go beyond the boundaries . . . of ourselves. When you look at someone, it's just bouncing light, or when you hear them, it's just sound waves, vibrating air, or touch is just nerve endings tingling. Know what a smell is?

JOE: It's . . . some sort of . . . No.

LOUIS: It's made of the molecules of what you're smelling. Some part of you, where you meet the air, is airborne.

(Louis steps carefully closer to Joe, who still seems ready, though not as ready, to bolt.)

LOUIS: Little molecules of Joe . . . *(Leaning in, inhaling deeply)* Up my nose.
Mmmm . . . Nice. Try it.

JOE: Try . . . ?

LOUIS: Inhale.

(Joe leans toward Louis, inhales.)

LOUIS: Nice?

JOE: Yes.
I should—

LOUIS *(Quietly)*: Sssshhhh.
Smelling. And tasting.
(Moving in closer) First the nose, then the tongue.

JOE *(Taking a half-step back, scared)*: I just don't—

LOUIS *(Stepping forward)*: They work as a team, see. The nose tells the body—the heart, the mind, the fingers the cock—what it wants, and then the tongue explores, finding out what's edible, what isn't, what's most mineral, food for the blood, food for the bones, and therefore most delectable.

(*Louis licks the side of Joe's cheek.*)

LOUIS: Salt.

(*Louis kisses Joe, who holds back a moment and then responds.*)

LOUIS: Mmm. Iron. Clay.

(*Louis slips his hand down the front of Joe's pants, groping him. Joe shudders. Louis pulls his hand out, smells and tastes his fingers, and then holds them for Joe to smell.*)

LOUIS: Chlorine. Copper. Earth.

(*They kiss again.*)

LOUIS: What does that taste like?
JOE: Um . . .
LOUIS: What?
JOE: Well . . . Nighttime.
LOUIS: Stay?
JOE: Yes.

(*They kiss again. Louis starts unbuttoning Joe's shirt.*)

JOE: Louis?
LOUIS: Hmmm?
JOE: What did that mean, ohblahdee ohblah—
LOUIS: Sssssh. Words are the worst things. Breathe. Smell.
JOE: But—
LOUIS: Or if you have to talk, talk dirty.

Scene 3

The same night. The sounds of wind and snow. Mr. Lies sits alone, still in his snowsuit, playing the oboe, in what's left of Harper's imaginary Antarctica, which is now bare, grim and grimy. Mr. Lies stops playing.

MR. LIES: The oboe: official instrument of the International Order of Travel Agents. If the duck was a songbird it would sing like this. Nasal, desolate, the call of migratory things.

(Harper enters dragging a small pine tree which she has felled, its slender stump-end shredded and splintered. The fantasy explorer gear from Act Three, Scene 3, of Millennium *is gone; she is dressed in the hastily assembled outfit in which she fled the apartment at the end of Act Two, Scene 9: a thin pullover, a skirt, torn tights, gloves. She's been outdoors for three days now and looks it—filthy and disheveled. Her previous pioneer determination, stretched thin, has become desperate and angry.)*

HARPER: I'm FREEZING!
MR. LIES *(Pointing to the tree)*: Where did you get that?
HARPER: From the great Antarctic pine forests. Right over that hill.
MR. LIES: There are no pine forests in Antarctica.
HARPER: I chewed this pine tree down. With my teeth. Like a beaver. I'm *hungry*, I haven't eaten in three days! I'm going to use it to build . . . something, maybe a fire.

(She takes a soggy box of matches from under her pullover. She strikes match after match; all dead.
  She gives up, and sits on the tree, heavy with despair.)

HARPER: I don't understand why I'm not dead. When your heart breaks, you should die. But there's still the rest of you. There's your breasts, and your genitals, and they're amazingly stupid, like babies or faithful dogs, they don't get it, they just want him. Want him.

(Joe enters the scene, dressed in his Temple garment, barefoot. He looks around, uncertain of where he is till he sees Harper.)

MR. LIES: The Eskimo is back.
HARPER: I know.
    I wanted a real Eskimo, someone chilly and reliable, not this, this is just . . . some lawyer, just—
JOE: Hey, buddy.
HARPER: Hey.
JOE: I looked for you. I've been everywhere.
HARPER: Well, you found me.
JOE: No, I . . . I'm not looking now. I guess I'm having an adventure.
HARPER: Can I come with you? This isn't working anymore. I'm cold.
JOE: I wouldn't want you to see.
HARPER: Think it's worse than what I imagine? It's not.
JOE: I should go.
HARPER: Bastard. You fell out of love with me.
JOE: That isn't true, Harper.
HARPER: Why did you come here? Leave me alone if you're so goddamned happy.
JOE: You want me here.

(She nods.)

HARPER: To see you again. Any way I can.
OH GOD I WISH YOU WERE— No I don't.
JOE: Please don't.
HARPER: DEAD.
Come back.

(Little pause.)

JOE: Oh, buddy, I wish so much that I could. But how can I?
I can't.

(He vanishes.
Mr. Lies plays the oboe—a brief, wild lament. The magic
Antarctic night fades away, replaced by a harsh sodium light and
the ordinary sounds of the park and the city in the distance.)

MR. LIES: Blues for the death of Heaven.
HARPER *(Shattered, scared)*: No . . .
MR. LIES: I tried to tell you. There are no Eskimo in
Antarctica.
HARPER: No. No trees either.
MR. LIES *(Pointing to the chewed-down pine tree)*: So where did
you get that?
HARPER: From the Botanical Gardens Arboretum. It's right
over there. Prospect Park. We're still in Brooklyn I guess.

(The lights of a police car begin to flash.)

MR. LIES *(Vanishing)*: The Law for real.
HARPER *(Raising her hands over her head)*: Busted. Damn.
What a lousy vacation.

Scene 4

The same night. In the Pitt apartment in Brooklyn. A telephone rings. Hannah, carrying the bags and wearing the coat she had on in Act Three, Scene 4, of Millennium Approaches, *enters the apartment, drops the bags, and runs for the phone.*

HANNAH *(Exhausted, grim)*: Pitt residence.
    No, he's out. This is his mother. No I have no idea where he is. I have no idea. He was supposed to meet me at the airport, but I don't wait more than three and three-quarters—
    I— Yes of course I know her, yes she lives here, what's—
    OH MY LORD! Is she— Wait, Officer, I don't— She did *what*, exactly?
    Why on earth would she chew down a pine tree?
    (Severe) You have no business laughing about it, you can stop that right now. That's ugly.
    Apology accepted.
    I don't know where that is, I just arrived from Salt Lake and I barely found Brooklyn, I had to give the superintendent money to let me into the— I'll take a . . . a taxicab.
    No! No hospital! She's not insane, she's just . . . bewildered, she—I don't see how it's any business of yours what she is.
    Tell her Mother Pitt is coming.

(Hannah hangs up.)

Scene 5

The same night. Prior in his bedroom, alone, asleep in his bed. The room is intact, no trace of the demolished ceiling. Prior is having a nightmare. He wakes up, frightened.

PRIOR: OH! *(He looks around)* Oh.
>*(He looks under the covers. He discovers that the lap of his pajamas is soaked in cum)*
>Will you look at this!
>First goddamn orgasm in months and I slept through it.

(He dials a number on his bedside telephone.
At Belize's workstation on the tenth floor of New York Hospital, a phone rings. Belize, in a colorful version of scrubs [his design and execution], is busy with paperwork.
Prior, while waiting for Belize to answer, grabs a box of Kleenex and, reaching under the covers, blots himself dry.
Belize answers.)

BELIZE: Ten East.
PRIOR: I am drenched in spooj.
BELIZE *(Continuing to work)*: Spooj?
PRIOR: Cum. Jiz. Ejaculate. I've had a wet dream.
BELIZE: Uh-huh, bound to happen, you've been abstemious to excess: Beaucoup de spooj.
PRIOR: It was a woman.
BELIZE *(Stops working)*: A woman.
PRIOR: Not a *conventional* woman.
BELIZE: Grace Jones.

(Prior looks at the ceiling.)

BELIZE: Hello?

PRIOR: An angel.

BELIZE: Oh FABULOUS.

PRIOR: I feel . . . lascivious. Come over.

BELIZE: I spent the whole day with you, I *do* have a life of my own, you know.

PRIOR: I'm sad.

BELIZE: I thought you were lascivious.

PRIOR: Lascivious sad. Wonderful and horrible all at once, like . . . like there's a war inside. My eyes are funny, I . . . *(He touches his eyes)* Oh.
  I'm crying.

BELIZE: Prior?

PRIOR: I'm scared. And also full of, I don't know, Joy or something.

(In the hospital, Henry, Roy's doctor, enters.)

PRIOR: Hope.

HENRY: Are you the duty nurse?

BELIZE *(To Henry)*: Yo.
  (To Prior) Look, baby, I have to go—

PRIOR: Oh no, not yet, I— Sing something first. Sing with me.

BELIZE *(To Prior)*: Wash up and sleep and—

HENRY *(Over the line above)*: Are you the duty nurse?

BELIZE *(To Henry)*: Yo, I said.

HENRY: Then why are you dressed like that?

BELIZE *(To Henry)*: You don't like it?
  (To Prior) I'll call you in the morning when I—

PRIOR: Just one little song. Some hymn?

HENRY: *Nurse. Hang up the fucking*—

BELIZE *(To Henry)*: One moment, *please.* This is an emergency.
(To Prior, singing:)
    Hark the herald angels sing—

(Prior joins in:)

PRIOR AND BELIZE:
    Glory to the newborn king.
    Peace on earth and mercy mild,
    God and sinners reconciled—
HENRY *(Over the last line above)*: What's your name?
PRIOR AND BELIZE *(Belize singing louder)*:
    JOYFUL all ye nations rise,
    Join the triumph of the skies!
    With angelic hosts proclaim:
    Christ is born in Bethlehem!
    Hark the herald angels sing,
    Glory to the newborn king!
BELIZE *(To Prior)*: Call you back. There's a man bothering me.
PRIOR: Je t'aime.

(Belize hangs up. He turns to Henry.)

BELIZE: May I help you?
HENRY: Nurses are supposed to wear white.
BELIZE: Doctors are supposed to be home, in Westchester, asleep.
HENRY: Emergency admit, Room 1013. Here are the charts.

(He hands medical charts to Belize. Belize scans the chart, reads the patient's name, raises his eyebrows, reads a little more. He looks up at Henry.)

HENRY: Start the drip, Gamma G and he'll need a CTM, radiation in the morning so clear diet and— What?

BELIZE: "Liver cancer."

HENRY: Just— Ignore that, just—

BELIZE: Oncology's on six, doll.

HENRY: This is the right floor.

BELIZE: It says liver can—

HENRY *(Lashing out)*: I don't give a *fuck* what it *says. I* said this is the right floor.

BELIZE: Ooooh, testy.

HENRY: He's a very important man.

BELIZE: Then I *shouldn't* fuck up his medication?

HENRY: Think you can manage that? And, maybe, you know, confidentiality, don't share this with your sewing circle.

BELIZE: Safe home.

(Henry leaves.)

BELIZE: Asshole.

(He looks at the chart, shakes his head; after a moment's hesitation he picks up the phone and dials. Prior answers.)

BELIZE: I have some piping hot dish.

PRIOR: How hot can it be at three in the—

BELIZE: Get out your oven mitts. *(Looking around to make sure no one is near, then:)*
    Don't tell anyone, but guess who just checked in with the troubles?
    The Killer Queen Herself. New York's number one closeted queer.

PRIOR: *Koch?*

BELIZE: *No,* not Koch. Better. *(He whispers into the receiver)*

PRIOR: The Lord moves in mysterious ways.

BELIZE: Oh indeed. Indeed She do.

Scene 6

The same night, continuous with Scene 5. Roy in his hospital bed, sick and very scared. Belize enters, putting on latex gloves.

ROY: Get outta here you, I got nothing to say to you.

BELIZE: Just doing my—

ROY: I want a white nurse. My constitutional right.

BELIZE: You're in a hospital, you don't have any constitutional rights.

(Belize begins preparing Roy's right arm for the insertion of an IV drip needle, palpating the vein, disinfecting the skin. He moves to insert the IV needle in Roy's arm.)

ROY *(Nervous)*: Find the vein, you moron, don't start jabbing that goddamned spigot in my arm till you find the fucking vein or I'll sue you so bad they'll repossess your teeth you dim black motherf—

BELIZE *(Had enough; very fierce)*: Watch. Yourself.

You don't talk that way to me when I'm holding something this sharp. Or I might slip and stick it in your heart. If you have a heart.

ROY: Oh I do. Tough little muscle.

BELIZE: I bet.

Now I've been doing drips a long time. I can slip this in so easy you'll think you were born with it. Or I can make it feel like I just hooked you up to a bag of Liquid Drano. So you be nice to me or you're going to be one sorry asshole come morning.

ROY: Nice.

BELIZE: Nice and quiet.

(Belize puts the drip needle, painlessly, in Roy's arm. Roy's impressed, but doesn't show it.)

BELIZE: There.

ROY *(Fierce)*: I *hurt.*

BELIZE: I'll get you a painkiller.

ROY: Will it knock me out?

BELIZE: I sure hope so.

ROY: Then shove it. Pain's . . . nothing, pain's life.

BELIZE: Sing it, baby.

ROY: When they did my facelifts, I made the anesthesiologist use a local. They lifted up my whole face like a dinner napkin and I was wide awake to see it.

BELIZE: Bullshit. No doctor would agree to do that.

ROY: I can get anyone to do anything I want. For instance: Let's be friends. Jews and coloreds, historical liberal coalition, right? My people being the first to sell retail to your people, your people being the first people my people could afford to hire to sweep out the store Saturday mornings, and then we all held hands and rode the bus to Selma. Not me of course, I don't ride buses, I take cabs. But the thing about the American Negro is, he never went Communist. Loser Jews did. But you people had Jesus so the reds never got to you. I admire that.

BELIZE: Your chart didn't mention that you're delusional.

ROY: Barking mad. Sit. Talk.

BELIZE: Mr. Cohn. I'd rather suck the pus out of an abscess. I'd rather drink a subway toilet. I'd rather chew off my tongue and spit it in your leathery face. So thanks for the offer of conversation, but I'd rather not.

(Belize starts to exit, turning off the light as he does.)

ROY: Oh forchristsake. Whatta I gotta do? Beg? I don't want to be alone.

(Belize stops.)

ROY: Oh how I fucking *hate* hospitals, nurses, this waste of time and . . . wasting and weakness, I want to kill the—
     'Course they can't kill this, can they?

(Belize says nothing.)

ROY: No. It's too simple. It knows itself. It's harder to kill something if it knows what it is. Like pubic lice. You ever have pubic lice?
BELIZE: That is none of your—
ROY: I got some kind of super crabs from some kid once, it took twenty drenchings of Kwell and finally shaving to get rid of the little bastards. *Nothing* could kill them. And every time I had to itch I'd smile, because I learned to respect them, these unkillable crabs, because . . . I learned to identify. You know? Determined lowlife. Like me.
     You've seen lots of guys with this.

(Little pause.)

BELIZE: Lots.
ROY: How do I look, comparatively?
BELIZE: I'd say you're in trouble.
ROY: I'm going to die. Soon.
     That was a question.
BELIZE: Probably. Probably so.
ROY: Hah.

I appreciate the . . . the honesty, or whatever . . .

If I live I could sue you for emotional distress, the whole hospital, but . . .

I'm not prejudiced, I'm not a prejudiced man.

(Belize just looks at him.)

ROY: These racist guys, simpletons, I never had any use for them—too rigid. You want to keep your eye on where the most powerful enemy really is. I save my hate for what counts.

BELIZE: Well. And I think that's a good idea, a good thing to do, probably.

(Little pause. Then, with great effort and distaste:)

This didn't come from me and I *don't* like you but let me tell you a thing or two:

They have you down for radiation tomorrow for the sarcoma lesions, and you don't want to let them do that, because radiation will kill the T-cells and you don't have any you can afford to lose. So tell the doctor no thanks for the radiation. He won't want to listen. Persuade him. Or he'll kill you.

ROY: You're just a fucking nurse. Why should I listen to you over my very qualified, very expensive WASP doctor?

BELIZE: He's not queer. I am.

(Belize winks at Roy.)

ROY: Don't wink at me.

You said "a thing or two." So that's one.

BELIZE: I don't know what strings you pulled to get in on the azidothymidine trials.

ROY: I have my little ways.

BELIZE: Uh-huh.

Watch out for the double blind. They'll want you to sign something that says they can give you M&Ms instead of the real drug. You'll die, but they'll get the kind of statistics they can publish in the *New England Journal of Medicine*. And you can't sue 'cause you signed. And if you don't sign, no pills. So if you have any strings left, pull them, because everyone's put through the double blind and with this, time's against you, you can't fuck around with placebos.

ROY: You hate me.

BELIZE: Yes.

ROY: Why are you telling me this?

BELIZE: I wish I knew.

(Pause.)

ROY *(Very nasty)*: You're a butterfingers spook faggot nurse. I think . . . you have little reason to want to help me.

BELIZE: Consider it solidarity. One faggot to another.

(Belize snaps, turns, exits. Roy calls after him:)

ROY: Any more of your lip, boy, and you'll be flipping Big Macs in East Hell before tomorrow night!
(He picks up his bedside phone)
And get me a real phone, with a hold button, I mean look at this, it's just one little line, now how am I supposed to perform basic bodily functions on *this*?
(He lifts the receiver, clicks the hang-up button several times)
Yeah who is this, the operator? Give me an outside line. Well then dial for me. It's a medical emergency,

darling, dial the fucking number or I'll strangle myself with the phone cord.

202-733-8525.

(Little pause)

Martin Heller. Oh hi, Martin. Yeah I know what time it is, I couldn't sleep, I'm busy dying. Listen, Martin, this drug they got me on, azido-methatalo-molamoca-whatchamacallit. Yeah. AZT.

I want my own private stash, Martin. Of serious Honest-Abe medicine. That I control, here in the room with me. No placebos, I'm no good at tests, Martin, I'd rather cheat. So send me my pills with a get-well bouquet, *PRONTO*, or I'll ring up CBS and sing Mike Wallace a song: *(Sotto voce, with relish)* "The Ballad of Adorable Ollie North and His Secret Contra Slush Fund."

(He holds the phone away from his ear; Martin is screaming)

Oh you only *think* you know all I know. *I* don't even know what all I know. Half the time I just make it up, and it *still* turns out to be true! We learned that trick in the fifties. Tomorrow, you two-bit scumsucking shitheel flypaper insignificant dried-out little turd. A nice big box of drugs for Uncle Roy. Or there'll be seven different kinds of hell to pay. *(He slams the receiver down)*

The Anti-
Migratory Epistle

(For Sigrid)

January 1986

Scene 1

*Three weeks after the end of Act One. Prior and Belize stand out-
side a dilapidated funeral parlor on the Lower East Side. They've
just left the funeral of a mutual friend, a major New York City
drag-and-style queen. Belize is in defiantly bright and beautiful clothing. Prior is dressed oddly, a long black coat over black
shirt and pants, and a large, fringed, black scarf draped like a hood
around his head, capped off with black sunglasses; the effect is disconcerting, vaguely suggesting adherence to a severe, albeit elegant,
religious discipline.*

Belize has been deeply moved by the service they've just attended. Prior is closed off in some place as dark as the costume he's wearing.

PRIOR: It was tacky.
BELIZE: It was divine.
He was one of the Great Glitter Queens. He couldn't be buried like a *civilian*. Trailing sequins and incense he came into the world, trailing sequins and incense he departed it. And good for him!
PRIOR: I thought the twenty professional Sicilian mourners were a bit much.
A great queen; big fucking deal. That ludicrous spectacle in there, just a parody of the funeral of someone who *really* counted. We don't; faggots; we're just a bad dream the real world is having, and the real world's waking up. And he's *dead*.

(Little pause.)

BELIZE *(Concerned, irritated)*: Lately, sugar, you have gotten very strange. Lighten up already.
PRIOR: Oh I *apologize*, it was only a for-God's-sake funeral, a cause for fucking *celebration*, sorry if I can't join in with the rest of you death-junkies, gloating about your survival in the face of that . . . of his ugly demise because unlike you I have nothing to gloat about. Never mind.

(Angry little pause.)

BELIZE: And you *look* like Morticia Addams.
PRIOR: Like the Wrath of God.
BELIZE: Yes.

PRIOR: That is the intended effect.

My eyes are fucked-up.

BELIZE: Fucked-up how?

PRIOR: Everything's . . . closing in. Weirdness on the periphery.

BELIZE: Since when?

PRIOR: For three weeks. Since the night when— *(He stops himself)*

BELIZE: Well what does the eye doctor say?

PRIOR: I haven't been.

BELIZE: Oh for God's sake. *Why?*

PRIOR: I was improving. Before.

Remember my wet dream.

BELIZE: The angel?

PRIOR: It wasn't a dream.

BELIZE: 'Course it was.

PRIOR: No. I don't think so. I think it really happened.

I'm a prophet.

BELIZE: Say what?

PRIOR: I've been given a prophecy. A Book. Not a *physical* book, or there was one but They took it back, but somehow there's still this Book. In me. A prophecy. It . . . really happened, I'm—almost completely sure of it.

(He looks at Belize)

Oh stop looking so . . .

BELIZE: You're scaring me.

PRIOR: It was after Louis left me. Every night I'd been having these horrible vivid dreams. And then . . .

(Little pause.)

BELIZE: Then . . . ?

PRIOR: And then She arrived.

Scene 2

Three weeks earlier. The Angel and Prior in Prior's bedroom. The wrecked ceiling, Prior in bed, the Angel in the air.

As the scene shifts, Prior changes out of his prophet garb and into his pajamas onstage. He does this quietly, deliberately, forcing himself back into memory, preparing to tell Belize his tale.

At first, Belize watches from the street, but soon he's drawn into the bedroom.

ANGEL: Greetings, Prophet!
    The Great Work Begins:
    The Messenger has arrived.
PRIOR *(Terrified)*: Go away.
ANGEL: Attend:
PRIOR *(Still terrified)*: Oh God there's a thing in the air, a thing, a thing.
ANGEL: I I I I
    Am the Bird of America, the Bald Eagle,
    Continental Principality,
    LUMEN PHOSPHOR FLUOR CANDLE!
    I unfold my leaves, Bright steel,
    In salutation open sharp before you:
    Prior WALTER
    Long-descended, well-prepared.
PRIOR *(Even more terrified)*: No, I'm not prepared, for anything, I have lots to do, I—
ANGEL *(With a gust of music)*: American Prophet tonight you become,
    American Eye that pierceth Dark,
    American Heart all Hot for Truth,

The True Great Vocalist, the Knowing Mind,
Tongue-of-the-Land, Seer-Head!
PRIOR: Oh, shoo! You're scaring the shit out me, get the fuck
out of my room. Please, oh please—
ANGEL: Now:
  Remove from their hiding place the Sacred Prophetic
  Implements.

  (Little pause.)

PRIOR: The *what?*
ANGEL: Remove from their hiding place the Sacred Prophetic
  Implements.
  (Little pause)
  Your dreams have revealed them to you.
PRIOR: What dreams?
ANGEL: You have had dreams revealing to you—
PRIOR: I haven't had a dream I can remember in months.
ANGEL *(Stern)*: No . . . *dreams*, you— Are you sure?
PRIOR: Yes. Well, the two dead Priors, they—
ANGEL: No not the heralds, not them. Other dreams.
  Implements, you must have—
  One moment.
PRIOR: *This*, this is a dream, obviously, I'm sick and so I—well
  OK it's a pretty spectacular dream but still it's just
  some—
ANGEL *(A flash of anger)*: Quiet. Prophet. A moment, please,
  I— *(Looking up, addressing unseen forces; severe)* The dis-
  organization is—
  (She coughs, looks up, rises higher in the air)
  Yes.
  (To Prior) In the kitchen. Under the tiles under the sink.

PRIOR: You want me to, to tear up the kitchen floor?

ANGEL: Get a shovel or an axe or some . . . *tool* for dislodging tile and, and grout and unearth the Sacred Implements.

PRIOR: No fucking way! The ceiling's bad enough, I'll lose the lease, I'll lose my security deposit, I'll wake up the downstairs neighbors, their hysterical dog, I—

Do it yourself.

ANGEL *(A tremendous, unearthly voice)*: SUBMIT, SUBMIT TO THE WILL OF HEAVEN!

(An enormous gust of wind knocks Prior over. He glares at her from the floor and shakes his head no. A standoff. The Angel coughs a little. There is a small explosion in the kitchen offstage. A cloud of plaster dust drifts in.)

PRIOR: What did you— What . . . ? *(Exits into the kitchen)*

ANGEL: And Lo, the Prophet was led by his nightly dreams to the hiding place of the Sacred Implements, and— Revision in the text: the Angel helped him to unearth them, for he was weak of body *(Pissed-off)* though not of will.

(Prior returns with an ancient leather suitcase, very dusty.)

PRIOR: You cracked the refrigerator, you probably released a whole cloud of fluorocarbons, that's bad for the, the environment.

ANGEL: My wrath is as fearsome as my countenance is splendid. Open the suitcase.

(Prior does. He reaches inside and produces a pair of bronze spectacles with rocks instead of lenses.)

PRIOR: Oh, look at this.

Like, wow, man, totally Paleozoic. *(He puts them on)*
This is—
(He stops suddenly. His head jerks up. He is seeing something)
OH! OH GOD NO! OH— *(Horror-stricken, he rips off the spectacles)*
That was terrible! I don't want to see that!

ANGEL: Remove the Book.

(Prior removes a large Book with bright steel pages from the suitcase. There is a really glorious burst of music, more light, more wind.)

ANGEL: From the Council of Continental Principalities
Met in this time of Crisis and Confusion:
Heaven here reaches down to disaster
And in touching you touches all of Earth.

(Music. She points to the spectacles.)

ANGEL: Peepstones.

(Prior retrieves them. He's understandably reluctant to put them on.)

ANGEL: Open me Prophet. I I I I am
The Book.
Read.

(Prior starts to put on the peepstones and then stops.)

PRIOR: Wait. Wait.
How come . . . How come I have this, um, erection?
It's very hard to concentrate.

ANGEL: The stiffening of your penis is of no consequence.

PRIOR: Well maybe not to you but—

ANGEL: READ!

(More music, more light. Prior puts the glasses on, and reads.)

ANGEL: You are Mere Flesh. I I I I am Utter Flesh,
   Density of Desire, the Gravity of Skin:
   What makes the Engine of Creation Run?
   Not Physics but Ecstatics Makes the Engine Run:
   (Continue below:)

(She begins to glow with intense sexual heat.)

PRIOR *(Hit by a wave of intense sexual feeling)*: Hmmmm . . .

ANGEL *(Continuous from above)*: The Pulse, the Pull, the Throb,
   the Ooze . . . *(Continue below:)*

PRIOR: Wait, please, I . . . Excuse me for just a minute, just a
   minute.
   OK I . . .

ANGEL *(Continuous from above)*: Priapsis, Dilation,
   Engorgement, Flow:
   The Universe Aflame with Angelic Ejaculate . . .
   (Continue below:)

PRIOR *(Losing control, he starts to hump the Book)*: Oh shit . . .

ANGEL *(Continuous from above)*: The Heavens a-thrum to the
   Seraphic Rut,
   The Fiery Grapplings . . . *(Continue below:)*

PRIOR: Oh God, I . . .

ANGEL *(Continuous from above)*: The Feathery Joinings of the
   Higher Orders,
   Infinite, Unceasing, the Blood-Pump of Creation!

(With a rough gesture, she causes Prior to flip over on his back. She's directly above and parallel to him, close.)

PRIOR: OH! OH! I . . . ANGEL: HOLY Estrus! HOLY
OH! Oh! Oh . . . oh . . . Orifice!
Ecstasis in Excelsis!
AMEN!

(Pause. The peepstones have fallen off, or he removes them.)

PRIOR: Oh. Oh God.

ANGEL: The Body is the Garden of the Soul.

PRIOR: What *was* that?

ANGEL: Plasma Orgasmata.

PRIOR: Yeah well no doubt.

BELIZE *(He's heard enough; stepping into the bedroom)*: Whoa whoa whoa wait a minute excuse me please. You fucked this angel?

PRIOR: She fucked me. She has . . . Well, She has eight vaginas.

ANGEL: REGINA VAGINA!

Hermaphroditically Equipped as well with a Bouquet of Phalli.

I I I I am Your Released Female Essence Ascendant!

BELIZE: The sexual politics of this are—

PRIOR: Very confusing. I know.

(As Belize challenges Prior, the Angel, unthreatened, intrigued, lands and listens closely.

From the moment Belize enters the bedroom, Prior is simultaneously with him, on the street, three weeks hence, trying to tell what happened, and present in the bedroom with the Angel, where he's very frightened, with no idea of what's about to happen.)

BELIZE: What . . . So what, um, *gender* is God? According to—

PRIOR: According to Her: male. God is a—

BELIZE: No shit? Seriously? You don't think that's sorta sexist or—

PRIOR: He's not an old man or anything, He's a—from what I gather He's a Hebrew letter.

ANGEL: THE ALEPH GLYPH.

PRIOR: A . . . *male* Hebrew letter.

ANGEL: Deus Erectus! Pater Omnipotens!

PRIOR *(To Belize)*: Each Angel is an infinite aggregate myriad entity, They're basically incredibly powerful bureaucrats, They have no imagination, They can *do* anything but They can't invent, create, They're sort of fabulous and dull all at once, and They copulate, *ceaselessly*, apparently, the Angels, They—I mean I—

BELIZE: They get fucked by a Hebrew letter.

ANGEL *(To Prior)*: READ ON.

(Prior gestures to the Angel to wait.)

PRIOR: When Angels cum They make something called, um— *(Continue below:)*

ANGEL: Plasma orgasmata!

PRIOR *(Continuous from above)*: —plasma orgasmata which makes some . . . other thing called— *(Continue below:)*

ANGEL: Protomatter.

PRIOR *(Continuous from above)*: —protomatter. Right. Which is what makes . . . Everything else.

ANGEL: Creation.

PRIOR: Creation. Heaven's, like, a lot, um, livelier than we were led to—

ANGEL: Heaven Is a City Much Like San Francisco.

(Prior puts on the peepstones and returns to the floor, reading at first from the Book, and then, as the Angel continues, he stops reading, removes the peepstones and listens to her. Belize is also listening, watching, bewildered and increasingly scared by the way Prior's sounding.)

ANGEL: House upon house depended from Hillside,
    From Crest down to Dockside,
    The green Mirroring Bay.
    Oh Joyful in the Buckled Garden,
    Undulant Landscape over which
    The Threat of Seismic Catastrophe hangs:
    More beautiful because imperiled.
    POTENT: yet DORMANT: The Fault Lines of
      Creation!
    (Coughs)
    When *He*, ALEPH,
    GLYPH From Whom All Words Descend,
    Tearing Glyph from Auto-Generative All-Adoring
      Gaze,
    He Would Come Down to Us ABLAZE!
    THEN: Heaven's Walls would Ring with the
    Glad mad moaning of the Winged Throng.
    Hot Wet FIRE would flood the Cosmos,
    And Igneous Gases Enflame the Voids,
    And lights revolve, and spheres resolve,
    As ALEPH Burns.
    He burns . . . forever, He . . .

(A deep sorrow wells up. She can't speak. Little pause. Prior looks at her.)

PRIOR *(Quietly, to the Angel)*:   BELIZE *(To Prior)*:
He what?   Let's go over to your place . . .
                                                             (Continue below:)
ANGEL: And then . . .   PRIOR *(Over Angel, to Belize)*:
(Pause)   No I don't like it there, it's—
HE . . . CHANGED.   BELIZE *(Continuous from
                                                             above)*: —make some tea
                                                             and talk about—

(A far-off, deep rumbling.)

PRIOR *(To the Angel, hearing something in her story that's recog-
      nizable)*: He changed.
BELIZE *(To Prior)*: God?

(Prior nods.)

BELIZE: Changed how, honey? If He's God, how can He—
PRIOR: I don't know. But He did. He—
ANGEL: He grew weary of Us.
        Our Songs and Fornications.
        His Angels: Who cannot Imagine, who lack that Faculty.
        Made for His Pleasure, We can only ADORE.
        Seeking something New,
        He split the World starkly in Two
        (A mounting fury directed at Prior:)
        And made YOU—
PRIOR *(To Belize)*: When God made people He created . . .
      division.
ANGEL: Human Beings:
        Uni-Genitalled: Female. Male.

PRIOR *(To Belize)*: He awakened a potential in the design for
    change—
ANGEL: In creating *You*—
PRIOR *(To Belize)*: —for random event.
ANGEL: Our Father-Lover Unleashed
    Eternal Creation's Potential for Change.
PRIOR *(To Belize)*: For movement forward.
ANGEL *(Bitter disgust, envy)*: In *YOU* the Virus of TIME began!
    YOU *Think*. And You *IMAGINE!*
    Migrate! Explore—
BELIZE: Uh-huh, but . . .
ANGEL: And when you do:
BELIZE: But so like you know none of this is, um, *real*, right?
ANGEL: Paradise itself Shivers and Splits—
PRIOR *(To Belize)*: I, I didn't say it was real, I said it was what
    She told me, and She's, well . . .
ANGEL: Each Day when *You* Awake—
PRIOR: Real *enough*, I guess, I don't know!
ANGEL *(Her fury now directed at Prior and Belize)*: As though
        WE are only
    The dream of *YOU*.
PRIOR: Everything's come unglued, right? So is . . . *(The room,
    the world) this* any less plausible than you know than—

*(A low but powerful tremor stops Prior. The Angel hears it,
too; Belize doesn't, but he sees Prior hearing it.)*

ANGEL *(With loathing)*: PROGRESS!
BELIZE *(To Prior)*: We're not supposed to *migrate*? To progress?

(Another tremor, louder and more powerful.)

ANGEL *(Again, with loathing)*: PRIOR *(To Belize)*: No, but,
MOVEMENT!   but there are *consequences!*
ANGEL *(Furious, with deep sorrow breaking through)*: Shaking
  HIM!
PRIOR *(To Belize)*: When we move around, heedless of, of—
  When the human race began to travel, intermingle, then—

  *(A much bigger, nearer, rolling tremor begins and builds. Belize
  hears it, or imagines that he hears something.)*

PRIOR *(To Belize)*: There began to be tremors in Heaven.
  Earthquakes or, or rather—
BELIZE *(To Prior)*: Intermingle?
PRIOR: Heavenquakes.
BELIZE: Are you hearing yourself?

  (Another deep, rolling tremor. All three look up.)

ANGEL: He . . . *began to*—! HE who never was begun, was
    always *IS* and
  Unbegun! He . . . *began* to
  Leave Us!
  Bored with His Angels, *Bewitched* by Humanity, in
    Mortifying Imitation of You, His least creation,
    He would sail off on Voyages, no knowing where.
    Quake follows quake, Absence follows Absence:
    Nasty Chastity and Disorganization; Loss of
    Libido; Protomatter Shortfall . . .

  (A huge tremor.)

ANGEL: UH. OH.
  Then:

PRIOR *(To Belize)*: April 18, 1906.

ANGEL: In that day:

PRIOR: It's the Great San Francisco Earthquake.

ANGEL: *In That Day*:
> Father-Lover of the Million Unutterable Names,
> Deus Ercctus, Pater Omnipotens, King of the Universe:
> He left—

PRIOR: He. Abandoned Them.

ANGEL: —And did not return.
> We do not know where He has gone.
> He may *never* . . .
> And bitter, cast-off, We wait, bewildered;
> Our finest houses, our sweetest vineyards,
> Made drear and barren, missing Him.

(She coughs. There's a pause, then:)

BELIZE *(To Prior)*: Abandoned.
> I smell a motif.

(Prior looks at Belize, then nods.)

PRIOR: Well it occurred to me.

BELIZE: The man that got away?
> And I think the time has come to let him go.

(Little pause.)

PRIOR *(To Belize, forlorn)*: And then?
> *(To the Angel)* And then what?

ANGEL: Surely you see towards what We are Progressing:

(Prior goes back to the Book. He takes up the peepstones but doesn't put them on.)

ANGEL: The fabric of the sky unravels:
    Angels hover, anxious fingers worry the tattered edge.
    Before the boiling of blood and the searing of skin
        comes the Secret catastrophe:
    Before Life on Earth becomes finally merely impossible,
    It will for a long time before have become completely
        unbearable.
    (Coughs, then, with great passion and force:)
    YOU HAVE DRIVEN HIM AWAY! YOU MUST
    STOP MOVING!

PRIOR *(Quiet, frightened)*: Stop moving.

ANGEL *(Softly, rapidly)*: Forsake the Open Road: Neither Mix
    Nor Intermarry
    Let Deep Roots Grow: If you do not MINGLE you
    will Cease to Progress. Seek Not to Fathom the
    World and its Delicate Particle Logic: You cannot
    Understand, You can only Destroy, You Do not
    "Advance," You only Trample.
    Poor blind Children, abandoned on the Earth,
    Groping terrified, misguided, over
    Fields of Slaughter, over bodies of the Slain:
    HOBBLE YOURSELVES!
    There is No Zion Save Where You Are!
    If you Cannot find your Heart's desire—

PRIOR: —In your own backyard—

ANGEL, PRIOR AND BELIZE: You never lost it to begin with.

(The Angel coughs. Prior is disturbed and confused by the cita-tion; she is confused and disturbed that humans know these lines. For Belize it's proof, of course, that this is a dream.)

ANGEL: Turn Back.

PRIOR: Please, please, whatever you are, angel or, or—

ANGEL: Undo.

PRIOR: I'm not a prophet, I'm a sick, lonely man, I—

ANGEL: Till He—

PRIOR: I don't . . . *understand* this visitation—

ANGEL: Till HE returns again.

(The Angel picks up the Book. Prior is now both terrified and very angry.)

PRIOR: Stop moving. That's what you want. Answer me! You want me dead.

(Pause. The Angel and Prior look at one another.)

PRIOR: Uh-huh, well *I. I'M TIRED!* Tired to death of, of being done to, um, *infected*, fucked-over and tortured by, by you, by this—

Is this, is this, disease, is the virus in me, is that the, the epistle, is that the prophecy? Is this just . . . *revenge*, because we, because you think we ruined . . .

No. No, I want you to go away, you go away or *I* will, I'll leave, I can leave, too, I'll—

(The Angel steps aside and gestures to Prior to leave. He hesitates and starts for the door. As he passes near her, the Angel touches him gently on the shoulder.)

ANGEL *(Leaning in, quiet, intimate)*: You can't Outrun your Occupation, Jonah.
Hiding from Me one place you will find me in another.

(She takes her hand from his shoulder.)

ANGEL: I I I I stop down the road, waiting for you.

(Tenderly, she puts her arm about his waist.)

ANGEL *(Almost a whisper)*: You Know Me Prophet: Your
    battered heart,
    Bleeding Life in the Universe of Wounds.

*(The Angel presses the Book against Prior's chest, then presses
her body against his. Together they experience something
unnameable—painful, joyful, in equal measure. There is a
terrible sound.)*

ANGEL: Vessel of the BOOK now: Oh Exemplum Paralyticum:
    On you in you in your blood we write have written:
    STASIS!
    The END.

*(She releases Prior, who sinks to the floor. In gales of music,
holding the Book aloft, the Angel ascends.)*

Scene 3

*The bedroom disappears. While this is happening, Prior stands,
and, again, with deliberate, unhurried pace, changes into his street
clothes. When he's ready he resumes his place beside Belize, who's
waiting, thinking, on the street in front of the funeral home.*

*Prior and Belize stare at one another, silent for a beat, and
then:*

BELIZE: Uh-huh. I . . .
    Well what do you want me to say?

PRIOR: It's . . . nuts.

BELIZE: It's . . . *worse* than nuts, it's— "Don't migrate"? "Don't mingle"? That's . . . kind of malevolent, isn't it, 'cause—
(Continue below:)

PRIOR: I hardly think it's appropriate for you to get *offended*, I didn't invent this shit it was *visited* on—

BELIZE *(Continuous from above)*: —you know, some of us didn't exactly *choose* to migrate, know what I'm saying, some of us— But it *is* offensive or at least monumentally confused and it's not . . . *visited*, Prior. By who? It *is* from you, what else is it?

PRIOR: Something else.

BELIZE: That's crazy.

PRIOR: Then I'm crazy.

BELIZE: No, you're—

PRIOR: Then it was an angel.

BELIZE: It was *not* an—

PRIOR: Then I'm crazy. The whole world is, why not me? It's 1986 and there's a *plague*, friends younger than me are dead, and I'm only thirty, and every goddamn morning I wake up and I think Louis is next to me in the bed and it takes me long minutes to remember . . . that this is *real*, it isn't just an impossible, terrible dream, so maybe yes I'm flipping out.

BELIZE *(Angry)*: Stop.

(Tough, harsh, very clear) This is not dementia. And this is not real. This is just you, Prior, afraid of . . . Of what's coming. Afraid of time.

But see that's just not how it goes, the world doesn't spin backwards.

(Prior starts to say something. Belize holds up his hand, forbidding, and Prior obeys.)

BELIZE: Listen to the world, to how fast it goes.

(They listen, and the sounds of the city grow louder and louder, filling the stage, sounds of traffic, whistles, alarms, people, all very fast and very complex and very determinedly moving ahead.)

BELIZE: That's New York traffic, baby, that's the sound of energy, the sound of time. Even if you're hurting, it can't go back.

You better fucking not flip out. There's no angel. You hear me? For me? *(Continue below:)*

THE ANGEL'S VOICE: Whisper into the ear of the World, Prophet. *(Continue below:)*

BELIZE *(Continuous from above)*: I can handle anything but not this happening to you.

THE ANGEL'S VOICE *(Continuous from above)*: Wash up red in the tide of its dreams,

And billow bloody words into the sky of sleep.

(Prior steps back from Belize, withdrawing.)

PRIOR: I'm sorry, baby, I . . . I've tried, really, but . . . I can't, it follows me, it won't let me go. So, maybe I'm a prophet. Not me, alone, all of us, the, the ones who're dying now. Maybe the virus is the prophecy? Be still. Maybe the world has driven God from Heaven. Because, because I do believe that, that over and over, I've seen the end of things. And *(He puts his hand near his eyes)* having seen, I'm going blind, as prophets do. Right? It makes a certain sense to me.

THE ANGEL'S VOICE: FOR THIS AGE OF ANOMIE: A NEW LAW! *(Continue below:)*

PRIOR: Oh, *oh God* how I hate Heaven. But I've got no resistance left.

THE ANGEL'S VOICE *(Continuous from above)*: Delivered this
    night, this silent night, from Heaven,
Oh Prophet, to You.

(Prior kisses Belize good-bye.)

PRIOR: Except to run.

(He limps away. Belize watches him go.)

ACT THREE:

Borborygmi

(The Squirming Facts Exceed the Squamous Mind)

January 1986

Scene 1

Several days after the end of Act Two. Split scene: Joe and Louis in bed in Louis's apartment, which is tidier, homier. Louis is sound asleep. Joe is awake, sitting up, watching Harper, who is in the living room of their Brooklyn apartment. She's dressed in a soiled nightgown. Returning Joe's stare, she removes her nightgown; she stands shivering, facing him in her bra, panties and stockings.

Hannah, in a bathrobe, enters the Brooklyn living room, carrying a dress over her arm and a pair of shoes. She puts the shoes down in front of Harper.

HANNAH: Good you're out of that nightdress, it was starting to smell.

HARPER: You're telling me.

HANNAH: Now let's slip this on.

(They put the dress on Harper.)

HANNAH: Good.
HARPER: I hate it.
HANNAH: It's pretty.
　　Shoes?

(Harper steps into them.)

HANNAH: Now let's see about the hair.

(Harper bends over; Hannah combs Harper's hair.)

HANNAH: It can be very hard to accept how disappointing life is, Harper, because that's what it is, and you have to accept it. With faith and time and hard work you reach a point where . . . where the disappointment doesn't hurt as much, and then it gets easy to live with. Quite easy. Which . . . is in its own way a disappointment. But. There.
HARPER: In my old life, my previous life, I never used to get up at five A.M.
　　(To Joe) This is a nightmare.
HANNAH: I said I'd open up.
HARPER *(Fake admiration)*: You volunteered.
HANNAH: I can't sit around, idle.
HARPER: You just got here, you could . . . sightsee, you could—
HANNAH: I didn't come for fun.
HARPER: You came to the right place.
HANNAH: I leave messages for him at work. They say he's not in but I know he is, but he won't take my calls. He's ashamed.

JOE: She's right.

HANNAH: I'll fix myself.

JOE: I am.

HANNAH: And we can go.

(Hannah exits.)

HARPER: You're in love with him.

(She crosses into Louis's bedroom. Joe shrinks from her, afraid, but he's careful not to wake Louis.)

JOE: I am?

HARPER: Don't ask *me*. Are you?

JOE: How're you doing?

HARPER: Huh. Maybe you're not in love with him. If you were, you wouldn't ask me that. You wouldn't be brave enough. You'd know.

LOUIS *(Still asleep, starting to wake)*: Joe . . . ?

JOE: Yeah, yeah, screwy stomach, nothing.   HARPER: Talk softer you're waking him up.

(Louis is asleep again.)

HARPER: I have terrible powers. Maybe I'm a witch.

JOE: You're not a—

HARPER: I see more than I want to see. You can't do that. I could be a witch. Why not? I married a fairy. Anything's possible, any awful thing.

JOE: Leave, Harper.

HARPER: I knew you'd be with someone. You think of yourself as so lonely all the time, but you've never been alone.

JOE: Oh that isn't . . . You don't know. I have felt very alone.

HARPER: Till now.

(Harper puts her hand under Louis's head, and pushes up; Louis startles awake.)

LOUIS: Who are you . . . ?
JOE *(To Louis)*: I— It's nothing, just . . .
          (To Harper) Go.

(She vanishes.)

JOE *(To Louis)*: Morning.
          Sleep well?
LOUIS: No.
          Did you?
JOE: Soundly.
LOUIS: How do you manage that? These fucking dreams, every . . .
          Don't you have—
JOE: I don't dream.
LOUIS: Everybody dreams.
JOE: I don't.
LOUIS: *Ever?*
JOE: Not that I can remember.
          Not since I started, um, being here, with you.
LOUIS *(A beat, then)*: You're a conundrum.
JOE: Solve me.
          (Embarrassed) Sorry, that was really—
LOUIS: But you can't—
JOE: Weird, that was really—
LOUIS: You can't *solve* conundrums, they're . . . bafflements, you can only, um . . .
JOE: Conjecture.

(Louis nods.)

JOE: So ask me something.
LOUIS: Like . . . ?
JOE: Something you've never asked me before.
  It should be easy, you haven't asked much.

(Louis looks around the room, as if not recognizing any of it, then he stares hard at Joe. A beat, then:)

LOUIS: Who *are* you?

Scene 2

Same day. Roy in his hospital room; near his bed, there's a mini-fridge with a locked door. He looks worse than before, gaunt, gray. The pain in his gut is now constant and it's getting worse. He's on the phone, a more elaborate model than the one in the previous scene; this phone has buttons.

ROY: No records no records what are you deaf I said I have no records for their shitty little committee, it's not how I work I—

(He has a severe abdominal spasm. He holds the phone away, grimaces terribly, curls up into a ball and then uncurls, making no sound, determined that the party on the line won't hear how much pain he's in.
  Ethel Rosenberg appears in her hat and coat. Roy sees her enter. He watches her walk to a chair and sit. He resumes his phone call, never taking his eyes off Ethel, who stares at him, silent, unreadable.)

ROY: Those notes were lost. LOST. In a fire, water damage, I can't do this any—

(Belize enters with a pill tray.)

ROY *(To Belize)*: I threw up fifteen times today! I *COUNTED*.
   (To Ethel) What are *you* looking at?
   (To Belize) Fifteen times. *(He goes back to the phone)* Yeah?
BELIZE: Hang up the phone, I have to watch you take these—
ROY: The LIMO thing? Oh for the love of Christ I was acquitted twice for that, they're trying to kill me dead with this *harassment*, I have done things in my life but I never killed anyone.
   (To Ethel) Present company excepted. And you *deserved* it.
   (To Belize) Get the fuck outta here.
   (Back to the phone) Stall. It can't start tomorrow if we don't show, so don't show, I'll pay the old harridan back. I have to have a—
BELIZE: Put down the phone.
ROY: Suck my dick, Mother Teresa, this is life and death.
BELIZE: Put down the—

(Roy grabs the pill cup off the tray and throws the pills on the floor. Belize reaches for the phone. Roy slams down the receiver and snatches the phone away, protecting it, cradling it.)

ROY: You touch this phone and I'll bite. And I got rabies.
   And from now on, I supply my own pills. I already told 'em to push their jujubes to the losers down the hall.
BELIZE: Your own pills.
ROY: No double blind. A little bird warned me. The vultures are—

(Another severe spasm. This time he makes noise)
Jesus God these cramps, now I know why women go
beserk once a— AH FUCK!

(He has another spasm. Ethel laughs.)

ROY: Oh good I made her laugh.
(The pain is slightly less. He's a little calmer)
I don't trust this hospital. For all I know Lillian fucking *Hellman* is down in the basement switching the pills
around. No, wait, she's dead, isn't she? Oh boy, memory,
it's— Hey, Ethel, didn't Lillian die, did you see her up
there, ugly, ugly broad, nose like a . . . like even a Jew
should worry mit a punim like that. You seen somebody
fitting that description up there in Red Heaven? Hah?
(To Belize) She won't talk to me. She thinks she's some
sort of a deathwatch or something.
BELIZE: Who are you talking to?

*(Roy looks at Ethel, realizing/remembering that Belize can't
see her.)*

ROY: I'm self-medicating.
BELIZE: With what?
ROY *(Trying to remember)*: Acid something.
BELIZE: Azidothymedine?
ROY: Gesundheit.

*(Roy retrieves a key on a ring from under his pillow and tosses
it to Belize.)*

BELIZE: AZT? You got . . . ?

(Belize unlocks the ice box; it's full of bottles of pills.)

ROY: One-hundred-proof elixir vitae.

Give me the key.

BELIZE: You scored.

ROY: Impressively.

BELIZE: Lifetime supply.

There are maybe thirty people in the whole country who are getting this drug.

ROY: Now there are thirty-one.

BELIZE: There are a hundred thousand people who need it.

Look at you. The dragon atop the golden horde. It's not fair, is it?

ROY: No, but as Jimmy Carter said, neither is life. And then we shipped him back to his peanut plantation. Put your brown eyes back in your goddamn head, baby, it's the history of the world, I didn't write it, though I flatter myself I am a footnote. And you are a nurse, so minister and skedaddle.

BELIZE: If you live fifty more years you won't swallow all these pills.

(Pause)

I want some.

ROY: That's illegal.

BELIZE: Ten bottles.

ROY: I'm gonna report you.

BELIZE: There's a nursing shortage. I'm in a union. I'm real scared.

I have friends who need them. Bad.

ROY: Loyalty I admire. But no.

BELIZE *(Amazed, off-guard)*: *Why?*

(Pause.)

ROY: Because you repulse me. *"WHY?"* You'll be begging for it next. *"WHY?"* Because I hate your guts, and your friends' guts, that's *why.* "Gimme!" So goddamned entitled. Such a shock when the bill comes due.

BELIZE: From what I read you never paid a fucking bill in your life.

ROY: *No one* has worked harder than me. To end up knocked flat in a—

BELIZE: Yeah well things are tough all over.

ROY: And you come *here* looking for *fairness? (To Ethel)* They couldn't *touch* me when I was alive, and now when I'm dying they try this: *(He grabs up all the paperwork in two fists)* Now! When I'm a— *(He can't find the word. Back to Belize)* That's fair? What am I? A dead man!

(A terrible spasm, quick and violent; he doubles up. Then, when the pain's subsided:)

Fuck! What was I saying Oh God I can't remember any . . . Oh yeah, dead.

I'm a goddamn dead man.

BELIZE: You expect *pity?*

ROY *(A beat, then)*: I expect you to hand over that key and move your nigger ass out of my room.

BELIZE: What did you say?

ROY: Move your nigger cunt spade faggot lackey ass out of my room.

BELIZE *(Overlapping, starting on "spade")*: Shit-for-brains filthy-mouthed selfish motherfucking cowardly cocksucking cloven-hoofed pig.

ROY *(Overlapping, starting on "cowardly")*: Mongrel. Dinge. Slave. Ape.

BELIZE: Kike.

ROY: *Now* you're talking!

BELIZE: Greedy kike.

ROY: Now you can have a bottle. But only one.

(Belize tosses the key at Roy, hard. Roy catches it. Belize takes a bottle of the pills, then another, then a third, and then leaves.
As soon as Belize is out of the room Roy is spasmed with pain he's been holding in.)

ROY: GOD! *(The pain subsides a little)* I thought he'd never go! *(It subsides a little more. Then to Ethel)* So what? Are you going to sit there all night?

ETHEL: Till morning.

ROY: Uh-huh. The cock crows, you go back to the swamp.

ETHEL: No. I take the 7:05 to Yonkers.

ROY: What the fuck's in Yonkers?

ETHEL: The disbarment committee hearings. You been hocking about it all week. I'll have a look-see.

ROY: They won't let you in the front door. You're a convicted and executed traitor.

ETHEL: I'll walk through a wall.

(She laughs. He joins her.)

ROY: Fucking SUCCUBUS!

(They're laughing, enjoying this.)

ROY: Fucking blood-sucking old bat!

(They continue to laugh as Roy picks up the phone, punches a couple of buttons and then stops dialing, his laughter gone. He stares at the phone, dejectedly, not noticing that Ethel has vanished.
Roy puts the receiver back in its cradle and puts the phone aside. He turns to the empty chair where Ethel had been sitting. He talks to the chair as if she's sitting in it.)

ROY: The worst thing about being sick in America, Ethel, is you are booted out of the parade. Americans have no use for sick. Look at Reagan: he's so healthy he's hardly human, he's a hundred if he's a day, he takes a slug in his chest and two days later he's out west riding ponies in his PJs. I mean *who does that?* That's America. It's just no country for the infirm.

Scene 3

Same day. The Diorama Room of the Mormon Visitors' Center. The room's a small proscenium theater; the diorama is hidden behind closed red velvet curtains. There are plush red theater seats for the audience, and Harper is slouched in one of them, dressed as she was in her previous scene. Empty potato chip and M&M bags and cans of soda are scattered around her seat. She stares with dull anger at the drawn stage curtains. She's been here a long time.
Hannah enters with Prior, dressed in his prophet garb.

HANNAH: This is the Diorama Room.
    (To Harper) I thought we agreed that you weren't—
    (To Prior) I'll go see if I can get it started.

(She exits. Prior sits. He removes his scarf and dark glasses. He wipes his face, startlingly pale and clammy with sweat, with the scarf. He breathes in and out, feeling tightness in his lungs.
    Harper watches this with a level stare and a flat affect— jaded, ironic disaffection she's self-protectively, experimentally assumed.
    The lights in the room dim. After a blare of feedback/static, a Voice on tape [the Angel's] intones:)

A VOICE: Welcome to the Mormon Visitors' Center Diorama Room. In a moment, our show will begin. We hope it will have a special message for you. Please refrain from smoking, and food and drink are not allowed. *(A chiming tone)* Welcome to the Mormon Visitors'—

(The tape lurches into very high speed, then smears into incomprehensibly low speed, then stops, mid-message, with a loud metallic blat, which frightens Prior. The lights remain dim.)

HARPER: They're having trouble with the machinery.

(She rips open a bag of M&Ms and offers them to Prior.)

PRIOR: No thanks, I—
        You're not supposed to eat in the—
HARPER: I can. I live here. Have we met before?
PRIOR: No, I don't . . . think so. You *live* here?
HARPER: There's a dummy family in the diorama, you'll see when the curtain opens. The main dummy, the big daddy dummy, looks like my husband, Joe. When they push the buttons he'll start to talk. You can't believe a word he says but the sound of him is reassuring. It's an *incredible* resemblance.
PRIOR: Are you a Mormon?
HARPER: Jack Mormon.
PRIOR: I beg your pardon?
HARPER: Jack Mormon. It means I'm flawed. Inferior Mormon product. Probably comes from jack rabbit, you know, I *ran*.
PRIOR: Do you believe in angels? In the Angel Mormon?
HARPER: Moroni, not Mormon, The Angel Moroni. Ask my mother-in-law, when you leave, the scary lady at the

reception desk: If its name was Moroni why don't they call themselves Morons. It's from comments like that you can tell I'm jack. You're not a Mormon.

PRIOR: No, I—

HARPER: Just . . . distracted with grief.

PRIOR (*Startled*): I'm not. I was just walking and—

HARPER: We get a lot of distracted, grief-stricken people here. It's our specialty.

PRIOR: I'm not . . . distracted, I'm doing research.

HARPER: On Mormons?

PRIOR: On . . . angels. I'm a . . . an angelologist.

HARPER: I never met an angelologist before.

PRIOR: It's an obscure discipline.

HARPER: I can imagine. Angelology. The field work must be rigorous. You'd have to drop dead before you saw your first specimen.

PRIOR (*A beat, then deciding to confide*): One . . . I saw one. An angel. It crashed through my bedroom ceiling.

HARPER: Huh. That sort of thing always happens to me.

PRIOR: I have a fever. I should be in bed but I'm too anxious to lie in bed.

You look *very* familiar.

HARPER: So do you. But—

But it's just not possible. I don't get out. I've only ever been here, or in some place a lot like this, alone, in the dark, waiting for the dummy.

(*Dramatic music as the house lights dim in the Diorama Room, the red curtains part and stage lights come up to reveal a brightly painted, brightly lit backdrop of the desert between Colorado and Utah, mountains looming in the distance. Posed before the backdrop, in silhouette, a family of Mormon pioneers, seated in a covered wagon.*)

A VOICE: In 1847, across fifteen hundred miles of frontier wilderness, braving mountain blizzards, desert storms, and renegade Indians, the first Mormon wagon trains made their difficult way towards the Kingdom of God.

(During the above, Harper noisily rips open a bag of Nacho-Flavored Doritos, which she holds out to Prior:)

HARPER: Want some Nacho-Flavored—

(She stops as, to the accompaniment of the sounds of a wagon train and the Largo from Dvořák's 9th Symphony, stage lights illuminate the Mormon family of costumed mannequins: two young sons, a mother and a daughter, and, driving the wagon, a father, who looks a lot like Joe.)

HARPER *(To the Mormon father)*: Hi Joe.

(The music and background sounds give way as the diorama scene begins. When either Caleb or Orrin speaks, his immobile face is hit with a pinspot; this has an unintentionally eerie effect. The father's face is animated, but not his body.)

CALEB *(Voice on tape)*: Father, I'm a-feard.
FATHER: Hush, Caleb.
ORRIN *(Voice on tape)*: The wilderness is so vast.
FATHER: Orrin, Caleb, hush. Be brave for your mother and your little sister.
CALEB: We'll try, Father, we want you to be proud of us. We want to be brave and strong like you.
ORRIN: When will we arrive in

HARPER: They don't have any lines, the sister and the mother. And only his face moves. That's not really fair.

Zion, Father? When will our great exodus finally be done? All this wandering . . .

FATHER: Soon, boys, soon, just like the Prophet promised. The Lord leads the way.

CALEB: Will there be lots to eat there, Father? Will the desert flow with milk and honey? Will there be water there?

FATHER: The Lord will provide for us, Son, he always has.

ORRIN: Well, not *always* . . .

FATHER: Sometimes He tests us, Son, that's His way, but—

CALEB: Read to us, Father, read us the story!

FATHER *(Chuckles)*: *Again?*

CALEB AND ORRIN: Yes! Yes! The story! The story! The story about the Prophet!

FATHER: Well, boys, well:

1823, the Prophet, who was a strapping lad, like everyone else in his time, was seeking God, there were many churches, disputatious enough, but who was Right? Could only be One True Church. All else darkness—

HARPER *(After "Zion")*: Never. You'll die of snake bite and your brother looks like scorpion food to me!

PRIOR: Sssshhhhh!

HARPER: No. Just sand. *(After "water")* Oh, there's a big lake but it's *salt*, that's the joke, they drag you on your knees through hell and when you get there the water of course is undrinkable. Salt.

It's a Promised Land, but *what* a disappointing promise!

(After the first "story") The story! The story! The story about the Prophet!

(Louis suddenly appears in the diorama. The lights onstage and in the dark auditorium shift, subtly.)

LOUIS: OK yeah yeah yeah but then answer me this: How can a fundamentalist theocratic religion function participatorily in a pluralist secular democracy? I can't *believe* you're a Mormon! I can't believe I've spent two whole weeks in bed with a Mormon!

JOE: Um, could you talk a little softer, I—

LOUIS: Are you busy?

JOE: I'm working, but— And it's closer to three weeks, almost, it's—

LOUIS: But you're a lawyer! A *serious* lawyer!

PRIOR *(Frightened)*: Oh my God, oh my God. What— *what is going on here?*	JOE: The Chief Clerk of the Chief Justice of the Supreme Court is a Mormon, Louis.
HARPER: You know him?	
PRIOR *(Closing his eyes)*: I'm delirious, I must be delirious.	LOUIS: He *is?*

(Joe nods yes.)

LOUIS: Jesus, Mormons everywhere, it's like *Invasion of the Body Snatchers.* I don't like cults.

JOE: The Church of Jesus Christ of Latter Day Saints is not a cult.

LOUIS: Any religion that's not at least two thousand years old is a cult. And I know people who would call *that* generous.

JOE: Are you upset about anything?

LOUIS: Oh, you, you noticed? Yeah, I'm . . . *(Continue below:)*

PRIOR: WHAT IS HE DOING IN THERE?

(Joe gets down from the wagon and goes to Louis.)

HARPER: Who? The little creep? He's in and out every day. I hate him. He's got absolutely *nothing* to do with the story.

LOUIS *(Continuous from above)*: I am, I'm upset about, about
. . . *(He starts to cry, then stops himself)* You . . . unsettle
me. You . . . abandoned your wife, and that's terrible, but
you're not a terrible person, and yet you seem so unboth-
ered by what you did, and that's terrible, too, but you're
so decent and openly kind and truly sweet in bed, and
I don't see how that's possible, but with you it seems to
be, so, so . . . *(Continue below:)*

PRIOR *(Standing, grabbing his things in a panic; to Harper)*: Can
you turn it off? The . . . I'm leaving, I can't . . .

LOUIS *(Continuous from above)*: Is it just that, you know,
belonging to a political party that's one half religious-
zealot-control-freak theocrats and one half ego-anarchist-
libertarian cowboys, you've had a lot of practice straddling
cognitive dissonance? Or, or what?
I can't . . .

(Joe kisses Louis.
Prior starts to leave, but the pain in his leg stops him; he's
too weak to run. He turns back to the diorama, and calls:)

PRIOR: Louis!

LOUIS *(Hearing him)*: Did you . . .

JOE: What?

LOUIS: Sssshh! I, I thought I heard . . .
(To himself) Fucking hell.
(To Joe) We have to talk.

JOE: I can't leave the office in the middle of the—

LOUIS: Fuck work! This is a, a crisis. Now.

(Louis exits. Joe follows.)

HARPER *(Alarmed)*: Oh! But the, but he— The dummy never *left* with the little creep, he never *left* before. When they come in and they see he's gone, they'll blame me.

(Harper rushes to the diorama stage and pulls its curtains closed. She turns back and sees that Prior is crying.)

HARPER *(Trying hard to sound hard)*: You shouldn't do that in here, this isn't a place for real feelings, this is just story-time here. *Stop.*

PRIOR: I never imagined losing my mind was going to be such hard work.

HARPER: Oh, it is.
    (Her tough veneer starts to crack) Find someplace else to be miserable in. This is *my* place and I don't want you to do that here!

PRIOR: I JUST SAW MY LOVER, MY . . . ex-lover, with a . . . with your husband, with that . . . window-display Ken doll, in that . . . *thing*, I saw him, I—

HARPER: OK OK don't have a hissy fit, I told you it wasn't working right, it's just . . . the magic of the theater or something. Listen, if you see the creep, tell him to bring Joe, to, to bring the mannequin back, they'll evict me and this is it, it's nothing but it's the last place on earth for me. I can't go sit in Brooklyn.

(Hannah enters with a flashlight.)

HANNAH: What on earth is going—
    (She sees Prior crying. She glares at Harper)
    What did you do to him?

HARPER: Nothing! He just can't *adjust*, is all, he just—

(Hannah goes to the diorama.)

HARPER: NO WAIT, don't—

*(Hannah yanks the curtain open. The father dummy is back—
a real dummy this time.)*

HARPER: Oh. *(To Prior)* Look, we . . . imagined it.

HANNAH: This is a favor, they let me work here as a favor,
but you keep making scenes, and look at this mess, it's a
garbage scow! *(Continue below:)*

HARPER *(To Prior)*: It doesn't look so much like him, now.
He's changed. Again. *(Continue below:)*

HANNAH *(Continuous from above)*: Are you just going to sit
here forever, trash piling higher, day after day till—well
till what? *(Continue below:)*

HARPER *(Continuous from above, to Hannah)*: You sound just
like him. You even grind your teeth in your sleep like
him.

HANNAH *(Continuous from above)*: If I could get him to come
back I would go back to Salt Lake tomorrow. *(Continue
below:)*

HARPER *(Continuous from above)*: You can't go back to Salt
Lake, you sold your house! *(Continue below:)*

HANNAH *(Continuous from above)*: But I know my duty when
I see it, and if you and Joe could say the same we—

HARPER *(Continuous from above, to Prior)*: My mother-in-law!
She sold her house! Her son calls and tells her he's a
homo and what does she do? She sells her house! And
she calls *me* crazy! *(To Hannah)* You have less of a place
in this world than *I* do if that's possible.

PRIOR *(To Harper)*: Am I dreaming this, I don't understand.

HARPER: He saw an angel.

HANNAH: That's his business.

HARPER: He's an angelologist.

PRIOR: Well don't go blabbing about it.

HANNAH *(Losing the little cool she came in with; to Prior)*: If you aren't serious you shouldn't come in here.

HARPER: Either that or he's nuts.

PRIOR *(To Hannah, also losing it)*: It's a *visitors'* center; I'm *visiting.*

HARPER: He has a point.

HANNAH *(To Harper)*: Quiet!

(To Prior) It's for serious visitors, it's a serious religion.

PRIOR: Do they like, *pay* you to do this?

HARPER: She volunteers.

PRIOR: Because you're not very hospitable. I did see an angel.

HANNAH *(Blowing up!)*: *And what do you want me to do about it? I have problems of my own.*

The diorama's closed for repairs. You have to leave.

(To Harper) Clean up this mess. *(She exits)*

(Harper and Prior look at each other.)

PRIOR: Oh God, I'm exhausted.

HARPER: You don't look well. You really should be home in bed.

PRIOR: I'll die there.

HARPER: Better in bed than on the street. Just ask anyone.

(Prior gathers his things. He looks around the Diorama Room, and then at the trash around Harper's seat, and then at Harper.)

PRIOR: Maybe you should leave, too.

HARPER: I'm waiting.

PRIOR: For what?

(Harper points to the Mormon Mother in the diorama.)

HARPER: His wife. His mute wife. I'm waiting for her to speak. Bet her story's not so jolly.

(Prior looks at Harper, afraid. He remembers where they've met.)

PRIOR: Dreaming used to be so . . . safe.
HARPER: It isn't, though, it's dangerous, imagining to excess. It can blow up in your face. Threshold of revelation.

(Prior startles; then, as he searches for something to say:)

HARPER: Till we meet again.

(Prior leaves.
Harper sits alone for a bit, then, addressing the Mormon Mother:)

HARPER: Bitter lady of the Plains, talk to me. Tell me what to do.

(The Mormon Mother turns to Harper, then stands and leaves the diorama stage. She gestures with her head for Harper to follow her.
Harper goes to the diorama, gets in the Mormon Mother's seat.)

HARPER *(To the dummy father)*: Look at us. So perfect in place. The desert the mountains the previous century. Maybe I could have believed in you then. Maybe we should never have moved east.
(To the Mormon Mother) I'm stuck. My heart's an anchor.
MORMON MOTHER: Leave it, then. Can't carry no extra weight.

HARPER: Was it a hard thing, crossing the prairies?

MORMON MOTHER: You ain't stupid. So don't ask stupid. Ask something for real.

HARPER *(A beat, then)*: In your experience of the world. How do people change?

MORMON MOTHER: Well it has something to do with God so it's not very nice.

God splits the skin with a jagged thumbnail from throat to belly and then plunges a huge filthy hand in, he grabs hold of your bloody tubes and they slip to evade his grasp but he squeezes hard, he *insists*, he pulls and pulls till all your innards are yanked out and the pain! We can't even talk about that. And then he stuffs them back, dirty, tangled and torn. It's up to you to do the stitching.

HARPER: And then get up. And walk around.

MORMON MOTHER: Just mangled guts pretending.

HARPER: That's how people change.

(They exit.)

Scene 4

Late that afternoon. Split scene: Joe and Louis at Jones Beach, and later, Prior in his apartment, and Louis at a Brooklyn payphone.

Joe and Louis are sitting shoulder to shoulder in the dunes, facing the ocean. It's cold. The sound of waves and gulls and distant Belt Parkway traffic. New York Romantic. Joe is very cold, Louis as always is oblivious to the weather.

LOUIS: The winter Atlantic. Wow, huh?

There used to be guys in the dunes even when it snowed. Nothing deterred us from the task at hand.

JOE: Which was?

LOUIS: Exploration. Across an unmapped terrain. The body of the homosexual human male. Here, or the Ramble, or the scrub pines on Fire Island, or the St. Mark's Baths. Hardy pioneers. Like your ancestors.

JOE: Not exactly.

LOUIS: And many have perished on the trail.

I fucked around a lot more than he did. No justice.

(Little pause.)

JOE: I love it when you can get to places and see what it used to be. The whole country was like this once. A paradise.

LOUIS: Ruined now.

JOE: It's still a great country. Best place on earth. Best place to be.

LOUIS *(Staring at him a beat, then)*: OY. A *Mormon.*

JOE: You never asked.

LOUIS: So what else haven't you told me?

Joe?

So the fruity underwear you wear, that's . . . ?

JOE: A temple garment.

LOUIS: *Oh my God.* What's it for?

JOE: Protection. A second skin. I can stop wearing it if you—

LOUIS: How can you stop wearing it if it's a skin? Your past, your beliefs, your—

JOE: I know how you feel, I keep expecting Divine Retribution for this, but . . .

I'm actually happy. Actually.

LOUIS: You're not happy, that's ridiculous, no one is happy. What am I doing? With you? With *anyone*, I should be exterminated but with *you*: I mean politically, and, and you're probably bisexual, and, and I mean I really *like* you a lot, but—

(Joe puts his hand over Louis's mouth.)

LOUIS: So, like, *this* is kind of hot . . .
JOE: Shut up, OK?

(Louis nods. Joe takes his hand off Louis's mouth and, after looking all around, kisses him, deeply.)

JOE: You know why you find the world so unsatisfying?

(Louis shakes his head no.)

JOE: Because you believe it's perfectible.
LOUIS: No I—
JOE: You tell yourself you don't, but you do, you cling to fantasies of perfection, and, and kindliness, and you never face the sorrow of the world, its bitterness. The parts of it that are bitter.
LOUIS *(Intrigued)*: Huh.
JOE: You have to reconcile yourself to the world's unperfectibility.
LOUIS *(Nodding)*: Reconcile. And . . . And how do you do that?

(Joe kisses Louis again, begins to unbutton Louis's shirt.)

JOE: By being thoroughly in the world but not of it.
LOUIS: You, you mean like a like an Emersonian kind of kind of thing? I don't see how that's um workable, practical, given, you know, *emotions* and—

(Joe bites Louis's nipple.)

LOUIS: Oh God . . .

JOE: You have to accept that we're not put here to make the entire earth into a heaven, you have to accept we can't. And accept as rightfully yours the happiness that comes your way.

LOUIS: But . . . *Rightfully?* That's . . . so . . . Republican, it's— Bite my nipple again.

(Joe does. Louis responds. Joe starts to unzip Louis's pants. Louis stops him.)

LOUIS: No, wait, fuck, I'm like lost in an ideological leather bar with you. I want my, my *clarity* back, what little I ever possessed, it's been stolen by, I mean, I mean I wish you weren't so, so . . .

JOE: Conservative.

LOUIS: No. So fucking gorgeous. *And conservative!* Though if you were gorgeous and your politics didn't horrifically suck I'd really be in trouble here, but yes, I do sort of wish you weren't responsible for everything bad and evil in the world.

JOE *(Not taking the bait, trying to keep the sex going forward)*: You give me way too much credit.

LOUIS: Right, I mean, Reagan deserves his fair share.

(Joe playfully pulls Louis's hair, but Louis shakes his hand away. Louis's withdrawal is beginning to make Joe apprehensive: something's up.)

JOE: You're obsessed, you know that? If people like you didn't have President Reagan to demonize, where would you be?

LOUIS: If he didn't have people like me to demonize where would *he* be? Upper-right-hand square on *The Hollywood Squares.*

JOE *(Seriously)*: I'm not your enemy. Louis.

LOUIS: I never said you were my—

JOE: Fundamentally, we both want the same thing.

(Little pause. Louis nods his head yes, then:)

LOUIS: I don't think that's true.

JOE: It is.

What you did . . . When you walked out on him, that was, it must've been hard. To do that. The world may not understand it or approve but . . . You did what you needed to do. And, and since I first met you, I . . . I consider you very brave. I don't think I've ever met anyone as—

LOUIS: Nobody does what I did, Joe. Nobody.

JOE: But maybe many want to.

This is so . . . This isn't . . . But.

(Beat)

I. I'm maybe . . . falling in—

(Louis laughs, embarrassed and alarmed.)

LOUIS: No you're not.

JOE *(Angry)*: Don't laugh at— Don't say that. I am. I'm—

LOUIS: You're not! You can't be, it's only been two weeks.
(Continue below:)

JOE: Three, actually, and what difference does that— I've never felt so, um, so happy to, so *hungry* for anyone before, it's like all the time I—

LOUIS *(Continuous from above)*: It takes *years* to . . . feel like that, love, love, ohmygod, *love*, if there even is such a

thing as, as— You *think* you do but that's just the, the
gay virgin thing, that's—

JOE: You and I, Louis, we're the same. We are. We both want
the same thing. We both—

LOUIS: I want to see Prior again.

(Joe freezes, then turns away.)

LOUIS: I miss him, I—

JOE: You want to go back to—

LOUIS: I just . . . need to see him again.

 It's like a, a bubble rising through rock, it's taken time,
these weeks, with you, but—

 Don't you . . . You must want to see your wife.

(Little pause.)

JOE: I miss her, I feel bad for her, I . . . I'm afraid of her.

LOUIS: Yes.

JOE: And I want more to be with—

LOUIS: I have to. See him.

 Please don't look so sad.

 Do you understand what I—

JOE: You don't want to see me anymore.

LOUIS *(Uncertainly)*: I—

JOE: Louis.

 Anything.

LOUIS: What?

JOE: Anything. Whatever you want. I can give up anything.

 My skin.

*(Joe starts to remove his clothes. When he realizes what Joe is
doing, Louis tries to stop him.)*

LOUIS: What are you doing, someone will see us, it's not a nude beach, it's freezing!

(Joe pushes Louis away, Louis falls, and Joe removes the rest of his clothing, tearing the temple garment off. He's naked.)

JOE: I'm flayed. No past now. I could give up anything. Maybe . . . in what we've been doing, maybe I'm even infected.

LOUIS: No you're—

JOE: I'm so . . . afraid of that. Of things I never knew I'd ever be afraid of, things I didn't even know existed until we— I'm afraid, now, maybe for the first time, really . . . um, scared.

Because I don't want to be sick. I want to live now. Maybe for the first time ever. And . . .

And I can be anything, anything I need to be. And I want to be with you.

(Louis starts to gather up Joe's clothes and dress him.)

JOE: You have a good heart and you think the good thing is to be guilty and kind always but it's not always kind to be gentle and soft, there's a genuine violence softness and weakness visit on people. You ought to think about that.

LOUIS: I will. Think about it.

JOE: You ought to think about—

LOUIS: Yeah, I will.

JOE: —about what you're doing to me. No, I mean— *(Continue below:)*

LOUIS: I'm sorry, I will, I, I tried to warn you that I—

JOE *(Continuous from above)*: *What you need.* Think about what you need. Be brave.

(Louis starts to walk away from Joe. Joe calls after him:)

JOE: And then you'll come back to me.

(Louis turns back to Joe, then turns again and leaves the beach. Joe starts to dress himself, then sinks to his knees in the sand.
Prior returns home to his apartment. He unwraps his layers of black prophet clothes. He is sweating heavily and feels very sick.
He goes to the sink, runs water, splashes a little on his face, shudders.
Joe, on the beach, looks up and yells:)

JOE: YOU'LL COME BACK TO ME!

(Joe remains, kneeling in the sand, trying to collect himself, unable to move.
Louis is now at a payphone at the edge of a parking lot near the beach.
Prior, in his apartment, takes one pill each from three different bottles, puts them in his mouth, then puts his mouth to the faucet.
Louis dials a number.
In Prior's apartment, the phone rings. Prior's still swallowing. He grabs the phone.)

PRIOR: Wait, I have a mouthful of pills and water, I—
LOUIS: Prior? It's Lou.

(Prior swallows.)

LOUIS: I want to see you.

ACT FOUR:

John Brown's Body

January 1986

Scene 1

Two days later. Roy and Joe in Roy's hospital room. Roy's in a big hospital chair, the kind that makes it possible for very sick people to sit upright briefly. The tube of an IV drip bag, hanging from a portable drip stand, runs into a vein in his arm. He's shockingly altered, in terrible shape. He wears a flimsy hospital bathrobe; under that, a backless hospital johnny gown, and under that, adult diapers. His legs are bare, fish-belly white, and there are disposable hospital slippers on his feet.

He forces himself to speak as normally as he can, using energy he doesn't have, to focus and stay connected.

Joe sits in an ordinary chair, facing Roy.

ROY: If you want the smoke and puffery you can listen to Kissinger and Schultz and those guys, but if you want to look at the heart of modern conservatism, you look at me.

Everyone else has abandoned the struggle, everything nowadays is just sipping tea with Nixon and Mao, that was *disgusting*, did you see that? Were you born yet?

JOE: Of course I—

ROY: My generation, we had *clarity*. Unafraid to look deep into the miasma at the heart of the world, what a pit, what a nightmare is there—*I* have looked, I have searched all my life for absolute bottom, and I found it, *believe* me: *Stygian*. How tragic, how brutal life is. How false people are. The immutable heart of what we are that bleeds through whatever we might become. All else is vanity.

I don't know the world anymore.

(He coughs)

After I die they'll say it was for the money and the headlines. But it was never the money: it's the moxie that counts. I never waivered. You: remember.

JOE: I will, Roy.

(Pause. Roy is sunk in silence. Joe is moved by what Roy's said, but he doesn't know how to respond. He clears his throat, then:)

JOE: I left my wife.

(Little pause)

I needed to tell you.

ROY: It happens.

JOE: I've been staying with someone. Someone else.

ROY: It happens.

JOE: With a . . .

I was afraid you wouldn't want to see me. If you'd forgive me. For letting you down.

ROY *(A shrug)*: I forgive you. But I don't forget. Or I forget but I don't forgive, I can't remember which, what does it—

(Suddenly looking around) You seen a lady around here, dumpy lady, stupid . . . hat? She . . . Oh boy. Oh boy, no she's off watching the hearings. Treacherous bitch.

JOE: Who?

ROY: Did you get a blessing from your father before he died?

JOE: A blessing?

ROY: Yeah.

JOE: No.

ROY: He should have done that. Life. That's what they're supposed to bless. Life.

(Roy motions for Joe to come over, then for him to kneel. Joe hesitates, then kneels.

Roy puts his hand on Joe's forehead. Joe leans the weight of his head into Roy's hand. They both close their eyes and enjoy it for a moment.)

JOE *(Quietly)*: Roy, I . . . I need to talk to you about—

ROY: Ssshah. Schmendrick. Don't fuck up the magic.

(He removes his hand) A *Brokhe.* You don't even have to trick it out of me, like what's his name in the Bible.

JOE: Jacob.

ROY: That's the one. A ruthless motherfucker, some bald runt, but he laid hold of his birthright with his claws and his teeth. Jacob's father—what was the guy's name?

JOE: Isaac.

ROY: Yeah. The sacrifice. That jerk.

My mother read me those stories.

See this scar on my nose? When I was three months old, there was a bony spur, she made them operate, shave it off. They said I was too young for surgery, I'd outgrow it but she insisted. I figure she wanted to toughen me up. And it worked.

I am tough. It's taking a lot . . . to dismantle me.
(He winces; he's having trouble masking the pain he's in)
Now you have to go.

(Joe stands, slowly, reluctant to leave.)

JOE: OK, I— But I.
The person I'm staying with?
It's not a . . .
(Forcing himself to say it) It's a . . . man.

(Pause.)

ROY: A man?
JOE: Yes.

(Little pause.)

ROY: You're with a man?
JOE: Yes I . . .

(He doesn't look at Roy. Roy however is looking hard at him.)

JOE: Yes. I, I guess I am, yes, it's someone I met, recently, we—for three weeks now, actually, we . . .
(He laughs, embarrassed)
Although I don't know if I, if he wants to, um, continue what . . .
And I'm going kinda crazy, a little, I can't, I don't know what I'll do if he, if he . . .

(Joe looks at Roy, who is now looking away.)

JOE: I guess it's a surprise to you, that I'm— I hope this is OK. There's no one I can talk to about it, I never wanted to talk about, about this, but now I'm going pillar to post, looking for, for oh Lord I don't know— *(Another laugh, angry, then, putting the word in air quotes)* "Sympathy"? I suppose? Which I never used to need, which I never wanted, never allowed or even, um *felt* for myself, I always found the whole idea of it just contemptible, just . . . repulsive— *(Continue below:)*

ROY *(Very soft, adrift, strange)*: Yeah . . .

JOE *(Not hearing Roy, continuous from above)*: —and I know how . . . preposterous this is, coming at you with this, but you . . .

I know you care for me. I know that. And I'm so—

(Roy starts to stand up.)

ROY: I gotta . . .

JOE: You . . . Oh I'm sorry, I'm— What, the . . . um, bathroom or . . . ?

(Roy walks unsteadily. The IV tube in his arm extends to its full length and then pulls. Roy looks down at it, remembering it's there. In a calm, disinterested manner he pulls it out of his arm, which starts bleeding profusely.)

ROY: Ow.

JOE: Roy, what are you—

(Joe starts for the door. Roy stands still, watching dark blood run down his arm.)

JOE *(Calling off)*: Um, help, please, I think he—

(Belize enters with the portable oxygen, and then sees Roy.)

BELIZE: Holy shit.

(Belize puts on rubber gloves, starts toward Roy.)

ROY *(To Belize)*: Get the fuck away from me.
JOE *(Going toward Roy)*: Roy, please, get back into—
ROY *(To Joe)*: SHUT UP!
    Now you listen to me.
BELIZE *(To Roy)*: Get your—
ROY *(To Belize)*: SHUT UP I SAID.
    (To Joe) I want you home. With your wife. Whatever else you got going, cut it dead.
JOE: Oh. Oh I, I *can't*, Roy, I need to be with him, I need to, I'm—

(Roy grabs Joe by the shirt, smearing it with blood.)

ROY: YOU NEED? *Listen to me. You do what I say. Or you will regret it.*

(Roy lets go of Joe's shirt, turning from him, disoriented, looking for the bed:)

ROY *(To Joe)*: And don't talk to me about it. *Ever again.*

(Belize moves in, takes Roy to the bed and begins bandaging the punctured arm.)

ROY *(To Joe)*: I . . . never saw that coming. You kill me.
BELIZE *(To Joe)*: Get somewhere you can take off that shirt and throw it out, and don't touch the blood.
JOE: Why? I don't unders—

ROY: OUT! OUT! You already got my blessing— WHAT MORE DO YOU WANT FROM ME?

(He has a terrible wracking spasm.)

BELIZE *(To Joe)*: Get the fuck outta here!
JOE *(To Roy)*: Please, wait, let me just wait till—
ROY *(Exhausted)*: Till *what?* You what, you want to stay and watch *this?* Well fuck you, too.

(Joe leaves.
Belize finishes bandaging Roy's arm, both of them silent for as long as this takes.
When he's finished with the arm, Belize straightens up a little. Roy looks blankly at the bandage, then:)

ROY: Every goddamn thing I ever wanted they have taken from me. Mocked and reviled, all my life.
BELIZE: Join the club.
ROY: I don't belong to any club you could get through the front door of.
    You watch yourself you take too many liberties.
    What's your name?
BELIZE *(A beat, then)*: Norman Arriaga. Belize to my friends, but you can call me Norman Arriaga.
ROY: Tell me something, Norman, you ever hire a lawyer?
BELIZE: No Roy. Never did.
ROY: Hire a lawyer, sue somebody, it's good for the soul.
    Lawyers are . . . the High Priests of America. We alone know the words that made America. Out of thin air. We alone know how to use The Words. The Law: the only club I ever wanted to belong to. And before they take that from me, I'm going to die.

(Roy has a series of awful spasms, the worst so far; they shake him violently. Roy grabs Belize by both arms. Belize tries to control Roy's body as he convulses in horrible pain. Roy hangs onto Belize; they're in a tight, desperate embrace, both shaken by Roy's agonized spasming.
During this seizure, Ethel appears.)

ROY: Sssshhh. Fire. Out.

(The pain subsiding a little, Roy forces the convulsions to abate. Through the remainder of the scene, with grim effort, conserving his resources, he just manages to keep his body under his control.)

ROY: God have mercy. This is a lousy way to go.
BELIZE: God have mercy.
ROY *(Seeing Ethel)*: Look who's back.
BELIZE *(Looking around, seeing no one)*: Who?
ROY: Mrs. Reddy Kilowatt.
      Fucking horror. How's . . . Yonkers?
BELIZE: I almost feel sorry for you.
ETHEL: A bad idea.
ROY: Yeah. Pity. Repulsive.
      (To Belize) You. Me. *(He snaps his fingers)* No. Connection.
      (Looking at Ethel) Nobody . . . with me now. But the dead.

Scene 2

Same day. Louis sitting alone, cold, on a park bench.
Prior enters and sits on the bench, as far as he can from Louis.

PRIOR: Oh this is going to be so much worse than I'd imagined.

LOUIS: Hello.

PRIOR: Fuck you you little shitbag.

LOUIS: Don't waste energy beating up on me, OK? I'm already taking care of that.

PRIOR: Don't see any bruises.

LOUIS: Inside.

PRIOR: You are one noble guy. *Inside.* Don't flatter yourself, Louis.

So. It's your tea party. Talk.

LOUIS: It's good to see you again. I missed you.

PRIOR: Talk.

LOUIS: I want to . . . try to make up.

PRIOR: Make up.

LOUIS: Yes. But—

PRIOR: Aha. But.

LOUIS: But you don't have to be so hostile. Don't I get any points for trying to arrive at a resolution? Maybe what I did isn't forgivable but—

PRIOR: It isn't.

LOUIS: But. I'm trying to be responsible. Prior. There are limits. Boundaries. And you have to be reasonable. *(Unable not to ask) Why are you dressed like that?*

PRIOR *(A challenging, cold smile)*: You were saying something about being reasonable.

LOUIS: I've been giving this a lot of thought. Yes I fucked up, that's obvious. But maybe you fucked up too. You never trusted me, you never gave me a chance to find my footing, not really, you were so quick to attack and . . . I think, maybe just too much of a victim, finally. Passive. Dependent. And what I think is that people do have a choice about how they handle—

PRIOR *(Cutting to the chase)*: You want to come back. Why? Atonement? Exoneration?

LOUIS: I didn't say I wanted to come back.

(Pause.)

PRIOR: Oh.
    No, you didn't.

LOUIS *(Softly, almost pleading)*: I can't. Move in again, start all over again. I don't think it'd be any different.

(Little pause. Prior looks hard at Louis.)

PRIOR: You're seeing someone else.

LOUIS *(Shocked)*: What? No.

PRIOR: You are.

LOUIS: I'M NOT. Well, occasionally a . . . He's a . . . just a pickup, how do you—

PRIOR: Threshold of revelation. Now: Ask me how I know he's a Mormon.

(Louis stares, shocked; Prior's as surprised as Louis.)

PRIOR: *Is* he a Mormon?
    (Little pause, then impressed and frightened:)
    Well, goddamn.
    Ask me how I knew.

LOUIS: How?

PRIOR *(Furious)*: Fuck you! I'm a prophet!

    Reasonable? Limits? Tell it to my *lungs*, stupid, tell it to my lesions, tell it to the cotton-woolly patches in my eyes!

LOUIS: Prior, I . . . haven't seen him for days now, I just—

PRIOR: I'm going, I have limits, too.

(Prior starts to leave. He has an attack of respiratory trouble. He sits heavily on the bench. Louis reaches out to him; Prior waves him away.

    Louis cries. Prior looks at Louis.)

PRIOR: You cry, but you endanger nothing in yourself. It's like the idea of crying when you do it. Or the idea of love.

    So. Your *boyfriend*—

LOUIS: He's not my—

PRIOR: Tell me where you met him.

LOUIS: In the park. Well, first at work, he—

PRIOR: He's a lawyer or a judge?

LOUIS: Lawyer.

PRIOR: A Gay Mormon Lawyer.

LOUIS: Yes. Republican too.

PRIOR: A Gay Mormon Republican Lawyer. *(With scathing contempt)* Louis . . .

LOUIS: But he's sort of, I don't know if the word would be . . . well, in a way sensitive, and I—

PRIOR: Ah. A *sensitive* gay Republican.

LOUIS: He's just company. Companionship.

(Pause.)

PRIOR: Companionship. Oh.

    You know just when I think he couldn't possibly say anything to make it worse, he does. Companionship. How *good*. I wouldn't want you to be *lonely*.

There are thousands of gay men in New York City with AIDS and nearly every one of them is being taken care of by . . . a friend or by . . . a lover who has stuck by them through things worse than my . . . So far. Everyone got that, except me. I got you. Why? What's wrong with me?

(Louis is crying again.)

PRIOR: Louis? Are you really bruised inside?

LOUIS: I can't have this talk anymore.

PRIOR: Oh the *list* of things you can't do. So fragile! Answer me: Inside: Bruises?

LOUIS: Yes.

PRIOR: Come back to me when they're visible. I want to see black and blue, Louis, I want to see blood. Because I can't believe you even *have* blood in your veins till you show it to me. So don't come near me again, unless you've got something to show.

(Prior leaves.)

Scene 3

Night of the following day. Roy's hospital room. There are several new machines, monitoring Roy's condition, which is considerably worse. Roy is sleeping a deep, morphine-induced sleep. Belize enters, carrying a tray and a glass of water. With some difficulty he wakes up Roy.

BELIZE: Time to take your pills.

ROY *(Waking, very disoriented)*: What? What time of . . .
　　Water.

(Belize gives him a glass of water. Roy takes a sip.)

ROY: Bitter.
　　Look out there. Black midnight.
BELIZE: You want anything?
ROY: Nothing that comes from there. As far as I'm concerned
　　you can take all that away.
　　(Seeing Belize) Oh . . .
BELIZE: What?
ROY: Oh. The bogeyman is here.
　　Lookit, Ma, a schvartze toytenmann.
　　Come in, sweetheart, what took you so long?
BELIZE: You're flying, Roy. It's the morphine. They put mor-
　　phine in the drip to stop the . . . You awake? Can you
　　see who I am?
ROY: Oh yeah, you came for my mama, years ago.
　　(Confiding, intimate) You wrap your arms around me
　　now. Squeeze the bloody life from me. OK?
BELIZE: Uh, no, it's not OK. You're stoned, Roy.
ROY: Dark strong arms, take me like that. Deep and sincere but
　　not too rough, just open me up to the end of me.
BELIZE *(A beat, then gently)*: Who am I, Roy?
ROY: The Negro night nurse, my negation. You've come to
　　escort me to the underworld. *(A serious sexual invitation)*
　　Come on.

*(A weight of sadness descends on Belize. He puts down the pill
tray and bends close over Roy:)*

BELIZE: You want me in your bed, Roy? You want me to take
　　you away.

ROY: I'm ready . . .

BELIZE: I'll be coming for you soon. Everything I want is in the end of you.

(Belize starts to move away from Roy.)

ROY: Let me ask you something, sir.

BELIZE: *Sir?*

ROY: What's it like? After?

BELIZE: After . . . ?

ROY: This misery ends.

BELIZE: Hell or Heaven?

ROY: Aw, come on . . . Jesus Christ, who has time for these . . . games . . .

BELIZE: Like San Francisco.

ROY: A city. Good. I was worried . . . it'd be a garden. I hate that shit.

BELIZE: Mmmm.

Big city, overgrown with weeds, but flowering weeds.

(Roy smiles and nods. Belize sits on the bed, next to Roy.)

BELIZE: On every corner a wrecking crew and something new and crooked going up catty-corner to that. Windows missing in every edifice like broken teeth, fierce gusts of gritty wind, and a gray, high sky full of ravens.

ROY: Isaiah.

BELIZE: Prophet birds, Roy.

Piles of trash, but lapidary like rubies and obsidian, and diamond-colored cow-spit streamers in the wind. And voting booths.

ROY: And a dragon atop a golden horde.

BELIZE: And everyone in Balenciaga gowns with red corsages, and big dance palaces full of music and lights and racial impurity and gender confusion.

(Roy laughs softly, delighted.)

BELIZE: And all the deities are Creole, mulatto, brown as the mouths of rivers.

(Roy laughs again.)

BELIZE: Race, taste and history finally overcome.
    And you ain't there.
ROY *(Shaking his head no in happy agreement)*: And Heaven?
BELIZE *(A beat, then)*: That *was* Heaven, Roy.
ROY: The fuck it was.
    (Suspicious, frightened) Who are you?

(Belize stands up.)

BELIZE *(Soft, calming)*: Your negation.
ROY: Yeah. I know you. Nothing. A stomach grumble that wakes you in the night.

(Ethel enters.)

BELIZE: Been nice talking to you. Go to sleep now, baby. I'm just the shadow on your grave.

Scene 4

The next day. Joe in his office at the courthouse in Brooklyn. He sits dejectedly at his desk. Prior and Belize enter the corridor outside.

PRIOR *(Whisper)*: That's his office.
BELIZE *(Whisper)*: This is stupid.
PRIOR *(Whisper)*: Go home if you're chicken.
BELIZE: *You're* the one who should be home.
PRIOR: I have a hobby now: haunting people. Fuck home. You wait here. I want to meet my replacement.

(Prior goes to Joe's door, opens it, steps in.)

PRIOR: Oh.
JOE: Yes, can I—
PRIOR: You look just like the dummy. She's right.
JOE: Who's right?
PRIOR: Your wife.

(Pause.)

JOE: What?
       Do you know my—
PRIOR: No.
JOE: You said my wife.
PRIOR: No I didn't.
JOE: Yes you did.
PRIOR: You misheard. I'm a Prophet.
JOE: What?
PRIOR: PROPHET PROPHET I PROPHESY I HAVE SIGHT I *SEE*.
       What do *you* do?

JOE: I'm a clerk.

PRIOR: Oh big deal. A clerk. You *what*, you file things? Well you better be keeping a file on the hearts you break, that's all that counts in the end, you'll have bills to pay in the world to come, you and your friend, the Whore of Babylon.
(*Little pause*)
Sorry wrong room.

(*Prior exits, goes to Belize.*)

PRIOR (*Despairing*): He's the Marlboro Man.

BELIZE: Oooh, I wanna see.

(*Joe is standing, perplexed, when Belize enters the office. Belize instantly recognizes Joe.*)

BELIZE: *Sacred* Heart of Jesus!

JOE: Now what is—
You're Roy's nurse. I recognize you, you're—

BELIZE: No you don't.

JOE: From the hospital. You're Roy Cohn's nurse.

BELIZE: No I'm not. Not a nurse. We all look alike to you. You all look alike to us. It's a mad mad world. Have a nice day.

(*Belize exits, runs back to Prior.*)

PRIOR: Home on the range?

BELIZE: Chaps and spurs. Now girl we *got* to get you home and into—

PRIOR: Mega-butch. He made me feel beyond nelly. Like little wispy daisies were sprouting out my ears. Little droopy wispy wilted—

225

(Joe comes out of his office.)

BELIZE: Run! Run!
JOE: Wait!

(They're cornered by Joe. Belize averts his face, masking his mouth and chin with his scarf.)

JOE: What game are you playing, this is a federal courthouse. You said . . . something about my wife. Now what . . . How do you know my—
PRIOR: I'm . . . Nothing. I'm a mental patient. He's my nurse.
BELIZE: Not his nurse, I'm not a n—
PRIOR: We're here because my will is being contested. Um, what is that called, when they challenge your will?
JOE: Competency? But this is an appellate court.
PRIOR: And I am *appealing* to anyone, anyone in the universe, who will listen to me for some . . . Charity . . . Some people are so . . . *greedy*, such pigs, they have everything, health, *everything*, and still they want more.
JOE: You said my wife. And I want to know, is she—
PRIOR: TALK TO HER YOURSELF, BULLWINKLE! WHAT DO I LOOK LIKE A MARRIAGE COUNSELOR?

(To Belize) Oh, nursey dear, fetch the medication, I'm starting to rave.
BELIZE: Pardons, Monsieur l'Avocat, nous sommes absolument Desolée.

(Prior blows a raspberry at Joe.)

BELIZE: Behave yourself, cherie, or nanny will have to use the wooden spoon.

(Prior exits.)

BELIZE *(To Joe, dropping scarf disguise)*: I am trapped in a world of white people. That's *my* problem. *(He exits)*

Scene 5

The next day. At the Bethesda Fountain in Central Park. It's cold, and as the scene progresses a storm front moves in and the sky darkens. Louis is sitting on the fountain's rim. Belize enters and sits next to him.

BELIZE: Nice angel.

LOUIS: What angel?

BELIZE: The fountain.

LOUIS *(Looking)*: Bethesda.

BELIZE: What's she commemorate? Louis, I'll bet you know.

LOUIS: The . . . Croton Aqueduct, I think. Right after the Civil War. Prior loves this—

BELIZE: The Civil War. I knew you'd know.

LOUIS: I know all sorts of things. The sculptress was a lesbian.

BELIZE: Ooh, a sister! That a fact? You are nothing if not well informed.

LOUIS: Listen. I saw Prior yesterday.

BELIZE: Prior is *upset*.

LOUIS: This guy I'm seeing, I'm not seeing him now. Prior misunderstood, he jumped to—

BELIZE: Oh yeah. Your new beau. Prior and me, we went to the courthouse. Scoped him out.

LOUIS: *You had no right to do that.*

BELIZE: Oh did we violate your *rights.* *(Continue below:)*

LOUIS: Yeah, sort of, and, and— Couldn't you have done this on the phone, you needed to, what? Extract every last drop of, of schadenfreude, get off on how unhappy I am, how—

BELIZE *(Continuous from above)*: You walk out on your lover. Days don't pass before you are out on the town with somebody new. But this— *"Schadenfreude"? (Continue below:)*

LOUIS: I'm *not* out on the— I want you to tell Prior that I—

BELIZE *(Continuous from above)*: *This* is a record low: sharing your dank and dirty bed with Roy Cohn's buttboy.

(Pause.)

LOUIS: Come again?

BELIZE: Doesn't that bother you at all?

LOUIS: *Roy Cohn?* What the fuck are you— I am not sharing my bed with Roy Cohn's . . .

BELIZE: Your little friend didn't tell you, huh? You and Hoss Cartwright, it's not a verbal kind of thing, you just kick off your boots and hit the hay.

LOUIS: Joe Pitt is not Roy Cohn's— Joe is a very moral man, he's not even *that* conservative, or, well not that *kind* of a . . . And I don't want to continue this.

BELIZE *(Starting to go)*: Bye-bye.

LOUIS: It's not my fault that Prior left you for me.

BELIZE: I beg your pardon.

LOUIS: You have always hated me. Because you are in love with Prior and you were when I met him and he fell in love with me, and so now you cook up this . . . I mean how do you know this? That Joe and *Roy Cohn* are—

BELIZE: I don't know whether Mr. Cohn has penetrated more than his *spiritual* sphincter. All I'm saying is you better hope there's no GOP germ, Louis, 'cause if there is, you got it.

LOUIS: *I don't believe you.* Not . . . *Roy Cohn.* Joe wouldn't— Not *Roy Cohn.* He's, he's like the polestar of human evil, he's like the worst human being who ever lived, the, the damage he's done, the years and years of, of . . . criminality, that whole era, that— Give me fucking credit for *something*, please, some little moral shred of, of, of *something*, OK sure I fucked up, I fucked up everything, I didn't want to, to face what I needed to face, what life was insisting I face but I don't know, I've always, I've always felt you had to, to take *action*, not sit, not to be, to be trapped, um, stuck, paralyzed by— Even if it's hard, or really terrifying, or even if it does damage, you have to keep moving, um, forward, instead of— I can't just, you know, sit around *feeling* shit, or feeling *like* shit, I . . . cry way too easily, I fall apart, I'm no good unless I, I *strike out* at— Which is easy because I'm so fucking *furious* at my— So I fucked up spectacularly, totally, I've ruined my life, and his life, I've hurt him so badly but but still, even I, even I am not so utterly lost inside myself that I— I wouldn't, um, *ever*, like, *sleep* with someone who . . . someone who's *Roy Cohn's* . . . *(He stops himself)*

BELIZE: Buttboy.

LOUIS *(In complete despair, quietly)*: Oh no.

BELIZE: You know what your problem is, Louis? Your problem is that you are so full of piping hot crap that the mention of your name draws flies. You don't even know Thing One about this guy, do you?

(Louis shakes his head no.)

BELIZE: Uh-huh. Well ain't that pathetic.

Just so's the record's straight: I love Prior but I was never in love with him. I have a man, uptown, and I have since *long* before I first laid my eyes on the sorry-ass sight of you.

LOUIS: I . . . I didn't know that you—

BELIZE: No 'cause you never bothered to ask.

Up in the air, just like that angel, too far off the earth to pick out the details. Louis and his Big Ideas. Big Ideas are all you love. "America" is what Louis loves.

(Louis is looking at the angel, not at Belize.)

LOUIS: So what? Maybe I do. You don't know what I love. You don't.

BELIZE: Well I hate America, Louis. I hate this country. It's just big ideas, and stories, and people dying, and people like you.

The white cracker who wrote the National Anthem knew what he was doing. He set the word "free" to a note so high nobody can reach it. That was deliberate. Nothing on earth sounds less like freedom to me.

You come with me to room 1013 over at the hospital, I'll show you America. Terminal, crazy and mean.

(A rumble of thunder. Then the rain comes. Belize has a collapsible umbrella, and he raises it. Louis stands in the rain.)

BELIZE: I *live* in America, Louis, that's hard enough, I don't have to love it. You do that. Everybody's got to love something.

(Belize leaves.)

LOUIS *(Quiet, resolved)*: Everybody does.

Scene 6

Same day. Hannah sits alone at the Visitors' Center reception desk.
It's dark outside, and raining steadily. Distant thunder.
   Joe enters.
   They look at each other for a long moment.

JOE: You shouldn't have come.

HANNAH: You already made that clear as day.

JOE: I'm sorry. I . . . I . . . don't understand why you're here.

HANNAH: For more than two weeks. You can't even return a simple phone call.

JOE: I just don't . . . have anything to say. I have nothing to say.

HANNAH: You could tell me so I could tell her where you are. You've been living on some rainy rooftop for all we knew. It's cruel.

JOE: Not intended to be.

HANNAH: You're sure about that.

JOE: I'm taking her home.

HANNAH: You think that's best for her, you think that she should—

JOE: I know what I'm doing.

HANNAH: I don't think you have a clue. You can afford not to. You're a man, you botch up, it's not a big deal, but she's been—

JOE: Just being a man doesn't mean . . . anything.
   It's still a big deal, Ma. Botching up.
   (Tough, cold, angry, holding it in) And nothing works. Not all my . . . oh, you know, my *effortful* clinging to the good, to what's right, not pursuing . . . freedom, or happiness. Nothing, nothing works anymore, nothing I try

fixes anything at all, nothing, I've got nothing, now, my whole life, all I've done is make . . . botches. Just . . .

(He looks down, shakes his head; he can't continue. Then:)

I'm really . . . um . . . *(This is not the word he wants to say)* bewildered . . .

(Little pause. Hannah looks at him; he wants consolation, but something stops her.)

HANNAH *(Quietly but firmly)*: Being a woman's harder. Look at her.

(Little pause.)

JOE: You and me. It's like we're back in Salt Lake again. You sort of bring the desert with you.
      Is she . . . ?
HANNAH: She's not here.
JOE: But . . . I went to the apartment. She isn't . . .
HANNAH: Then she's escaped.
      I think maybe motion's better for her right now, being out and away from—
JOE: It's raining. She can't be out on her own.
HANNAH: Can I help look for—
JOE: There's nothing you can do. You should go, Ma, you should go back home. It's a terrible time. You never wanted to visit before. You shouldn't—
HANNAH: You never asked me.
JOE: You didn't have to—
HANNAH: I didn't and I shouldn't and I don't know *why* I did, but I'm here, so let me help.
JOE: *She's my responsibility. Ma.* Fly home. Please.

HANNAH: I . . . can't.

JOE: Why?

HANNAH: I . . .

Aunt Libby thought she'd smelled radon gas in the basement.

JOE: What?

HANNAH: Of the house.

JOE: You can't smell radon gas, it has no smell, and since when do you listen to, to Libby? I can't— *(Continue below:)*

HANNAH: I acted on impulse, and I . . . *(She decides against telling him that she's sold the house)*

JOE *(Continuous from above)*: I can't, um, could we talk about this another—

HANNAH: That thing you told me, that night. On the telephone, from Central Park. When you were drinking.

JOE: No, we can't do that. Not now. I don't want to— *(Continue below:)*

HANNAH: You said you thought you—

JOE *(Continuous from above)*: I don't want to talk about it. Forget it.

HANNAH: But I think maybe now we ought to, we ought to—

JOE *(Suddenly scarily enraged)*: NO!! And do what?! PRAY TOGETHER?! *NO.* I couldn't . . . *stomach* the prospect!

(Hannah turns away. He stares, baffled; it takes several moments for him to realize she might be crying.)

JOE: Are you . . . ?

I'm sorry. Don't cry.

HANNAH *(Not turning to face him)*: Don't be stupid.

And if I ever do. I promise you you'll not be privileged to witness it.

JOE: I should . . .

(Still facing away, she nods yes.)

JOE: Is there radon gas in the—
HANNAH: Just go.

(Little pause.)

JOE: I'll pay to change your ticket.

(Joe exits. Hannah sits. She's alone for several moments. There's a peal of thunder.
Prior enters, wet, in his prophet garb, dark glasses on, despite the dark day outside. He's breathless, manic.)

PRIOR: That man who was just here.
HANNAH *(Not looking at him)*: We're closed. Go away.
PRIOR: He's your son.

(Hannah looks at Prior. Little pause. Prior turns to leave.)

HANNAH: Do you know him. That man?
How . . . How do you know him, that he's my—
PRIOR: My ex-boyfriend, he knows him. I, I shadowed him, all the way up from— I wanted to, to . . . warn him about *later*, when his hair goes and there's hips and jowls and all that . . . human stuff, that poor slob there's just gonna wind up miserable, fat, frightened and *alone* because Louis, he can't handle bodies.

(Little pause.)

HANNAH: Are you a . . . a homosexual?
PRIOR: Oh is it *that* obvious? Yes. I am. What's it to you?

HANNAH: Would you say you are a typical . . . homosexual?

PRIOR: Me? Oh I'm *stereotypical*. What, you mean like am I a hairdresser or . . .

HANNAH: *Are* you a hairdresser?

PRIOR: Well it would be *your* lucky day if I was because frankly . . .

(Little pause.)

PRIOR: I'm sick. I'm sick. It's expensive.
   (He starts to cry)
   Oh shit now I won't be able to stop, now it's started. I feel really terrible, do I have a fever?

(Hannah doesn't touch his forehead. He offers it again, impatiently.)

PRIOR: *Do I have a fever?*

(She hesitates, then puts her hand on his forehead.)

HANNAH: Yes.

PRIOR: How high?

HANNAH: There might be a thermometer in the—

PRIOR: Very high, very high. Could you get me to a cab, I think I want . . .
   (He sits heavily on the floor)
   Don't be alarmed, it's worse than it looks, I mean—

HANNAH: You should . . . Try to stand up, or . . . Let me see if anyone can—

PRIOR *(Listening to his lungs)*: Sssshhh.
   Echo-breath, it's . . . *(He shakes his head "no good")* I . . . overdid it. I'm in trouble again.

235

Take me to Saint Vincent's Hospital, I mean, help me to a cab to the . . .

(Little pause, then Hannah exits and reenters with her coat on.)

HANNAH: Can you stand up?
PRIOR: You don't . . . Call me a—
HANNAH: I'm useless here.

(She helps him stand.)

PRIOR: Please, if you're trying to convert me this isn't a good time.

(Distant thunder. Prior looks up, startled.)

HANNAH: Lord, look at it out there. It's pitch-black. We better move.

(They exit. Thunder.)

Scene 7

Same day, late afternoon. Rain is coming down in sheets, an icy wind has picked up. Harper is standing at the railing of the Promenade in Brooklyn Heights, watching the river and the Manhattan skyline. She is wearing the dress she wore in Act Three, Scene 3, inadequate for the weather, and she's barefoot.
Joe enters with an umbrella. Harper turns to face him.

HARPER: The end of the world is at hand. Hello, paleface. *(She turns back to the skyline)*

Nothing like storm clouds over Manhattan to get you in the mood for Judgment Day.

(Thunder.)

JOE: It's freezing, it's raining, where are your shoes?

HARPER: I threw them in the river.

The Judgment Day. Everyone will think they're crazy now, not just me, everyone will see things. Sick men will see angels, women who have houses will sell their houses, dime store dummies will rear up on their wood-putty legs and roam the land, looking for brides.

JOE: Let's go home.

HARPER: Where's that?

(Pointing toward Manhattan) Want to buy an island? It's going out of business. You can have it for the usual cheap trinkets. Fire sale. The prices are insane.

JOE: Harper.

HARPER: Joe. Did you miss me?

JOE: I . . . I've come back.

HARPER: Oh I know.

Here's why I wanted to stay in Brooklyn. The Promenade view.

Water won't ever accomplish the end. No matter how much you cry. Flood's not the answer, people just float.

Let's go home.

Fire's the answer. The Great and Terrible Day. At last.

Scene 8

That night. Rain and thunder outside. Prior, Hannah and Emily (Prior's nurse-practitioner) in an examination room in Saint Vincent's emergency room. Emily is listening to Prior's breathing, while Hannah sits in a nearby chair.

EMILY: You've lost eight pounds. Eight pounds! I know people who would kill to be in the shape you were in, you were *recovering*, and you threw it away.

PRIOR: This isn't about WEIGHT, it's about LUNGS, UM . . . PNEUMONIA.

EMILY: We don't know yet.

PRIOR: THE FUCK WE DON'T ASSHOLE YOU MAY NOT BUT I *CAN'T BREATHE.*

HANNAH: You'd breathe better if you didn't holler like that.

PRIOR *(Looks at Hannah, then)*: This is my ex-lover's lover's Mormon mother.

(Little pause. Emily nods, then:)

EMILY: Keep breathing. Stop moving. STAY PUT.

(Prior startles at her last two words, and stares hard at Emily as she exits.)

HANNAH *(Standing to go)*: I should go.

PRIOR: I'm not insane.

HANNAH: I didn't say you—

PRIOR: I saw an angel.

(She doesn't respond.)

PRIOR: That's insane.

HANNAH: Well, it's—

PRIOR: Insane. But I'm not insane. Do I *seem* insane?

HANNAH: You . . . I'm not sure I—

PRIOR: Oh for pityfuckingsake just answer the fucking—

HANNAH: No. *Driven*, and, and rude, but—

PRIOR: But then why did I do this to myself? Because I have
been driven insane by . . . your son and by that lying . . .
Because I'm consumed by this ice-cold, razorblade terror
that shouts and shouts, "Don't stay still get out of bed
keep moving! Run!" And I've run myself into the ground.
Right where She said I'd eventually be.

What's happened to me?

She seemed so real.

HANNAH: Who?

Oh, the . . . *(Angel gesture)*

(Prior nods yes.

Hannah hesitates, then:)

HANNAH: Could be you had a vision.

PRIOR: A vision. Thank you, Maria Ouspenskaya.

HANNAH: People have visions.

PRIOR: No they— Not sane people.

HANNAH *(A beat before deciding to say this)*: One hundred and
seventy years ago, which is recent, an angel of God
appeared to Joseph Smith. In Upstate New York, not
far from here.

PRIOR: But that's ridiculous, that's—

HANNAH: It's not polite to call other people's beliefs
ridiculous.

PRIOR: I didn't mean to—

HANNAH: I *believe* this. He had great need of understanding. Our Prophet. His desire made prayer. His prayer made an angel. The angel was real. I believe that.

PRIOR: I don't. And I'm sorry but it's repellent to me. So much of what you believe.

HANNAH: What do I believe?

PRIOR: I'm a homosexual. With AIDS. I can just imagine what you—

HANNAH: No you can't. Imagine. The things in my head. You don't make assumptions about me, mister; I won't make them about you.

PRIOR *(A beat; he looks at her, then)*: Fair enough.

HANNAH: My son is . . . well, like you.

PRIOR: Homosexual.

HANNAH *(A nod, then)*: I flew into a rage when he told me, mad as August hornets. At first I assumed it was about his . . . *(She shrugs)*

PRIOR: Homosexuality.

HANNAH: But that wasn't it. Homosexuality. I don't find it an appetizing notion, two men, together, but men in *any* configuration . . . That wasn't it. Stupidity gets me cross, but that wasn't it either. I flew into a rage, filled with rage, then the rage . . . lifted me up; I felt . . . Truly I felt lifted up, into the air, and . . .

   (She laughs to herself)
   And I flew.

PRIOR: I wish you would be more true to your demographic profile.

(Little pause. Hannah smiles. They both laugh, a little. Prior's laugh brings on breathing trouble. Trying to find a comfortable position, he begins to panic.)

HANNAH: Just lie still. You'll be all right.

PRIOR: No. I won't be. My lungs are getting tighter. The fever mounts and you get delirious. And then days of delirium and awful pain and drugs; you start slipping and then. I really . . . fucked up.

(Losing it, crying) I'm scared. I can't do it again.

HANNAH: You shouldn't talk that way. You ought to make a better show of yourself.

PRIOR: Look at this . . . horror.

(He lifts his shirt; his torso is spotted with several lesions) See? See that? That's not human. That's why I run.

(Hannah's shocked but doesn't show it; it's hard to look at, but she manages.)

HANNAH: It's a cancer. Nothing more. Nothing more human than that.

(She puts a hand on his shoulder. He calms down. They're silent for a moment.)

PRIOR: Do Mormons read the you know the Bible? Or just the—

HANNAH *(Tight, trying not to take offense)*: The Book of Mormon is a part of the—

PRIOR: Don't get technical, you know what I mean, the other parts, the Old Testament part.

HANNAH: I've read the—

PRIOR: The prophets in the Bible, do they . . . ever refuse their visions?

HANNAH *(Considering, then)*: One did. There might be others, I—

PRIOR: And what does God do to them? When they do that?
HANNAH: He . . . feeds them to whales.

(Prior laughs, Hannah joins him, they're both a little hysterical. The laughter subsides.)

PRIOR: Stay with me.
HANNAH: Oh no, I—
PRIOR: Just till I sleep? You comfort me.
HANNAH: Oh, I—
PRIOR: You do, you . . . *(A little Katharine Hepburn)* stiffen my spine.

(Little pause.)

HANNAH: I'm not needed elsewhere, I suppose I . . .
(She thinks for a moment, then sits in a chair)
When I got up this morning this is not how I envisioned the day would end.
PRIOR: Me neither.

(He lies back, and she settles into her chair.)

HANNAH: An angel is a belief. With wings and arms that can carry you. If it lets you down, reject it.

(Prior looks at her.)

PRIOR: Huh.
HANNAH: There's scriptural precedent.
PRIOR: And then what?
HANNAH *(A little shrug, then)*: Seek something new.

Scene 9

That night, the rain's still falling. The Pitt apartment in Brooklyn. Joe and Harper's clothing is strewn about the floor.

Joe enters from the bedroom in a pair of boxers. He picks up his shirt, puts it on and starts to button it. He stops when Harper enters, wrapped in a bedsheet, naked underneath. He hesitates a beat, then resumes buttoning.

HARPER: When we have sex. Why do you keep your eyes closed?

JOE: I don't.

HARPER: You always do. You can say why, I already know the answer.

JOE: Then why do I have to—

HARPER: You imagine things.
Imagine men.

JOE: Yes.

HARPER: Imagining, just like me, except the only time I wasn't imagining was when I was with you. You, the one part of the real world I wasn't allergic to.

JOE: Please. Don't.

HARPER: But I only *thought* I wasn't dreaming.

(Joe picks up his pants. Harper watches him as he puts them on, then:)

HARPER: Oh. Oh. Back in Brooklyn, back with Joe.

JOE *(Still dressing, not looking at Harper)*: I'm going out. I have to get some stuff I left behind.

HARPER: Look at me.

(He doesn't. He puts on his socks and shoes.)

HARPER: Look at me.
>Look at me.
>*Here! Look here at—*
JOE *(Looking at her)*: What?
HARPER: What do you see?
JOE: What do I . . . ?
HARPER: What do you see?
JOE: *Nothing,* I—
>*(Little pause)*
>I see nothing.
HARPER *(A nod, then)*: Finally. The truth.
JOE *(A beat, then)*: I'm going. Out. Just . . . Out.

(He exits.)

HARPER: It sets you free.
>Good-bye.

Scene 10

Later that night. Louis is in his apartment, sitting on the floor; all around him are Xeroxed pages stapled together in thick packets. Louis is reading one of these.
>*There's a knock at the door.*

JOE *(Outside the apartment)*: Louis.
>Please let me in.

(Louis looks at the Xeroxed packets, fixes a grim little smile on his face, stands, unlocks the door, then immediately returns to his place on the floor.)

LOUIS: You're in.

(A little pause, then Joe turns the knob, opens the door and enters. He looks at Louis, who's ignoring him, continuing to read.)

JOE: You weren't at work. For three days now. You . . . I wish you'd get a phone.

> I'm staying in a hotel, near Fulton Street. It's kind of—

> You said you'd call me, or—

LOUIS *(Still reading)*: No I never.

JOE: Or OK I expected you to call me, I hoped you'd—

LOUIS *(Finally looking at Joe)*: "Have you no decency, sir?"

> Who said that?

JOE: I'm having a very hard time. With this. Please, can we—

LOUIS: "At long last? Have you no sense of decency?"

> *(Fake pleasant teasing)* Come on, who said it?

JOE: Who said . . . ?

LOUIS: Who said, "Have you no—"

JOE: I don't . . . I'm not interested in playing guessing games, Louis, please stop and let me—

LOUIS: You *really* don't know who said, "Have you no decency?"

JOE: I want to tell you something, I want to—

LOUIS: OK, second question: *Have* you no decency?

(Joe doesn't respond. Louis gathers the Xeroxed packets and stands up.)

LOUIS: Guess what I spent the rainy afternoon doing?

JOE: What?

LOUIS: Research at the courthouse. Look what I got:

> *(Holding out the papers)* The Decisions of Justice Theodore Wilson, Second Circuit Court of Appeals. 1981–1984. The Reagan Years.

(Little pause.)

JOE: You, um, you read my decisions.

LOUIS: *Your* decisions. Yes.

(The fake pleasantness fading) The librarian's gay, he has all the good dish, he told me that Justice Wilson didn't write these opinions any more than Nixon wrote *Six Crises*—

JOE: Or Kennedy wrote *Profiles in Courage.*

LOUIS: Or Reagan wrote *Where's the Rest of Me?* Or you and I wrote the Book of Love.

These gems were ghostwritten. By you: his obedient clerk.

JOE: OK, OK so we can talk about the decisions, if that's what you want, or, or Prior, if you want to talk about— If you saw him, I'm— Well I'm relieved you're here. I was scared you'd have moved back, I mean out. I'm . . . Oh God it's so good to see you again.

(Joe tries to touch Louis. Louis puts a hand on Joe's chest and firmly pushes him back.)

JOE: Hey!

LOUIS: Naturally I was eager to read them.

(Louis starts flipping through the files, looking for one in particular.)

JOE: Free country.

LOUIS *(Finding it, leafing through the pages)*: I love the one where you found against those women on Staten Island who were suing the New Jersey factory, the toothpaste makers whose orange-colored smoke was *blinding children*—

JOE: Not blind, just minor irritation.

(Louis holds the decision right up to Joe's face, open to the relevant page.)

LOUIS: Three of them had to be hospitalized. Joe.

(Joe looks away from the paper.)

LOUIS: It's sort of brilliant, in a satanic sort of way, how you conclude— *(Continue below:)*
JOE: I don't believe this.
LOUIS *(Continuous from above)*: —How you concluded that these women had no right to sue under the Air and Water Protection Act because—
JOE: My opinions are being criticized by the guy who changes the coffee filters in the secretaries' lounge!
LOUIS: Because the Air and Water Protection Act doesn't protect *people*, but actually only *air and water*. That's like— *(Continue below:)*
JOE: It's not your fault that you have no idea what you're talking about— *(Continue below:)*
LOUIS *(Continuous from above)*: That's like fucking *creative*, or something.
  (Under his breath while flipping through the cases) Have you no decency, have you no—
JOE *(Continuous from above)*: —but it's unbelievable to me how total ignorance is no impediment for you in forming half-baked uninformed snap judgments masquerading as adult opinions, you, you . . . *child.*

(Joe snatches at the papers. Louis dodges, at the same time locating the case he's been looking for.)

LOUIS: But my *absolute favorite* is this:
Stephens versus the United States.

JOE: Of course. I was waiting for that. It's a complicated case, you don't—

LOUIS: The army guy who got a dishonorable discharge—for being gay. Now as I understand it, this Stephens had told the army he was gay when he enlisted, but when he got ready to retire they booted him out. Cheat the queer of his pension.

JOE: Right. And he sued. And he won the case. He got the pension back. And then the—

LOUIS: The first judges gave him his pension back, *yes*, because: they ruled that gay men are members of a legitimate minority, entitled to the special protection of the Fourteenth Amendment of the U.S. Constitution. Equal Protection under the Law.

I can just imagine how that momentary lapse into you know *sanity* was received! So then all the judges on the Second Circuit were *hastily* assembled, and—

JOE: And they found for the guy again, they—

LOUIS: But but but!

On an equitable estoppel. I had to look that up, I'm Mr. Coffee, I can't be expected to know these things. They didn't change the *decision*, they just changed the *reason for* the decision. Right? They gave it to him on a technicality: the army knew Stephens was gay when he enlisted. That's all, that's why he won. Not because it's unconstitutional to discriminate against homosexuals. Because homosexuals, they write, are *not* entitled to equal protection under the law.

JOE: Not, not insofar as precedence determines the—which is how law works, as opposed to— The definition of a suspect class, which you probably've never—

LOUIS: Actually *they* didn't write this.

(He goes right up to Joe; speaking softly) You did. They gave this opinion to Wilson to write, which since they *know* he's a vegetable incapable of writing do-re-mi, was quite the vote of confidence in his industrious little sidekick. This is an important bit of legal fag-bashing, isn't it? They trusted you to do it. And you didn't disappoint.

JOE: It's law not justice, it's power, not the merits of its exercise, it's not an expression of the ideal, it's—

LOUIS: So who said, "Have you no decency?"

JOE: I didn't come here to— I'm leaving.

(Joe starts toward the door. Louis gets in his way.)

LOUIS: You moron, how can you not know that?

JOE: I'm leaving, you . . . son of a bitch, get out of my—

LOUIS: It's only the greatest punchline in American history.

JOE *(Very angry, threatening)*: Out of my way, Louis.

LOUIS: *"Have you no decency, at long last, sir, have you no decency at all?"*

JOE: I DON'T KNOW WHO SAID IT! Why are you doing this to me?! *I love you!* Please believe me, please, *I love you. Stop hurting me like*—

LOUIS: *Joseph Welch!* The Army/McCarthy hearings!

Ask Roy. He'll tell you. He knows. He was *there.*

(Little pause)

Roy Cohn. What I want to know is, did you fuck him?

JOE: Did I what?

LOUIS: How often has the latex-sheathed cock I put in my mouth been previously in the mouth of the most evil, twisted, vicious bastard ever to snort coke at Studio 54, because lips that kissed those lips will never kiss mine.

JOE: Don't worry about that, just get out of the—

(Joe tries to push Louis aside; Louis pushes back, forcefully.)

LOUIS: Did you fuck him, did he pay you to let him—
JOE: MOVE!

(Louis throws the Xeroxes in Joe's face. They fly everywhere. Joe pushes Louis, Louis grabs Joe.)

LOUIS: You *lied* to me, you *love* me, well fuck you, you cheap piece of—

(Joe shoves Louis aside. Louis stumbles as Joe starts for the door.)

LOUIS: He's got AIDS!

(Joe stops.)

LOUIS: Did you even *know* that?

(Joe starts again for the door, but Louis grabs him. They struggle.)

LOUIS: Stupid closeted bigots, you probably never figured out that each other was—
JOE: Shut up.

(Joe slugs Louis in the stomach, hard. Louis goes to his knees. Again Joe tries to leave, but Louis grabs his leg and won't let go. Louis pulls himself up, using Joe's leg and jacket, as Joe struggles to free himself.)

LOUIS: Fascist hypocrite lying filthy—

(Joe punches Louis in the face. Louis drops to the floor, clutching his eye. Joe stands over him.)

JOE: Now stop. Now stop. I . . .

LOUIS: Oh jeeesus, aw jeez, oh . . .

JOE: Please. Say you're OK, please. *Please.*

LOUIS: That . . . Hurt.

JOE: I never did that before, I never hit anyone before, I—

(Louis sits up. One eye has been cut. Blood's running down his face.)

JOE: Can you open it? Can you see?

LOUIS: I can see blood.

JOE: Let me get a towel, let me—

LOUIS: I could have you arrested you . . . Creep.

They'd think I put you in jail for beating me up.

JOE: I never hit anyone before, I—

LOUIS: But it'd really be for those decisions.

(Laughing) It was like a sex scene in an Ayn Rand novel, huh?

JOE: I hurt you. I'm sorry, Louis, I never hit anyone before, I . . .

(Joe tries to touch Louis. Louis shoves Joe's hand away.)

LOUIS: Yeah yeah get lost. Before I really lose my temper and hurt you back.

I just want to lie here and bleed for a while. Do me good.

(Joe stands still, not knowing what to do. He looks at his hand, which he's hurt in the fight; there's blood on it.

*He looks at Louis, then starts to leave, then stops. He stares
at Louis, unable to move.
Then he leaves.)*

Scene 11

*Later that night. Roy in a very serious hospital bed, monitoring
machines and IV drips galore. Ethel appears.*

ROY *(Very weak, singing to himself)*:
> John Brown's body lies a-moulderin' in the grave,
> John Brown's body lies a-moulderin' in the grave,
> John Brown's body lies a-moulderin' in the grave,
> His truth is marching on . . .

ETHEL: Look at that big smile. What you got to smile about,
Roy?

ROY: I'm going, Ethel. Finally, finally done with this world, at
long long last. All mine enemies will be standing on the
other shore, mouths gaping open like stupid fish, while
the Almighty parts the Sea of Death and lets his Royboy
cross over to Jordan. On dry land and still a lawyer.

ETHEL: Don't count your chickens, Roy.
It's over.

ROY: Over?

ETHEL: I wanted the news should come from me.
The panel ruled against you Roy.

ROY: No, no, they only started meeting two days ago.

ETHEL: They recommended disbarment.

ROY: The Executive still has to rule . . . on the recommendation, it'll take another week to sort it out and before
then—

PERESTROIKA

ETHEL: The Executive was waiting, and they ruled, one two three. They accepted the panel's recommendation.

ROY *(A beat, then)*: I'm . . .

ETHEL: One of the main guys on the Executive leaned over to his friend and said, "Finally. I've hated that little faggot for thirty-six years."

ROY: I'm . . . They . . . ?

ETHEL: They won, Roy. You're not a lawyer anymore.

ROY: But am I dead?

ETHEL: No. They beat you. You lost.

(Pause)

I decided to come here so I could see could I forgive you. You who I have hated so terribly I have borne my hatred for you up into the heavens and made a needle-sharp little star in the sky out of it. It's the star of Ethel Rosenberg's Hatred, and it burns every year for one night only, June Nineteen. It burns acid green.

(Roy has turned his face away from her, looking in the opposite direction.)

ETHEL: I came to forgive but all I can do is take pleasure in your misery. Hoping I'd get to see you die more terrible than I did. And you are, 'cause you're dying in shit, Roy, defeated. And you could kill me, but you couldn't ever defeat me. You never won. And when you die all anyone will say is: Better he had never lived at all.

(Pause. Roy slowly turns his head back to stare at Ethel.)

ROY: Ma?
     Muddy? Is it . . . ?
     Ma?

253

ETHEL *(Uncertain, then)*: It's Ethel, Roy.

ROY: Muddy? I feel bad.

ETHEL *(Looking around)*: Who are you talking to, Roy, it's—

ROY: Good to see you, Ma, it's been years.

   I feel bad. Sing to me.

ETHEL: I'm not your mother, Roy.

ROY: It's cold in here, I'm up so late, past my time.

   Don't be mad, Ma, but I'm scared . . . ? A little.

   Don't be mad. Sing me a song. Please.

ETHEL: I don't want to Roy, I'm not your—

ROY: Please, it's scary out here. *(He starts to cry)*

   (He sinks back) Oh God. Oh God, I'm so sorry . . .

(Little pause.)

ETHEL *(Singing softly)*:

   Shteyt a bocher
   Un er tracht,
   Tracht un tracht
   A gantze nacht:
   Vemen tzu nemen
   Um nit farshemen
   Vemen tsu nemen,
   Um nit farshem.
   Tum-ba-la, tum-ba-la, tum-balalaike,
   Tum-ba-la, tum-ba-la, tum-balalaike,
   Tum-balalaike, shpil balalaike—

(Roy is completely still, his eyes closed. He's not breathing. Ethel watches him; then, quietly:)

ETHEL: Roy . . . ? Are you . . . ?

(She crosses to the bed, looks at him. Goes back to her chair.)

ETHEL: That's it.

(Belize enters, goes to the bed.)

BELIZE: Wake up, it's time to—
Oh.
Oh, you're—

(Roy's eyes pop open and he sits bolt upright!)

ROY: No I'm *NOT*!
(Shaking with some terrible, jubilant, hateful joy) I fooled you, Ethel! I knew who you were all along! I can't believe you fell for that Ma stuff!! I just wanted to see if I could finally, *finally* make Ethel Rosenberg sing! *I WIN!*
(Something very bad happens in his head—he's thrown a pulmonary clot, and it strikes his brain—and he falls back on the bed)
Oh fuck, oh fuck me I—
(In a faraway voice, to Belize) Next time around: I don't want to be a man. I wanna be an octopus. Remember that, OK? A fucking— *(Punching an imaginary button with his finger)* Hold.

(Roy dies.)

ACT FIVE:

Heaven,
I'm in Heaven

January 1986

Scene 1

Very late, same night. Prior has been moved to a proper hospital room. He's standing on his bed, a pillow covering his crotch. There's an eerie light on him. Hannah is sleeping in a chair, a flimsy hospital blanket covering her lap and legs. She stirs, moans a little, wakes up suddenly, sees Prior.

PRIOR: She's approaching.
HANNAH: What are you . . . ?
　　　She is?
PRIOR: Modesty forbids me explaining exactly *how* I know, but . . . I have an infallible barometer of Her proximity. And it's rising.

HANNAH: Oh, nonsense, that's—

PRIOR: She's on Her way.

(The lights drain to black.)

HANNAH: Turn the lights back on, turn the lights—

(There is the sound of a silvery trumpet in the dark, and a tattoo of faraway drums. Silence. Thunder. Then all over the walls, Hebrew letters appear, writhing in flames. The scene is lit by their light. The Angel is there, suddenly. She is dressed in black and looks terrifying. Hannah screams and buries her face in her hands.)

ANGEL: I I I I Have Returned, Prophet,
> *(Thunder!)*
> And not according to Plan.

PRIOR: Take it back.
> *(Big thunderclap)*
> The Book, whatever you left in me, I won't be its repository, I reject it.
> *(Thunder. To Hannah:)*
> Help me out here. HELP ME!

HANNAH *(Closing her eyes tight, trying to shut it all out)*: I don't, I don't— *(Pulling the blanket over her head)* This is a dream it's a dream it's a—

PRIOR: I don't think that's really the point right at this particular—

HANNAH *(Under the blanket)*: I don't know what to—

PRIOR: Well it was *your* idea, reject the vision you said and—
> *(Continue below:)*

HANNAH: Yes but I thought it was more a . . . metaphorical . . . I—

PRIOR *(Continuous from above)*: You said scriptural precedent, you said—

(Prior tries to yank the blanket away from Hannah, who hangs on to it.)

PRIOR: WHAT AM I SUPPOSED TO—

HANNAH: You, you wrestle her.

PRIOR: SAY *WHAT*?

HANNAH: It's an angel, you just . . . grab hold and say . . . oh what was it, wait, wait, umm . . . OH! Grab her, say, "I will not let thee go except thou bless me!"

PRIOR: And then what?

HANNAH: Then wrestle with her till she gives in.

PRIOR *(A beat, then)*: YOU wrestle Her, I don't know how to wrestle, I—

(Prior faces the Angel, who has been waiting for him, blazing with menace. She opens her arms, challenging, terrifying. Prior draws as deep a breath as he can; then, to his and her and Hannah's surprise, he charges at the Angel. He throws his arms around her waist. She emits a terrible, impossibly loud, shuddering eagle-screech.)

PRIOR: I . . . will not let thee go except thou bless me.

(She tries to pry him off, but he hangs on. Prior and the Angel begin to wrestle. It is a life-and-death struggle, fierce, violent and deadly serious. The Angel at first is far stronger and has a clear upper hand. But she cannot pry Prior loose. As they struggle:)

PRIOR: Take back . . . your Book. Anti-Migration, that's . . . so . . . *feeble*, I can't believe . . . you couldn't do better than that!

(Prior's tenacity begins to tire and panic her. She screeches again, then unable to shake him off, she opens her wings wide and begins to beat them, battering Prior. He loses his grip for an instant; she rises immediately into the air. Prior leaps up, grabs her right leg and pulls down with all his might and weight. She beats her wings more furiously, rising higher, lifting him up off the ground, but he won't let go.)

PRIOR: Free me! Unfetter me! Bless me or whatever . . . but *I will be let go.*

(The Angel is straining Heavenward but can't ascend higher; Prior's weight causes her to lose altitude.)

ANGEL *(Her voice a whole chorus of voices)*: I I I I Am the
CONTINENTAL PRINCIPALITY OF
AMERICA, I I I I
AM THE BIRD OF PREY I Will NOT BE
COMPELLED, I—

(They descend. Prior's feet touch earth first, and he redoubles his grasp, first on her leg and then her torso, wrapping himself tightly around her. Helpless, she stretches her wings to their utmost, screams the eagle-screech again, and stops fighting.

Instantly there is a great blast of music. The fiery letters fade and the room is sunk in blue murk. A second blast of music, even louder, and, from above, a column of incredibly bright white light stabs through the blue. Within the column of light, a ladder of even brighter, purer light appears, reaching up into infinity. At the conjunctions of each rung there are flaming Alephs.)

ANGEL: Entrance has been gained. Return the Text to Heaven.
PRIOR *(Terrified)*: Can I come back? I don't want to go unless—

ANGEL *(Very angry)*: You have prevailed, Prophet. You . . . *Choose!*

Now release me.

I have torn a muscle in my thigh.

PRIOR: Big deal, my leg's been hurting for months.

(He releases the Angel. He hesitates. He looks at Hannah, asking her: "Should I go?" Frightened as she is, she manages to hold her hand out, bidding him to stay.

Prior, suddenly very sad, shakes his head no, and turns to the ladder. After one last look at the Angel, he puts his hands on the rungs, then one foot, then the other, and begins climbing. The column of bright light intensifies as he ascends, till Prior and the ladder are entirely subsumed within its blinding radiance and can no longer be seen.

Then abruptly the column of light disappears, and the room is drowned in semi-darkness. The ladder and Prior are gone. The Angel turns to Hannah.)

HANNAH: What? What? You've got no business with me, I didn't call you, you're *his* fever dream not mine, and he's gone now and you should go, too, I'm waking up right . . . NOW!

(Nothing happens. The Angel spreads her wings. The room becomes red hot. The Angel extends her hands toward Hannah. Hannah walks toward her, torn between immense unfamiliar desire and fear. Hannah kneels. The Angel kisses her on the forehead and then the lips—a long, hot kiss.)

ANGEL: The Body is the Garden of the Soul.

(Hannah has an enormous orgasm, as the Angel flies away to the accompanying glissando of a baroque piccolo trumpet.)

Scene 2

Prior Walter is in Heaven. He wears new prophet robes, red, dark brown and white stripes, reminiscent of Charlton Heston's Moses-parting-the-Red-Sea drag in The Ten Commandments. *Beneath the robe, Prior's wearing his flimsy white hospital gown. He's carrying the Book of the Anti-Migratory Epistle.*

Heaven looks like San Francisco after the Great Quake: deserted streets, beautiful buildings in ruins, toppled telegraph poles, downed electrical cables, rubble strewn everywhere.

On a nearby street corner, Harper sits on a wooden crate, holding and petting a cat.

HARPER: Oh! It's you! My imaginary friend.

PRIOR: What are you doing here? Are you dead?

HARPER: No, I just had sex, I'm not dead! Why? Where are we?

PRIOR: Heaven.

HARPER: Heaven? I'm in Heaven?

PRIOR: That cat! That's Little Sheba!

HARPER: She was wandering around. Everyone here wanders. Or they sit on crates, playing card games. Heaven. Holy moly.

PRIOR: How did Sheba die?

HARPER: Rat poison, hit by a truck, fight with an alley cat, cancer, another truck, old age, fell in the East River, heartworms and one last truck.

PRIOR: Then it's true? Cats really have nine lives?

HARPER: That was a joke. I don't know how she died, I don't talk to cats I'm not that crazy. Just upset. Or . . .

We had sex, and then he . . . had to go. I drank an enormous glass of water and two Valiums. Or six. Maybe I overdosed, like Marilyn Monroe.

Did you die?

PRIOR: No, I'm here on business.
I can return to the world. If I want to.

HARPER: Do you?

PRIOR: I don't know.

HARPER: I know. Heaven is depressing, full of dead people and all, but life.

PRIOR: To face loss. With grace. Is key, I think, but it's impossible. All you ever do is lose and lose.

HARPER: But not letting go deforms you so.

PRIOR: The world's too hard. Stay here. With me.

HARPER: I can't. I feel like shit but I've never felt more alive. I've finally found the secret of all that Mormon energy. Devastation. That's what makes people migrate, build things. Devastated people do it, people who have lost love. Because I don't think God loves His people any better than Joe loved me. The string was cut, and off they went. Ravaged, heartbroken, and free.

(Little pause)

I have to go home now. I hope you come back. *Look* at this place. Can you imagine spending eternity here?

PRIOR: It's supposed to look like San Francisco.

HARPER *(Looking around)*: Ugh.

PRIOR: Oh but the real San Francisco, on earth, is unspeakably beautiful.

HARPER: Unspeakable beauty.
That's something I would like to see.

(Harper and Sheba vanish.)

PRIOR: Oh! She . . . She took the cat. Come back, you took the—

(Little pause)

Good-bye, Little Sheba. Good-bye.

(The Angel is standing there.)

ANGEL: Greetings, Prophet. We have been waiting for you.

Scene 3

Two A.M. Same night as Scene 1. Roy's hospital room. Roy's body is on the bed. Ethel is sitting in a chair. Belize enters, then calls off in a whisper:

BELIZE: Hurry.

(Louis enters wearing an overcoat and dark sunglasses, carrying an empty knapsack.)

LOUIS: Oh my God, oh my God it's—oh this is too weird for words, it's Roy Cohn! It's . . . so *creepy* here, I hate hospitals, I—

BELIZE: *Stop whining.* We have to move fast, I'm supposed to call the duty nurse if his condition changes and . . . *(He looks at Roy)* It's changed.
    Take off those glasses you look ridiculous.

(Louis takes off the glasses. He has a black eye, with a nasty-looking cut above it.)

BELIZE: What happened to *you?*

(Belize touches the swelling near Louis's eye.)

LOUIS: OW OW! *(He waves Belize's hand away)* Expiation. For my sins. What am I doing here?

(Belize takes the knapsack from Louis.)

BELIZE: Expiation for your sins. I can't take the stuff out myself, I have to tell them he's dead and fill out all the forms, and I don't want them confiscating the medicine. I needed a packmule, so I called you.

LOUIS: Why me? You hate me.

BELIZE: I needed a Jew. You were the first to come to mind.

LOUIS: What do you mean you needed—

(Belize has opened Roy's refrigerator and begins putting all the bottles of AZT into the knapsack.)

BELIZE: We're going to thank him. For the pills.

LOUIS: *Thank him?*

BELIZE: What do you call the Jewish prayer for the dead?

LOUIS: The Kaddish?

BELIZE: That's the one. Hit it.

LOUIS: Whoah, hold on.

BELIZE: Do it, do it, they'll be in here to check and he—

(Belize has filled the knapsack and closed the empty refrigerator.)

LOUIS: I'm not— Fuck no! For *him*?! No fucking way! The drugs OK, sure, fine, but no fucking way am I praying for *him*. My New Deal Pinko Parents in Schenectady would never forgive me, they're already so disappointed, "He's a fag, he's an office temp, and *now look*, he's saying Kaddish for Roy Cohn." I can't believe you'd actually pray for—

BELIZE: Louis, I'd even pray for you.

He was a terrible person. He died a hard death. So maybe . . . A queen can forgive her vanquished foe. It isn't easy, it doesn't count if it's easy, it's the hardest thing. Forgiveness. Which is maybe where love and justice finally meet. Peace, at least. Isn't that what the Kaddish asks for?

LOUIS: Oh it's Hebrew or Aramaic or something, who knows what it's asking.

(Little pause. Louis and Belize look at each other, and then Louis looks at Roy, staring at him unflinchingly for the first time.)

LOUIS: I'm thirty-two years old and I've never seen a dead body before.
It's . . .

(Louis touches Roy's forehead.)

LOUIS: It's so heavy, and small.
(Little pause)
I know probably less of the Kaddish than you do, Belize, I'm an intensely secular Jew, I didn't even Bar Mitzvah.

BELIZE: Do the best you can.

(Louis hesitates, then puts a Kleenex on his head.)

LOUIS: Yisgadal ve'yiskadash sh'mey rabo, sh'mey de kidshoh, uh . . . Boray pre hagoffen. No, that's the Kiddush, not the . . . Um, shema Yisroel adonai . . . This is silly, Belize, I can't—

ETHEL *(Standing, softly)*: B'olmo deevro chiroosey ve'yamlich malchusey . . .

LOUIS: B'olmo deevro chiroosey ve'yamlich malchusey . . .

ETHEL: Bechayeychon uv'yomechechon uvchayey d'chol beys Yisroel . . .

LOUIS: Bechayeychon uv'yomechechon uvchayey d'chol beys
Yisroel . . .

ETHEL: Ba'agolo uvizman koriv . . .

LOUIS: Ve'imroo omain.

ETHEL: Yehey sh'mey rabo m'vorach . . .

LOUIS AND ETHEL: L'olam ulolmey olmayoh. Yisborach
ve'yishtabach ve'yispoar ve'yisroman ve'yisnasey ve'yis'-
hadar ve'yisalleh ve'yishallol sh'mey dekudsho . . .

ETHEL: Berich hoo le'eylo min kol birchoso veshiroso . . .

ETHEL AND LOUIS: Tushbchoso venechemoso, daameeron
b'olmo ve'imroo omain. Y'he sh'lomo rabbo min sh'mayo
v'chayim olenu v'al kol Yisroel, v'imru omain.

ETHEL: Oseh sholom bimromov, hu ya-aseh sholom olenu v'al
col Yisroel . . .

LOUIS: Oseh sholom bimromov, hu ya-aseh sholom olenu v'al
col Yisroel . . .

ETHEL: V'imru omain.

LOUIS: V'imru omain.

ETHEL: You sonofabitch.

LOUIS: You sonofabitch.

(Ethel vanishes.
Belize hands Louis the knapsack.)

BELIZE: Thank you, Louis. You did fine.

LOUIS: Fine? What are you talking about, fine? That was . . .
fucking miraculous.

Scene 4

Two A.M. Joe enters the empty Brooklyn apartment.

JOE: I'm back. Harper?
> *(He switches on a light)*
> Harper?

> *(Roy enters from the bedroom, dressed in a fabulous floor-length black velvet robe de chambre. Joe starts with terror, turns away, then looks again. Roy's still there. Joe's terrified. Roy does not move.)*

JOE: What are you doing here?
ROY: Dead Joe doesn't matter.
JOE: No, no, you're not here, you . . .
> *(Joe closes his eyes, willing Roy away. He opens his eyes. Roy's still there)*
> You *lied* to me! You said cancer, you said—
ROY: You could have read it in the papers. AIDS. I didn't want you to get the wrong impression.
> You feel bad that you beat somebody.
JOE: I want you to—
ROY: He deserved it.
JOE: No he didn't, he—
ROY: Everybody does. Everybody could use a good beating.
JOE: No, no, that's— I want you to go Roy, you're really frightening me. *Get out.* You don't belong here—
> He didn't *deserve* what I did to him! I *hurt* him, Roy! I made him *bleed*! He . . . He won't ever see me again.

(Realizing that this is true) Oh no, oh no . . . What did
I do that for? What did I do? What did I— *(Joe starts to
cry. He stops himself, violently shaking his head)*
Tell me what to do now.

(Roy doesn't respond.)

JOE: I thought I was doing what I was supposed to do,
I thought I'd find my way, the way you did, to the, to the
heart of the things, to the heart of the world, I imagined
myself . . . safe there, in the hollow of . . . but . . .
(Little pause)
I'm . . . above nothing. I'm . . . *of* the world. Whatever
. . . that means, whatever God thinks of the world, I think
He must think the same of me.
Tell me what I do now.

(Roy shrugs.)

JOE: I'm a liar. I lied. I never told you how much you frighten
me, Roy.

(He walks toward Roy.)

JOE: I'm not blind, not . . . blind as I tried to be. I've always
seen, *known* what you are. And, and I'm not like that.
Not like you. But I've lied and lied and lied . . .

*(Joe is facing Roy. He puts his head against Roy's chest, lost. Roy's
surprised, pleased, moved. He puts his arms around Joe, a tender,
careful embrace. Joe raises his head. They look at one another.)*

ROY *(Gently)*: Show me a little of what you've learned, baby
Joe. Out in the world.

(They kiss, intimate, uncertain, as affectionate as it is sexual.)

ROY: Damn.

   I gotta shuffle off this mortal coil.

   (Looking up at the ceiling, warning the Powers Above:)
   I hope they have something for me to do in the Great
   Hereafter, I get bored easy.

   (To Joe) You'll find, my friend, that what you love will
   take you places you never dreamed you'd go.

   (Roy vanishes. Joe doesn't move, eyes closed.
   He opens them when Harper enters. They stare at one
   another.)

HARPER: Hope you didn't worry.
JOE: Harper?
   Where . . . Were you—
HARPER: A trip to the moon on gossamer wings.
JOE: What?
HARPER: You ought to get your hearing checked, you say that
   a lot.
   I was out. With a friend. In Paradise.

Scene 5

Heaven: in the Council Room of the Hall of the Continental
Principalities. As the scene is being set, a Voice proclaims:

A VOICE: In the Hall of the Continental Principalities; Heaven,
   a City Much Like San Francisco. Six of Seven Myriad
   Infinite Aggregate Angelic Entities in Attendance, May

Their Glorious Names Be Praised Forever and Ever, Hallelujah. Permanent Emergency Council is now in Session.

(Power for the great chamber is supplied by an unseen immense generator, the rhythmic pulsing as well as the occasional surges and wavers of which are visible in the unsteady lights, and audible continuously underneath the scene until its cessation [indicated in the text].

At the center of the room is a very large round table covered with a heavy tapestry on which is woven a seventeenth-century map of the world. The tabletop is covered with ancient and broken astronomical, astrological, mathematical and nautical objects of measurement and calculation, cracked clay tablets, dulled styli, dried inkpots, split quill pens, disintegrating piles of parchment, and old derelict typewriters. On the table and all around the room are heaps and heaps and heaps of books, bundles of yellowing newspapers and dusty teetery stacks of neglected and abandoned files.

On one side of the table, a single bulky radio, a 1940s model in very poor repair, is switched on, its dial and tubes glowing. The six present Continental Principalities are gathered about it, sitting and standing. The Angel of Asiatica is seated nearest to the radio; the Angel of Antarctica is farthest away.

The Principalities are dressed uniformly in elegant, flowing, severely black robes that look like what justices, judges, magistrates wear in court.

All six sound very much alike, as if speaking with a single voice. Their speech is always careful, a little slow, and soft, like mild old people; in everything they say there's a distinct tone of quiet, enduring desolation and perplexity. This tone doesn't vary; even when they argue they sound tentative, careful, broken.

They're almost completely still, but as they listen they turn slightly, slowly, looking to one another for comfort. Asiatica and Africanii intermittently hold hands.

The Principalities are aghast, frightened and grief-stricken at the news they're hearing on the radio—which they're not supposed to be using. They listen intently to the dim, crackly signal.)

RADIO *(In a British accent)*: . . . one week following the explosion at the number four reactor, the fires are still burning and an estimated . . . *(Static)* . . . releasing into the atmosphere fifty million curies of radioactive iodine, six million curies of caesium and strontium rising in a plume over eight kilometers high, carried by the winds over an area stretching from the Urals to thousands of kilometers beyond Soviet borders, it . . . *(Static)*

ANTARCTICA: When?

OCEANIA: April 26th. Three months from today.

ASIATICA: Where is this place? This reactor?

EUROPA: Chernobyl. In Belarus.

(The static intensifies.)

ASIATICA: We are losing the signal.

(The Angels make mystic gestures. The signal returns.)

RADIO: . . . falling like toxic snow into the Dnieper River, which provides drinking water for thirty-five million— *(Static, then)* . . . is a direct consequence of the lack of safety culture caused by Cold War isolation— *(Static, then)* . . . Radioactive debris contaminating over three hundred thousand hectares of topsoil for a minimum of thirty years, and . . . *(Static)* . . . now hearing of thousands of workers who have absorbed fifty times the lethal dose of . . . *(Static)* . . . BBC Radio, reporting live from Chernobyl, on the eighth day of the . . .

(The radio signal is engulfed in white noise and fades out.)

EUROPA: Hundreds, thousands will die.

OCEANIA: Horribly. Hundreds of thousands.

AFRICANII: Millions.

ANTARCTICA: Let them. Uncountable multitudes. Horrible. It is by their own hands. I I I will rejoice to see it.

AUSTRALIA: That is forbidden us.

Silence in Heaven.

ASIATICA: This radio is a terrible radio.

AUSTRALIA: The reception is too weak.

AFRICANII: A vacuum tube has died.

ASIATICA: Can it be fixed?

AUSTRALIA: It Is Beyond Us.

ASIATICA: However, I I I I I I I would like to know. What is a vacuum tube?

OCEANIA: It is a simple diode.

ASIATICA: Aha.

AFRICANII: Within are an anode and a cathode. The positive electrons travel from the cathode across voltage fields—

OCEANIA: The cathode is, in fact, negatively charged.

AFRICANII: No, positive, I I I I— *(She begins carefully to examine the works in the back of the radio)*

EUROPA: This device ought never to have been brought here. It is a Pandemonium.

AUSTRALIA: I I I I agree. In diodes we see manifest the selfsame Divided Human Consciousness which has engendered the multifarious catastrophes to which We are impotent witness. But—

AFRICANII *(Having concluded her examination, to Oceania)*: You are correct, it is negative. Regardless of the charge, it is the absence of resistance in a vacuum which—

ANTARCTICA: I I I do not weep for them, I I I weep for the vexation of the Blank Spaces, I I I weep for the Dancing Light, for the irremediable wastage of Fossil Fuels, Old Blood of the Globe spilled wantonly or burned and jettisoned into the Crystal Air—

AUSTRALIA: But it is a Conundrum, and We cannot solve Conundrums. If only He would return. I I I I do not know whether We have erred in transporting these dubious Inventions, but . . .

(Opening a huge dusty Book) If We refer to His Codex of Procedure, I I I I cannot recall which page but—

(There is an enormous peal of thunder and a blaze of lightning.
The Angel of America ushers Prior into the chamber. Terrified and determined, he stands before the council table.
The Principalities stare at Prior.)

ANGEL: Most August Fellow Principalities, Angels Most High: I regret my absence at this session, I was detained.

(Pause.)

AUSTRALIA: Ah, this is . . . ?
ANGEL: The Prophet. Yes.
AUSTRALIA: Ah.

(Exchanging brief, concerned glances with one another, the Angels bow to Prior.)

EUROPA: We were working.
AFRICANII: Making Progress.

(Thunderclap. Prior's startled. Then, realizing they're waiting for him to speak, he musters his courage and says in a small, uncertain voice:)

PRIOR: I . . . I want to return this.

(He holds out the Book. No one takes it from him.)

AUSTRALIA: What is the matter with it?
PRIOR: It just . . . It just . . .

(They wait, anxious to hear his explanation. A beat, then:)

PRIOR: We can't just stop. We're not rocks. Progress, migration, motion is . . . modernity. It's *animate*, it's what living things do. We desire. Even if all we desire is stillness, it's still desire *for*. *(On "for" he makes a motion with his hand: starting one place, moving forward)* Even if we go faster than we should. We can't *wait*. And wait for what? God—

(Thunderclap.)

PRIOR: God—

(Thunderclap.)

PRIOR: He isn't coming back.
    And even if He did . . .
    If He ever did come back, if He ever *dared* to show His face, or his Glyph or whatever in the Garden again. If after all this destruction, if after all the terrible days of

275

this terrible century He returned to see . . . how much suffering His abandonment had created, if all He has to offer is death . . .

You should *sue* the bastard. That's my only contribution to all this *Theology*. Sue the bastard for walking out. How dare He. He oughta pay.

(All stand, frozen, then the Angels exchange glances. Then:)

ANGEL: Thus spake the Prophet.

PRIOR *(Holding out the Book)*: So thank you . . . for sharing this with me, but I don't want to keep it.

OCEANIA: He wants to live.

PRIOR *(Grief breaking through)*: Yes! *(Pushing the sorrow back, determined to stay composed)* I'm thirty years old, for God-sake—

(A softer rumble of thunder.)

PRIOR: I haven't *done* anything yet, I—I want to be healthy again! And this plague, it should stop. In me and everywhere. Make it go away.

AUSTRALIA: Oh We have tried.
We suffer with You but
We do not know. We
Do not know how.

(Prior and Australia look at each other.)

EUROPA: This is the Tome of Immobility, of respite, of cessation.

Drink of its bitter water once, Prophet, and never thirst again.

PRIOR: I . . . can't.

(Prior puts the Book on the table. He removes his prophet robes, revealing the hospital gown underneath. He places the robe by the Book.)

PRIOR: I still want . . . My blessing. Even sick. I want to be alive.

ANGEL: You only think you do.
　　　Life is a habit with you.
　　　You have not *seen* what is to come:
　　　We *have*:
　　　What will the grim Unfolding of these Latter Days
　　　　　bring
　　　That you or any Being should wish to endure them?
　　　Death more plenteous than all Heaven has tears to
　　　　　mourn it,
　　　The slow dissolving of the Great Design,
　　　The spiraling apart of the Work of Eternity,
　　　The World and its beautiful particle logic
　　　All collapsed. All dead, forever,
　　　In starless, moon-lorn onyx night.

(The Angel goes to Prior.)

ANGEL: We are failing, failing,
　　　The Earth and the Angels.
　　　Look up, look up.

(Prior and the Angel are looking up.)

ANGEL: It is Not-to-Be Time.

(The sound of the enormous generator begins to slow and then to fail. The lights in the chamber dim.)

ANGEL (*Asking Prior a real question, mystified by his persistence*):
Oh who asks of the Orders Blessing
With Apocalypse Descending?
Who demands: More Life
When Death like a Protector Blinds our eyes,
    shielding from tender nerve
More horror than can be borne?

(*She returns to stand with the other Principalities, all facing Prior.*)

ANGEL: Let any Being on whom Fortune smiles
Creep away to Death
Before that last dreadful daybreak
When all your ravaging returns to you
With the rising, scorching, unrelenting Sun:
When morning blisters crimson
And bears all life away,
A tidal wave of Protean Fire
That curls around the planet
And bares the Earth clean as bone.

(*Pause.*)

PRIOR: But still. Still.
Bless me anyway.
I want more life. I can't help myself. I do.
I've lived through such terrible times, and there are people who live through much much worse, but . . . You see them living anyway. When they're more spirit than body, more sores than skin, when they're burned and in agony, when flies lay eggs in the corners of the eyes of their children, they live. Death usually has to *take* life

away. I don't know if that's just the animal. I don't know if it's not braver to die. But I recognize the habit. The addiction to being alive. We live past hope. If I can find hope anywhere, that's it, that's the best I can do. It's so much not enough, so inadequate but . . . Bless me anyway. I want more life.

(He turns away to leave. When his back is turned, the Angels silently make mystical signs.

Prior stops, suddenly feeling sick again: leg pain, constricted lungs, cloudy vision, febrile panic and under that, dreadful weakness.

He gathers his strength, then turns again, with a new calm, to face them.)

PRIOR: You haven't seen what's to come. You've only seen what you're afraid is coming. Until it arrives—please don't be offended but . . . all you can see is fear.

I'm leaving Heaven to you now. I'll take my illness with me, and. And I'll take my death with me, too.

The earth's my home, and I want to go home.

Scene 6

Seven A.M. Prior descends from Heaven and slips into his hospital bed.

Belize is sleeping in a chair.

PRIOR *(Waking)*: Oh.
    I'm exhausted.
BELIZE *(Waking)*: You've been working hard.

PRIOR: I feel terrible.

BELIZE: Welcome back to the world.

PRIOR: From where, I . . .

Oh. Oh I—

(Emily enters.)

EMILY: Well look at this. It's the dawn of man.

BELIZE: Venus rising from the sea.

PRIOR: I'm wet.

EMILY: Fever broke. That's a good sign, they'll be in to change you in—

PRIOR *(Looking around)*: Mrs. Pitt? Did she—

BELIZE: Elle fait sa toilette. Elle est *tres* formidable, ça. Where did you find her?

PRIOR: We found each other, she—

I've had a remarkable dream. And *(To Belize)* you were there, and *(To Emily)* you.

(Hannah enters.)

PRIOR: And you.

HANNAH: I what?

PRIOR: And some of it was terrible, and some of it was wonderful, but all the same I kept saying I want to go home. And They sent me home.

HANNAH *(To Prior)*: What are you talking about?

PRIOR *(To Hannah)*: Thank you.

HANNAH: I just slept in the chair.

PRIOR *(To Belize)*: She saved my life.

HANNAH: I did no such thing, I slept in the chair. Being in hospital upsets me, it reminds me of things.

I have to go home now. I had the most *peculiar* dream.

(There's a knock on the door. It opens. Louis enters.)

LOUIS: Can I come in?

(Brief tense pause; Prior looks at Louis and then at Belize.)

EMILY: I have to start rounds.
　　(To Prior) You're one of the lucky ones. I could give you a rose. You rest your weary bones.
PRIOR *(To Louis)*: What are you . . .
　　(He sees Louis's cuts and bruises) What happened to *you?*
LOUIS: Visible scars. You said—
PRIOR: Oh, Louis, you're so goddamned literal about everything.
HANNAH *(A quick glance at Louis when Prior says his name, then)*: I'm going now.
PRIOR: You'll come back.
HANNAH *(A beat, then)*: If I can. I have things to take care of.
PRIOR: Please do.
　　I have always depended on the kindness of strangers.
HANNAH: Well that's a stupid thing to do.

(Hannah exits.)

LOUIS: Who's she?
PRIOR *(A beat, then)*: You really don't want to know.
BELIZE: Before I depart. A homecoming gift.

(Belize puts his shoulder bag on Prior's lap. Prior opens it; it's full of bottles of pills.)

PRIOR *(Squinting hard)*: What? I can't read the label, I—
　　My eyes. Aren't any better.

(*Squints even harder*) AZT?

Where on earth did you . . . These are hot pills. I am shocked.

BELIZE: A contribution to the get-well fund. From a bad fairy.

LOUIS: These pills, they . . . They make you better.

PRIOR: They're poison, they make you anemic.

This is my life, from now on, Louis. I'm not getting "better."

(*To Belize*) I'm not sure I'm ready to do that to my bone marrow.

BELIZE (*Taking the bag*): We can talk about it tomorrow. I'm going home to nurse my grudges. Ta, baby, sleep all day. Ta, Louis, you sure know how to clear a room.

(*Belize exits.*)

LOUIS: Prior.

I want to come back to you.

Scene 7

Same morning. Split scene: Louis and Prior in Prior's hospital room, continuous from Scene 6. Harper and Joe in Brooklyn. Joe sits in a chair; Harper enters from the bedroom, dressed for traveling, carrying a small suitcase.

HARPER: I want the credit card.

That's all. You can keep track of me from where the charges come from. If you want to keep track. I don't care.

JOE: I have some things to tell you.

HARPER: Oh we shouldn't talk. I don't want to do that anymore.

Credit card.

JOE: I don't know what will happen to me without you. Only
you. Only you love me. Out of everyone in the world.
I have done things, I'm ashamed. But I have changed.
I don't know how yet, but . . . Please, please, don't leave
me now.

Harper.

You're my good heart.

(She looks at him, she walks up to him and slaps him, hard.)

HARPER *(Quietly)*: Did that hurt?

(Joe nods yes.)

HARPER: Yes. Remember that. Please.

If I can get a job, or something, I'll cut the card to
pieces. And there won't be charges anymore. Credit card.

(Joe takes out his wallet, gives her the card.)

JOE: Call or . . . Call. You have to.

HARPER: No. Probably never again. That's how bad.

Sometimes, maybe lost is best. Get lost. Joe. Go
exploring.

*(Harper takes a bottle of Valium from a coat pocket. She
shakes out two pills, goes to Joe, takes his hand and puts the
Valium in his open palm.)*

HARPER: With a big glass of water.

(Harper leaves.)

LOUIS: I want to come back to you.

You could . . . respond, you could say something, throw me out or say it's fine, or it's not fine but sure what the hell or . . .
(Little pause)
I really failed you. But . . . This is hard. Failing in love isn't the same as not loving. It doesn't let you off the hook, it doesn't mean . . . you're free to not love.

PRIOR: I love you Louis.

LOUIS: Good. I love you.

PRIOR: I really do.

But you can't come back. Not ever.
I'm sorry. But you can't.

Scene 8

That night. Louis and Prior remain from the previous scene. Joe is sitting alone in Brooklyn. Harper appears. She is in a window seat on board a jumbo jet, airborne.

HARPER: Night flight to San Francisco. Chase the moon across America. God! It's been years since I was on a plane!

When we hit thirty-five-thousand feet, we'll have reached the tropopause. The great belt of calm air. As close as I'll ever get to the ozone.

I dreamed we were there. The plane leapt the tropopause, the safe air, and attained the outer rim, the ozone, which was ragged and torn, patches of it threadbare as old cheesecloth, and that was frightening . . .

But I saw something only I could see, because of my astonishing ability to see such things:

Souls were rising, from the earth far below, souls of the dead, of people who had perished, from famine, from war, from the plague, and they floated up, like skydivers in reverse, limbs all akimbo, wheeling and spinning. And the souls of these departed joined hands, clasped ankles, and formed a web, a great net of souls, and the souls were three-atom oxygen molecules, of the stuff of ozone, and the outer rim absorbed them, and was repaired.

Nothing's lost forever. In this world, there is a kind of painful progress. Longing for what we've left behind, and dreaming ahead.

At least I think that's so.

EPILOGUE:

Bethesda

January 1990

Prior, Louis, Belize and Hannah sitting on the rim of the Bethesda Fountain in Central Park. It's a bright day, but cold.

    Prior is heavily bundled, and he has thick glasses on. He supports himself with a cane. Hannah is noticeably different—she looks like a New Yorker, and she's reading an issue of The Nation. *Louis and Belize are arguing. The Bethesda Angel is above them all.*

LOUIS: The Berlin Wall has fallen. The Ceaușescus are out. He's building democratic socialism. The New Internationalism. Gorbachev is the greatest political thinker since Lenin.

BELIZE: I don't think we know enough yet to start canonizing him. The Russians hate his guts.

LOUIS: Yeah but. Remember back four years ago? The whole time we were feeling everything everywhere was stuck, while in Russia! Look! Perestroika! The Thaw! It's the end of the Cold War! The whole world is changing! Overnight!

HANNAH: I wonder what'll happen now in places like Yugoslavia.

LOUIS: Yugoslavia?

PRIOR *(To audience)*: Let's just turn the volume down on this, OK?

They'll be at it for hours. It's not that what they're saying isn't important, it's just . . .

This is my favorite place in New York City. No, in the whole universe. The parts of it I have seen.

On a day like today. A sunny winter's day, warm and cold at once. The sky's a little hazy, so the sunlight has a physical presence, a character. In autumn, those trees across the lake are yellow, and the sun strikes those most brilliantly. Against the blue of the sky, that sad fall blue, those trees are more light than vegetation. They are Yankee trees, New England transplants. They're barren now.

It's January 1990. I've been living with AIDS for five years. That's six whole months longer than I lived with Louis.

LOUIS: Whatever comes, what you have to admire in Gorbachev, in the Russians is that they're making a leap into the unknown. You can't wait around for a theory. The sprawl of life, the weird . . .

HANNAH: Interconnectedness.

LOUIS: Yes.

BELIZE: Maybe the sheer size of the terrain.

LOUIS: It's all too much to be encompassed by a single theory now.

BELIZE: The world is faster than the mind.

LOUIS: That's what politics is. The world moving ahead. And only in politics does the miraculous occur.

BELIZE: But that's a theory.

HANNAH: You can't live in the world without an idea of the world, but it's living that makes the ideas. You can't wait for a theory, but you have to have a theory.

LOUIS: Go know. As my grandma would say.

PRIOR *(Turning the sound off again)*: This angel. She's my favorite angel. I like them best when they're statuary. They commemorate death but they suggest a world without dying. They are made of the heaviest things on earth, stone and iron, they weigh tons but they're winged, they are engines and instruments of flight.

This is the angel Bethesda. Louis will tell you her story.

LOUIS: Oh. Um, well, she was this angel, she landed in the Temple Square in Jerusalem, in the days of the Second Temple, right in the middle of a working day she descended and just her foot touched earth. And where it did, a fountain shot up from the ground.

When the Romans destroyed the Temple, the fountain of Bethesda ran dry.

PRIOR: And Belize will tell you about the nature of the fountain, before its flowing stopped.

BELIZE: If anyone who was suffering, in the body or the spirit, walked through the waters of the fountain of Bethesda, they would be healed, washed clean of pain.

PRIOR: They know this because I've told them, many times. Hannah here told it to me. She also told me this:

HANNAH: When the Millennium comes—

PRIOR: Not the year two thousand, but the capital-M Millennium—

HANNAH: Right. The fountain of Bethesda will flow again. And I told him I would personally take him there to bathe. We will all bathe ourselves clean.

LOUIS: Not literally in Jerusalem, I mean we don't want this to have sort of Zionist implications, we—

BELIZE: Right on.

LOUIS: But on the other hand we *do* recognize the right of the state of Israel to exist.

BELIZE: But the West Bank should be a homeland for the Palestinians, and the Golan Heights should—

LOUIS: Well not *both* the West Bank and the Golan Heights, I mean no one supports Palestinian rights more than I do but—

BELIZE: Oh yeah right, Louis, like not even the Palestinians are more devoted than—

PRIOR: I'm almost done.

The fountain's not flowing now, they turn it off in the winter, ice in the pipes. But in the summer it's a sight to see. I want to be around to see it. I plan to be. I hope to be.

This disease will be the end of many of us, but not nearly all, and the dead will be commemorated and will struggle on with the living, and we are not going away. We won't die secret deaths anymore. The world only spins forward. We will be citizens. The time has come.

Bye now.

You are fabulous creatures, each and every one.

And I bless you: *More Life.*

The Great Work Begins.

END OF PLAY

Notes

Acknowledgments

For Millennium Approaches

From the first edition, published in 1993:

I received generous support during the writing of this play in the form of grants from the National Endowment for the Arts, the Gerbode Foundation, and the Fund for New American Plays/American Express. Further financial and abundant emotional support came from my parents, Bill and Sylvia Kushner, Martha Deutscher, and Dot and Jerry Edelstien. Joyce Ketay the Wonder-Agent, and her associate Carl Mulert have been awesomely protective and farsighted; and from Jim Nicola of New York Theatre Workshop I have gotten wonderfully smart advice.

Gordon Davidson and the staff of the Mark Taper Forum provided the play and its author with the best circumstances for development and production any artist could hope for.

Richard Eyre and the staff of the National Theatre made a timorous and occasionally querulous visitor to British theater feel at home. Declan Donnellan and Nick Ormerod made the play dance.

Millennium Approaches has benefited from the dramaturgical work of Roberta Levitow, Philip Kan Gotanda, Leon Katz and Ellen McLaughlin; K. C. Davis contributed dramaturgy, dedication and Radical Queerness.

Bill Anderson, Andy Holland, Ian Kramer, Peter Minthorn, Sam Sommer and John Ryan (of blessed memory) are everywhere in this play.

David Esbjornson helped shape the final version of *Millennium* and brought it, fabulously, to San Francisco.

Tony Taccone brought craft, clarity and menschlichkeit to Los Angeles.

For Perestroika

From the first edition, published in 1994:

Abundant emotional support was provided by my aunt, Martha Deutscher. Dot and Jerry Edelstien, and Marcia, Tony and Alex Cunha made homes away from home for me. My assistant, Michael Petshaft, helped keep me sane.

Jim Nicola of New York Theatre Workshop has encouraged and advised me all the way, and so has Rosemarie Tichler of the New York Shakespeare Festival. Together they shed blood for the play, literally; they have won my purple heart.

Gordon Davidson has been the most open-hearted and -handed producer/shepherd any playwright could ever want, and the whole staff of the Taper has been sensational, fabulous, divine.

The National Theatre staff has also been immensely supportive, and I'm particularly grateful to Richard Eyre and Giles Croft for believing in the play even in its scruffiest stages.

I am also indebted to Rocco Landesman, Jack Viertel, Paul Libin, Margo Lion, Susan Gallin, Herb Alpert, Fred Zollo and the angelic hosts of brave and honorable producers who gambled on this outrageous experiment on Broadway.

Mary K. Klinger stage-managed the show both in Los Angeles and in New York, unshakable in the face of many tempests.

The play has benefited from the dramaturgical work of Leon Katz and K. C. Davis, as well as the directors and actors who have participated in its various workshops and productions.

Stephen Spinella, Joe Mantello and Ellen McLaughlin have made invaluable suggestions on shaping and editing.

David Esbjornson, who directed the play in its first draft in San Francisco, has listened to and commented on its stories ever since.

Tony Taccone made invaluable structuring suggestions during his work on the play in Los Angeles.

Declan Donnellan and Nick Ormerod directed and designed the play at the National Theatre in London. Their early insights and responses have been challenging and helpful and have goaded me to keep trying to make the play better.

George C. Wolfe has been an inspiring and indefatigable collaborator on this final stage of shaping the play; he's been brilliantly insightful, respectful and galvanizing. The last step was the hardest, and I wouldn't have managed it without him.

Acknowledgments

From the revised edition, published in 1996:

While making the most recent revisions in the text, I've been particularly indebted to Michael Mayer, Mark Wing-Davey, Brian Kulick and Tess Timoney.

For this edition:

In 2007 Rupert Goold and the Headlong theater production of *Angels* toured England and played for six weeks at the Lyric Hammersmith in London. The director, Daniel Kramer, in preparation for the production, asked me many questions, and engaged me in a series of delightful, pointed and challenging discussions, which got me back to work on *Perestroika* for the first time in several years.

In 2009, I saw the first revival of Ivo van Hove's 2008 production of *Angels* with the Toneelgroep Amsterdam. As is so often the case in the work of this extraordinary theater artist, Ivo found a new, boldly imaginative form of stage life for *Angels* through a serious, meticulous, deep exploration of its text. Ivo and I didn't discuss alterations to the plays, but his production and his company's performances changed my understanding of what I'd written and powerfully impacted my thinking about further revisions for *Perestroika*.

Those revisions began in earnest when Jim Houghton and the Signature Theatre Company wanted to include *Angels* as one of the three plays for my Signature season, in 2010–2011. Because of Jim's enormous, indefatigable generosity, enthusiasm and patience, as well as the devotion and endless kindness of Beth Whitaker, Kirsten Bowen and the whole Signature staff, it was possible for me to dig into *Perestroika*, accompanied every step along the way by our director, the great Michael

Greif, and the dazzling company of actors he assembled. I was able to experiment with new scenes, talk and argue about them with colleagues whose passion, acuity and talent made exhilarating the scary business of attempting to improve a script that for many years had worked just fine. They bravely allowed me to flounder around, to fine-tune what worked before many preview audiences, and finally to come close to feeling that I'd truly completed a play—at least for the time being. My gratitude extends to Michael and every actor in the company, and most particularly to Bill Heck, who had to incorporate the largest number of changes and who was dedicated, energetic, gracious and fearless throughout.

I'm deeply indebted to Harold Bloom's reading of the Jacob story, which I first encountered in his introduction to Olivier Revault d'Allonnes's *Musical Variations on Jewish Thought*, in which Bloom translates the Hebrew word for "blessing" as "more life." Bloom expands on his interpretation in *The Book of J.*

Yiddish translations were graciously provided by the late Joachim Neugroschel, and additionally by Jeffrey Salant.

The late Ian Kramer, Esq. provided essential information about the juridical mischief of the Reagan–era federal bench. The court cases in Act Four, Scene 10, are actual cases with some of the names and circumstances changed.

Sigrid Wurschmidt

Act Two of *Perestroika* is dedicated to Sigrid Wurschmidt, a radiantly intelligent, passionate and beautiful actor and a member of the Eureka Theatre Company. The part of the Angel was originally written for her. While I was writing the play, Sigrid was diagnosed with breast cancer. Anticipating her hair falling out during chemotherapy, she shaved her head, which is one reason the Angel refers to herself as "the bald eagle."

Angels was originally meant to be a two-hour-long play. In the fall of 1988, having finished the first draft of two acts and most of a third act that covered less than half of the narrative I'd outlined, I flew to San Francisco to read what I'd written with the Eureka actors and Oskar Eustis. The purpose of the reading was to help Oskar and me decide what could be cut to bring the play down to a normal length. After the reading, which lasted nearly three hours, everyone walked to Sigrid's house for a discussion over lunch. On the way, Sigrid took my arm and asked me to tell her what I imagined would happen in the rest of the play. I told her. When we reached her house I showed her a sketch in my notebook for Harper's final speech about her night flight to San Francisco. Sigrid read it, and told me that the play needed to be long enough to include it. I responded that the play was already so long that I didn't see how I'd be able to fit much more in. "Well you have to use this speech," Sigrid replied, and then added, matter-of-factly, "make the play two evenings long." That possibility hadn't occurred to me, at least not consciously, and I took it as being one of those silly things you say to comfort a playwright in trouble. But she made sure I understood: she meant it.

Sigrid played the Angel in the first-ever public reading of *Millennium Approaches*, at Mark Taper Forum's Taper Too in Los Angeles, in the fall of 1989. After that reading, too ill to continue, she handed the role over to her close friend and mine, the divine Ellen McLaughlin. Sigrid died in 1990.

And finally:

My friends and indispensable colleagues Antonia Grilikhes-Lasky and Kyle Warren, in addition to epic note-taking and endless proofreading, were tireless, supportive, and offered sage advice throughout this process.

My agent, Joyce Ketay, took me on as a client in 1984, when I'd written one play that had yet to receive a professional production. She's protected me and my work through many perilous passages; her advice, attention and acumen prevented *Angels* from killing its author and vice versa. She's one of my dearest friends. I rely on her too often and for far too much and she never complains, though sometimes she makes faces.

My existence since birth has been bracketed by my extraordinary sister and brother, Lesley and Eric, who keep the world glued together for me, and for whose support I'm more thankful than it's my ability or any sibling's obligation to fully express.

I met my husband, Mark Harris, after much of my work on *Angels* had been completed, but for the play's ongoing life, as he has for everything in my ongoing life, he's provided wise counsel, a writer's unerring ear, a sharp editor's eye, and more happiness than I ever expected to find in this ongoing life. And also he's very very funny.

A few months after I started work on *Perestroika* in 1990, my mother, Sylvia Deutscher Kushner, died of cancer. She's a mighty presence in the play.

My father, William David Kushner, died in March 2012. He was a great artist and a great father and he, too, is everywhere in these pages.

Oskar Eustis commissioned *Angels in America* and has been intimately involved in every stage of its development. Without his great intelligence, talent, friendship and determination, the project would have been neither begun nor completed. I began *Angels* as a conversation, real and imaginary, between Oskar and myself; that conversation has never stopped, and never will.

Without Mark Bronnenberg, my first lover, my forever friend, and one of my favorite homosexuals, I wouldn't have known any of the things I needed to know to write *Angels*.

Kimberly T. Flynn taught me much of what I now believe to be true about life: theory and practice. Her words and ideas are woven through the work, and our friendship formed its bedrock. This is her play as much as it's mine.

Production History

The actors, directors and designers who have worked with me on *Angels in America* have transformed it. The following list includes those productions that significantly contributed to the play's development.

Millennium Approaches was first performed in a workshop production presented by Center Theatre Group/Mark Taper Forum in Los Angeles, in May 1990. It was directed by Oskar Eustis. Sets were designed by Mark Wendland, costumes by Lydia Tanji, lights by Casey Cowan and Brian Gale, and music by Nathan Birnbaum. The cast was as follows:

ROY COHN	Richard Frank
JOE PITT	Jeffrey King
HARPER PITT	Lorri Holt
BELIZE	Harry Waters, Jr.
LOUIS IRONSON	Jon Matthews
PRIOR WALTER	Stephen Spinella

HANNAH PITT	Kathleen Chalfant
THE ANGEL	Ellen McLaughlin

The world premiere of *Millennium Approaches* was presented by the Eureka Theatre Company in San Francisco, in May 1991. It was directed by David Esbjornson. Sets were designed by Tom Kamm, costumes by Sandra Woodall, and lights by Jack Carpenter and Jim Cave. The cast was as follows:

ROY COHN	John Bellucci
JOE PITT	Michael Scott Ryan
HARPER PITT	Anne Darragh
BELIZE	Harry Waters, Jr.
LOUIS IRONSON	Michael Ornstein
PRIOR WALTER	Stephen Spinella
HANNAH PITT	Kathleen Chalfant
THE ANGEL	Ellen McLaughlin

Perestroika was first performed in a staged reading by the Eureka Theatre Company in San Francisco, in May 1991. It was directed by David Esbjornson. Sets were designed by Tom Kamm, costumes by Sandra Woodall and lights by Jack Carpenter and Jim Cave. The cast was as follows:

ROY COHN	John Bellucci
JOE PITT	Michael Scott Ryan
HARPER PITT	Anne Darragh
BELIZE	Harry Waters, Jr.
LOUIS IRONSON	Michael Ornstein
PRIOR WALTER	Stephen Spinella
HANNAH PITT	Kathleen Chalfant
THE ANGEL	Ellen McLaughlin

Millennium Approaches opened in London, at the Royal National Theatre of Great Britain, in January 1992. It was directed by Declan Donnellan. It was designed by Nick Ormerod, lights by Mick Hughes, and music by Paddy Cunneen. The cast was as follows:

ROY COHN	Henry Goodman
JOE PITT	Nick Reding
HARPER PITT	Felicity Montagu
BELIZE	Joseph Mydell
LOUIS IRONSON	Marcus D'Amico
PRIOR WALTER	Sean Chapman
HANNAH PITT	Rosemary Martin
THE ANGEL	Nancy Crane
THE RABBI, HENRY, MARTIN HELLER, PRIOR I	Jeffrey Chiswick

Perestroika was further developed in a workshop at Center Theatre Group/Mark Taper Forum in Los Angeles, in May 1992. Oskar Eustis and Tony Taccone directed the staged reading. The cast was as follows:

ROY COHN	Lawrence Pressman
JOE PITT	Jeffrey King
HARPER PITT	Cynthia Mace
BELIZE	Harry Waters, Jr.
LOUIS IRONSON	Joe Mantello
PRIOR WALTER	Stephen Spinella
HANNAH PITT	Kathleen Chalfant
THE ANGEL	Ellen McLaughlin

The world premiere of *Angels in America, Parts One and Two*, was presented at Center Theatre Group/Mark Taper Forum in Los Angeles, in November 1992. It was directed by Oskar Eustis and Tony Taccone. Sets were designed by John Conklin, costumes by Gabriel Berry, lights by Pat Collins, and music by Mel Marvin. The cast was as follows:

ROY COHN	Ron Leibman
JOE PITT	Jeffrey King
HARPER PITT	Cynthia Mace
BELIZE	K. Todd Freeman
LOUIS IRONSON	Joe Mantello
PRIOR WALTER	Stephen Spinella
HANNAH PITT	Kathleen Chalfant
THE ANGEL	Ellen McLaughlin

Millennium Approaches opened at the Walter Kerr Theatre in New York, in April 1993, followed by *Perestroika* in November 1993. It was directed by George C. Wolfe. Sets were designed by Robin Wagner, costumes by Toni-Leslie James, lights by Jules Fisher, and music by Anthony Davis. The cast was as follows:

ROY COHN	Ron Leibman
JOE PITT	David Marshall Grant
HARPER PITT	Marcia Gay Harden
BELIZE	Jeffrey Wright
LOUIS IRONSON	Joe Mantello
PRIOR WALTER	Stephen Spinella
HANNAH PITT	Kathleen Chalfant
THE ANGEL	Ellen McLaughlin

Perestroika was presented at New York University/Tisch School of the Arts by the third-year students of the Graduate Acting Program, in April 1993. It was directed by Michael Mayer. Sets were designed by Tony Cisek and Andrew Hall, costumes by Robin J. Orloff, lights by Jack Mehler, and music by Michael Philip Ward. The cast was as follows:

ROY COHN	Ben Shenkman
JOE PITT	Robert Carin
HARPER PITT	Debra Messing
BELIZE	Mark Douglas
LOUIS IRONSON	Johnny Garcia
PRIOR WALTER	Daniel Zelman
HANNAH PITT	Vivienne Benesch
THE ANGEL	Jenna Stern

Angels in America, Parts One and Two, opened at the Royal National Theatre of Great Britain in London, in November 1993. It was directed by Declan Donnellan. Sets and costumes were designed by Nick Ormerod, lights by Mick Hughes, and music by Paddy Cunneen. The cast was as follows:

ROY COHN	David Schofield
JOE PITT	Daniel Craig
HARPER PITT	Clare Holman
BELIZE	Joseph Mydell
LOUIS IRONSON	Jason Isaacs
PRIOR WALTER	Stephen Dillane
HANNAH PITT	Susan Engel
THE ANGEL	Nancy Crane
THE RABBI, HENRY, MARTIN HELLER, PRIOR I, PRELAPSARIANOV	Harry Towb

PRODUCTION HISTORY

Angels was presented by the American Conservatory Theater in San Francisco, in September 1994. It was directed by Mark Wing-Davey. Sets were designed by Kate Edmunds, costumes by Catherine Zuber, and lights by Christopher Akerlind. The cast was as follows:

ROY COHN	Peter Zapp
JOE PITT	Steven Culp
HARPER PITT	Julia Gibson
BELIZE	Gregory Wallace
LOUIS IRONSON	Ben Shenkman
PRIOR WALTER	Garret Dillahunt
HANNAH PITT	Cristine McMurdo-Wallis
THE ANGEL	Lise Bruneau

The American national touring company of *Angels* began performances at the Royal George Theatre in Chicago, in September 1994. It was directed by Michael Mayer. Sets were designed by David Gallo, costumes by Michael Krass, lights by Brian MacDevitt, and music by Michael Philip Ward. The cast was as follows:

ROY COHN	Jonathan Hadary
JOE PITT	Philip Earl Johnson
HARPER PITT	Kate Goehring
BELIZE	Reg Flowers
LOUIS IRONSON	Peter Birkenhead
PRIOR WALTER	Robert Sella
HANNAH PITT	Barbara Robertson
THE ANGEL	Carolyn Swift

I continued my work on *Angels* during the rehearsals and previews of the productions mentioned above, sometimes making major changes, sometimes tweaking only a line or two. Most of the work was focused on the structure of *Perestroika*. After the national tour was launched, I decided to stop, at least for a time.

An English touring production of *Angels*, mounted by Headlong, premiered in Glasgow on April 20, 2007, arriving at the Lyric Hammersmith Theatre in London, on June 20, 2007. It was directed by Daniel Kramer. The sets were designed by Soutra Gilmour, costumes by Mark Bouman, lights by Charles Balfour, and sound by Carolyn Downing. The cast was as follows:

ROY COHN	Greg Hicks
JOE PITT	Jo Stone-Fewings
HARPER PITT	Kirsty Bushell
BELIZE	Obi Abili
LOUIS IRONSON	Adam Levy
PRIOR WALTER	Mark Emerson
HANNAH PITT	Ann Mitchell
THE ANGEL	Golda Rosheuvel

A new Dutch production of *Angels*, by Toneelgroep Amsterdam, with a translation by Carel Alphenaar, opened on March 5, 2008, at the Stadsschouwburg. It was directed by Ivo van Hove. The Toneelgroep's dramaturg for the production was Peter van Kraaij. The sets were designed by Jan Versweyveld, video by Tal Yarden, costumes by Wojciech Dziedzic, and music by Wim Selles. The cast was as follows:

ROY COHN	Hans Kesting
JOE PITT	Barry Atsma
HARPER PITT	Hadewych Minis
BELIZE	Roeland Fernhout
LOUIS IRONSON	Fedja van Huêt
PRIOR WALTER	Eelco Smits
HANNAH PITT	Marieke Heebink
THE ANGEL	Alwin Pulinckx

Perestroika was presented at the Paul Walker (of blessed memory!) Theatre by the second-year students of the Graduate Acting Program of New York University's Tisch School of the Arts, on October 30, 2009. It was directed by Janet Zarish. The sets were designed by James Bolenbaugh, costumes by Maria Hooper, and lighting by Jimmy Lawlor. The cast was as follows:

HENRY, LOUIS IRONSON, ASIATICA, PRELAPSARIANOV	Matt Citron
PRIOR WALTER	Alex Hurt
THE ANGEL, ETHEL ROSENBERG, EMILY, EUROPA	Megan Ketch
MR. LIES, ROY COHN	Derek Wilson
HARPER PITT, HANNAH PITT, OCEANIA	Clea Alsip
JOE PITT	Ansel Davis Brasseur
HANNAH PITT, THE MORMON MOTHER, HARPER PITT	Lesley Shires
ROY COHN, BELIZE, AFRICANII	Korey Jackson
BELIZE, THE ANGEL	Carra Patterson
LOUIS IRONSON, AUSTRALIA	Todd C. Bartels
PRIOR WALTER	Ben Cole

And finally (or at least for the time being):

Angels in America opened in New York City, on October 27, 2010, as the first production of the 2010–2011 Signature Theatre Company season. It was directed by Michael Greif. The sets were designed by Mark Wendland, costumes by Clint Ramos, additional costumes by Jeff Mahshie, lights by Ben Stanton, music by Michael Friedman and Chris Miller, and projections by Wendall K. Harrington. The cast was as follows:

ROY COHN	Frank Wood
JOE PITT	Bill Heck
HARPER PITT	Zoe Kazan
BELIZE	Billy Porter
LOUIS IRONSON	Zachary Quinto
PRIOR WALTER	Christian Borle
HANNAH PITT	Robin Bartlett
THE ANGEL	Robin Weigert

A Few Notes from the Playwright About Staging

In General

Millennium Approaches and *Perestroika* are two parts of a single play, but at the same time they're two rather different plays, each with its own structure and character. *Millennium* has three acts and *Perestroika* has five. Three acts make a tauter, cleaner play, the gestures and rhythms of which will feel more inexorable, more destination-driven; a five-act play is likely to provide a more expansive, exploratory and ultimately open-ended and unresolved experience. Perhaps it can be said that *Millennium* is a play about security and certainty being blown apart, while *Perestroika* is about danger and possibility following the explosion. The events in *Perestroika* proceed from the wreckage made by the Angel's traumatic entry at the end of *Millennium*. A membrane has broken; there is disarray and debris. All of which is to suggest that, especially when the two parts of *Angels* are produced in repertory, the differences should be visible and palpable onstage.

The plays benefit from a pared-down style of presentation, with scenery kept to an evocative and informative minimum. There are a lot of scenes and a lot of locations; an informative minimum means providing what's needed to enable the audience to know, as quickly as possible, where a scene is set. Actors need to help by playing the reality of these locations: How loud can you get, really, in a fancy restaurant?

I recommend rapid scene shifts (no blackouts!), employing the cast as well as stagehands in shifting the scene. This must be an actor-driven event.

Intermissions

Audiences are said to have grown increasingly impatient and unwilling to sit through long evenings in the theater. The people of whom this is true will likely seek out shorter plays than *Angels in America*. I believe that, once engaged, audiences rediscover the rewards of patience and effort and the pleasures of an epic journey. An epic play *should* be a little fatiguing; a rich, heady, hard-earned fatigue is among a long journey's pleasures and rewards.

That said, the audience has to be given chances along the way to gather its strength and attention. *Millennium Approaches* is a long play, and *Perestroika* is longer. Each play is meant to have two intermissions, after Act One and Act Two of *Millennium*, and after Act Three and Act Four of *Perestroika*. These segments are shaped to function as coherent single events as well as successions of scenes.

The temptation to take only one intermission in each of the two parts should, in my opinion, be resisted. Although one intermission shortens the running time, the demands it puts on the audience's attention and the pressures it puts on the scenes immediately before the single intermission or near the end of the play are unnecessary, detrimental and counter-productive—the running time may be shorter, but it will feel much longer.

Magic

The moments of magic, such as the appearance and disappearance of Mr. Lies, the ghosts, Prior's fiery Book hallucination and the Angel's arrival, ought to be fully imagined and realized, as wonderful *theatrical* illusions—which means it's OK if the wires show, and maybe it's good that they do, but the magic should at the same time be thoroughly thrilling, fantastical, amazing.

It's easy to stage a person's (or a ghost's) magical disappearance by simply having the actor exit into the wings, but I don't think that's a strong choice. Not only is it *not* thoroughly thrilling, fantastical, amazing or fun to watch a person walk offstage, it's also pedestrian, literally and figuratively. Walking offstage is slow, and therefore it lacks one very important aspect of *vanishing*—namely that it's abrupt. In a world in which young people by their thousands sicken and, with obscene speed, die (in other words, the world of this play), vanishing abruptly is particularly upsetting, even frightening. The magic ought to be fun for the audience, but also disturbing. For Prior, it's increasingly terrifying.

There's more magic in *Perestroika*, and as the play progresses, the magic gets grander. It's hard to make this happen: long, two-part plays are enormously demanding of resources, time and energy, and there's always the risk that invention, attention to detail, time and cash will run out just when they're needed most, in the play's home stretch. *Perestroika*'s fifth-act Heaven scenes should, whether or not the stage directions are followed, at the very least resemble nothing on Earth; the Hall of the Continental Principalities in Act Five, Scene 5, ought to be the high point of the stage magic of *Angels*.

Split Scenes

In the split scenes, two separate events occur more or less simultaneously in different locations—for example, Act One, Scene 8, of *Millennium Approaches*, in which we observe Harper and Joe in their living room in Brooklyn and Louis and Prior in their Alphabetland bedroom. Both events are intended to continue, active and alive, throughout the entire split scene, with focus going where the story needs it to go. Stopping one of the two events in its tracks by artificially freezing it is an easy but again, in my opinion, not a strong choice. The trick is to work out psychologically coherent (hence playable), compellingly dramatic reasons why the characters in one event become still and quiet when the action that the audience should be attending to shifts to the other event and onto other characters.

When a character chooses to stop talking, to be still and quiet, for reasons having to do with the conflict he or she is in during a scene, an active choice is being made, and hence the character stays alive onstage—as opposed to being put in suspended animation by the director. Finding concurrent, complementary vitality in the two events of a split scene gives them their particular dynamism; they'll be much more fun to play, and to watch.

Language

The engine of the play is the struggle in which the characters engage to change unendurable circumstances—*all* the characters, *all* the time we're watching them. The circumstances the characters face, the world they inhabit, and the characters themselves are in a very important sense made up of words. Words are important, and they're specific. We speak to produce effects, to catalyze, to engender consequences. We choose words strategically, precisely, whether or not we do so consciously.

If the character you're playing says something that strikes you, the actor, as odd, large, artificial, you should assume it strikes your character that way as well. If a character opposite yours says something that sounds ornate, awkward, a non-sequitur to you, the actor, it probably sounds that way to your character too.

I advise taking very seriously and working hard to answer the question that you, the actor, and probably also the character you're playing, are longing to ask: Why am I/Why is this other person talking this way? That question is important. When the language in the play is strange, in other words, its strangeness is always an action. A sentence is no less an action than a blow with a broadsword or a passionate kiss. And the degree and kind of strangeness matter enormously.

The characters in the play are fighting for survival; the stakes are very high. They talk to make things happen, to advance an agenda, to defend, to enlist, to seduce, to punish. Sometimes they speak in an effort to understand how or what they're feeling. But never speak solely to announce your character's distress, hoping for pity. The characters in the play are tougher than that; the world of the play, like the world outside the theater, is a tough place.

Two Notes Regarding Pronunciation

On page 156, Roy's coinage, "azido-methatalo-molamoca-whatchamacallit" is pronounced "aZIDOmuhTHATUHLO-moluhmocuh-whatchamacallit." The "I" in "ZIDO" is short, as in "in," and the "TH" in "*THA*TUHLO" is soft, as in "*TH*istle."

On page 224, Prior is using the verb "prophesy," which is pronounced "proph-uh-sigh," *not* the noun "prophecy" which is pronounced "proph-uh-see."

Nine Notes Regarding the Angel

The Angel, who is related to humans but isn't human, is arguably the most challenging character in *Angels*, and Act Two of *Perestroika* is inarguably the most challenging sequence. After two decades of struggling with her and watching others struggle, I'm offering these thoughts, which I hope will be helpful.

1) *Metaphysics:* I'll begin by repeating: The Angel is related to humans but isn't human. That's the primary challenge in acting, directing and designing her. For starters, she refers to herself in the plural (I I I I) because she isn't a single thing: She is a Principality, which is, depending on which angelological ordering system you subscribe to, the highest or one of the highest types among the angelic orders. She is four Divine Emanations—Lumen (blue), Candle (gold), Phosphor (green) and Fluor (purple)—manifest as an aggregate entity, the Continental Principality of America. I have no advice about how to play four nonhuman beings amalgamated into one nonhuman being. I only know that while she should be comprehensible to the audience, she should also be terribly unfamiliar.

2) *Appearance:* She should be extraordinary to behold, and her wings are of paramount importance—they should move and they should move us. She shouldn't look like Botticelli painted her, or any other Italian Renaissance painter, or any European of any period, or like a traditional Christmas tree ornament. She should look breathtaking, severe, scary, powerful, and magnificently American.

3) *Her Cough:* The Angel's cough is a manifestation of cosmic unwellness, but she controls it, and she is a creature of unimaginable strength and discipline. She doesn't want Prior to sense any weakness, disorder or confusion on her part, and her cough ought to be a single, dry bark, *not* prolonged wracking emphysemic spasms. Ellen McLaughlin, who created the role, based her brusque, even angry rap of a cough on a cat hacking up a furball. It was startling, sharp, simple—one *hack*, not ten—and effectively nonhuman, not funny as much as disconcerting and ominous, and always always *dignified*. It did not make her seem frail.

4) *She's Not Joking, and She's No Joke:* Some of what happens between Prior and the Angel is supposed to be funny, but it's essential for the play, and, for that matter, for the comedy, that the Angel's dignity and her unequivocally serious purpose are never—as in *not for one single second!*—compromised by schticky winking at the audience. Prior's terror at being in her presence and/or at the possibility that he's going mad never (as in not for one single second) abandons him. As Prior has his first full encounter with the Angel, and simultaneously relates it to Belize three weeks later, we're watching a cosmically high-stakes encounter between a badly frightened but very brave human being and his furious, grief-stricken, frightened and frighteningly powerful nonhuman visitor/intruder.

Apologies if I'm sounding strident, but I've learned that there are dire consequences if this reality is parodied or traduced. People can enjoy pratfalls, mugging and easy laughs, even while determining that they won't be fooled again into deep investment in what's proved to be unserious. Once faith in the seriousness of what's onstage has been withdrawn, however briefly, it's unlikely to return fully.

5) *Her Arrival:* If at all technically feasible, the Angel should arrive in Prior's bedroom by crashing through the ceiling. This is harder than bringing her through a crack in the rear wall, which is what's usually done. But she's coming down from Heaven, not from across town; it's a drop-down-on-your-head explosive revelation, rather than the sneaky, sideways kind. If at all possible, she should arrive in dust and noise as the ceiling rains down on Prior's head. I didn't know, when I wrote the play, that so few theaters have fly space.

6) *Flying Versus Rehearsing:* I also didn't know how difficult stage flying would prove to be. Originally I imagined that the Angel would fly during Act Two of *Perestroika*, doing spectacular aerial stunts as she spoke. I've seen many productions of *Perestroika*, and I've never seen this happen. What I've seen instead is many valuable hours of rehearsal and tech time lost, and much money spent hiring stage-flying specialists, trying to make this happen.

I've come to the conviction that attempting extensive flying is not only unwise, because it lies beyond the technical and temporal means of most theaters, it's a distraction from the real business at hand. The Anti-Migratory Epistle sequence in Act Two won't be solved by Angelic midair somersaults—which, trust me, will never materialize. The effectiveness of this long and difficult scene depends entirely on getting its complex realities clear, specific and playable, and that means time-consuming, painstaking, actor-director rehearsal-room work, for which there is no substitute.

7) *Unhooking the Angel:* There *should* be flying, of course: The Angel should fly in, and fly out, carrying the Epistle. In between her entrance and her exit, she has to be able to move around the stage, so that she can interact fully with Prior and, when appropriate, with Belize. This most likely means that she will have to be unhooked from her flying rig onstage while the scene is in progress, and then hooked back up. Stagehands, visible to the audience, can do this. Her fly-wires show, so why not visible stagehands? Stagehands ought to help Prior out of his prophet garb and into his pajamas in the transition from the street to his bedroom and back again.

Openly including the crew in the stage life in Act Two (when necessary for the storytelling, not as an embellishment) seems to me consonant with the act's mixing narrated and dramatized storytelling, an amalgam which occurs at no other point in *Angels*. Moments when the crew takes active part in the dramatic event should be staged—interesting to watch, specific and unapologetic, not artificially slow but not rushed and frantic. Prior's change of clothes, from prophet drag to pajamas, is part of a transition he's chosen to undertake. He's stepping into a violent memory because telling Belize isn't enough; Prior has to show him. When the stagehands unhook the Angel, they should do so respectfully; it goes without saying that they wouldn't touch her without her willing them to do so.

8) *Staging the Anti-Migratory Epistle:* Act Two confronts directors, actors and designers with the formidable (but, I hope, exciting and enjoyable) challenge of staging three characters

occupying two locations that are separated, albeit permeably and not cleanly, by distance and time.

This is a scene involving *three* characters: Prior, the Angel and Belize. There's a temptation to sideline Belize to a stationary spot on the outskirts and leave him there for the duration, tossing in quips, irrelevant to the action. This is a tempting choice because it makes the scene easier to stage. The problem is that without Belize's active involvement, the scene makes no sense. The overarching actions are the Angel's arrival, the delivery of the Epistle, Prior's refusal of it, and then his unwilling acceptance of or forced submission to it. But the scene takes place in the present as well as in the past, and integral to the event is the in-the-bedroom/on-the-street contest between Belize and the Angel for Prior's attention and soul, a battle of three strong wills that propels/pulls Belize into Prior's bedroom, into his awful dream—where, once he's entered, the Angel seems intermittently to be aware of Belize's presence.

Belize is tough, but Prior unfolds for him what must sound, to a nurse with considerable experience dealing with AIDS, like a wholly unfamiliar form of dementia, far more coherent than anything Belize has heard from his patients. He's bewildered, grief-stricken, and, when Prior's delusions assume uncharacteristically, deeply disturbing reactionary, even racist overtones, Belize becomes frightened and then angry. Thus Prior's desperate attempt to end his loneliness by telling his best friend about the waking nightmare in which he's trapped results in even greater isolation.

9) *Her Broken Heart:* The Angel's power and purpose semi-successfully conceal an abandoned lover's determination to get her lost love to return before everything falls apart. Prior is supposed to be useful, as surrogate for his species, the last fragile hope of averting universal extinction. But to the heart-

broken lover that this heavenly emissary also is, he's a hateful, guilty homewrecker who also happens to be her kin and her ward. In this predicament the Angel is recognizable to Prior, to Belize and to us, and she grows more familiar as the Epistle progresses, but only to a point. As I began, so I'll end: the Angel isn't human.

Two Omitted Scenes from Perestroika

In previous published versions of *Perestroika* I included two scenes which were almost always cut in production. In preparing this new version, I decided it was time to acknowledge the verdict of twenty-two years of production history and remove the scenes from the play. I'm including them here for whatever enjoyment and interest they provide readers; the play in production unquestionably works better without them.

This scene, formerly Act Five, Scene 6, immediately followed the scene in which Prior confronts the Angels in the Hall of the Principalities.

Act Five, Scene 6

On the streets of Heaven. Rabbi Isidor Chemelwitz and Sarah Ironson are seated on wooden crates with another crate between them. They are playing cards. Prior enters.

PRIOR: Excuse me, I'm looking for a way out of this, do . . .
Oh! You're . . .

SARAH IRONSON *(To the Rabbi)*: Vos vil er? [What does he
want?]

RABBI ISIDOR CHEMELWITZ: Di goyim, zey veysn nisht vi zikh
oyftsufirn. [These Gentiles, they have no manners.]

PRIOR: Are you Sarah Ironson?

(She looks up at him.)

PRIOR: I was at your funeral! You look just like your grandson,
Louis. I know him. Louis. He never wanted you to find
out, but did you know he's gay?

SARAH IRONSON *(Not understanding)*: Vi? [What?]

RABBI ISIDOR CHEMELWITZ: Dein aynickl, Louis? [Your
grandson, Louis?]

SARAH IRONSON: Yeah?

RABBI ISIDOR CHEMELWITZ *(Sotto voce)*: Er iz a feygele.

SARAH IRONSON: A *feygele?* Oy.

RABBI ISIDOR CHEMELWITZ *(To Sarah)*: Itst gistu. [You deal.]

PRIOR: Why does everyone here play cards?

RABBI ISIDOR CHEMELWITZ: Why? *(To Sarah)* Dos goy vil
visnfar-Vos mir shpiln in kortn. [The goy wants to know
why we play cards.]

OK.

Cards is strategy but mostly a game of chance. In
Heaven, everything is known. To the Great Questions
are lying about here like yesterday's newspaper all the
answers. So from what comes the pleasures of Paradise?
Indeterminacy! Because mister, with the Angels, may
their names be always worshipped and adored, it's all
gloom and doom and give up already. But still is there
Accident, in this pack of playing cards, still is there the

Unknown, the Future. You understand me? It ain't all so much mechanical as they think.

You got another question?

PRIOR: I want to go home.

RABBI ISIDOR CHEMELWITZ: Oh simple. Here. To do this, every Kabbalist on earth would sell his right nut. Penuel, Peniel, Ja'akov Beth-Yisroel, Killeeyou, kill-eemee, OOO-ooooooo-OOOO-oooooohmayn!

(The ladder, the music and the lights. Prior starts to descend.)

SARAH IRONSON: Hey! Zogt Loubeleh az di Bobbe zogt:

RABBI ISIDOR CHEMELWITZ: She says tell this Louis Grandma says:

SARAH IRONSON: Er iz tomid geven a bissele farblonjet, shoin vi a boytshikl. Ober siz nisht keyn antshuldigunk.

RABBI ISIDOR CHEMELWITZ: From when he was a boy he was always mixed up. But it's no excuse.

SARAH IRONSON: *He should have visited!* But I forgive. Tell him: az er darf ringen mit zain Libm Nomen. Yah?!

RABBI ISIDOR CHEMELWITZ: You should struggle with the Almighty.

SARAH IRONSON: Azoi toot a Yid.

RABBI ISIDOR CHEMELWITZ: It's the Jewish way.

END OF SCENE

Two Omitted Scenes

In earlier versions of *Perestroika*'s Act Five, this scene followed Scene 7 and preceded Scene 8 (in the current version's numbering).

Roy, in Heaven, or Hell or Purgatory—standing waist-deep in a smoldering pit, facing a great flaming Aleph, which bathes him and the whole theater in a volcanic, pulsating red light. Underneath, a basso-profundo roar, like a thousand Bessemer furnaces going at once, deep underground.

ROY: Paternity suit? Abandonment? Family court is my particular metier, I'm an absolute fucking demon with Family Law. Just tell me who the judge is, and what kind of jewelry does he like? If it's a jury, it's harder, juries take more talk but sometimes it's worth it, going jury, for what it saves you in bribes. Yes I will represent you, King of the Universe, yes I will sing and eviscerate, I will bully and seduce, I will win for you and make the plaintiffs, those traitors, wish they had never heard the name of . . .
(Huge thunderclap)
Is it a done deal, are we on? Good, then I gotta start by telling you you ain't got a case here, you're guilty as hell, no question, you have nothing to plead but not to worry, darling, I will make something up.

END OF SCENE

With a Little Help
from My Friends

This essay was originally published in the New York Times
*on November 21, 1993, and was included in the two previous
published versions of* Perestroika.

Angels in America, Parts One and Two, has taken five years to
write, and as the work nears completion I find myself thinking a great deal about the people who have left their traces in
these texts. The fiction that artistic labor happens in isolation,
and that artistic accomplishment is exclusively the provenance
of individual talents, is politically charged and, in my case at
least, repudiated by the facts.

   While the primary labor on *Angels* has been mine, over
two dozen people have contributed words, ideas and structures
to these plays: actors, directors, audiences, one-night stands,
my former lover and many friends. Two in particular, my closest
friend, Kimberly T. Flynn (*Perestroika* is dedicated to her), and
the man who commissioned *Angels* and helped shape it, Oskar

Eustis, have had profound, decisive influences. Had I written these plays without the participation of my collaborators, they would be entirely different—would, in fact, never have come to be.

Americans pay high prices for maintaining the myth of the Individual: We have no system of universal health care, we don't educate our children, we can't pass sane gun control laws, we elect presidents like Reagan, we hate and fear inevitable processes like aging and death. Way down close to the bottom of the list of the evils Individualism visits on our culture is the fact that in the modern era it isn't enough to write; you must also be a Writer, and play your part as the protagonist in a cautionary narrative in which you will fail or triumph, be in or out, hot or cold. The rewards can be fantastic; the punishment dismal; it's a zero-sum game, and its guarantor of value, its marker is that you pretend you play it solo, preserving the myth that you alone are the wellspring of your creativity.

When I started to write these plays, I wanted to attempt something of ambition and size even if that meant I might be accused of straying too close to ambition's ugly twin, pretentiousness. Given the bloody opulence of this country's great and terrible history, given its newness and its grand improbability, its artists are bound to be tempted towards large gestures and big embraces, a proclivity de Tocqueville deplored as a national artistic trait nearly two hundred years ago. Melville, my favorite American writer, strikes inflated, even hysterical, chords on occasion. It's the sound of the Individual ballooning, overreaching. We are all children of "Song of Myself." And maybe in this spacious, under- and depopulated, as yet only lightly inscribed country, the Individual will finally expand to its unstable, insupportably swollen limits, and pop. (But here I risk pretentiousness, and an excess of optimism to boot— another American trait.)

Anyone interested in exploring alternatives to Individualism and the political economy it serves, Capitalism, has to be willing to ask hard questions about the ego, both as abstraction and as exemplified in oneself.

Bertolt Brecht, while he was still in Weimar-era Berlin and facing the possibility of participating in a socialist revolution, wrote a series of remarkable short plays, his *Lehrstücke*, or learning plays. The principal subject of these plays was the painful dismantling, as a revolutionary necessity, of the individual ego. This dismantling is often figured, in the learning plays, as death.

Brecht, who never tried to hide the dimensions of his own titanic personality, didn't sentimentalize the problems such personalities present, or the process of loss involved in letting go of the richness, and the riches, that accompany successful self-creation.

Brecht simultaneously claimed and mocked the identity he'd won for himself, "a great German writer," raising important questions about the means of literary production, challenging the sacrosanctity of the image of the solitary artist and, at the same time, openly, ardently wanting to be recognized as a genius. That he was a genius is inarguably the case. For a man deeply committed to collectivity as an ideal and an achievable political goal, this blazing singularity was a mixed blessing at best and at worst, an obstacle to a blending of radical theory and practice.

In the lower right-hand corner of the title page of many of Brecht's plays you will find, in tiny print, a list of names under the heading "collaborators." Sometimes these people contributed little, sometimes a great deal. One cannot help feeling that those who bore those minuscule names, who expended the considerable labor the diminutive typography conceals, have gotten a bum deal. Many of these effaced collaborators, Ruth Berlau, Elisabeth Hauptmann, Margarete Steffin, were women. In the question of shared intellectual and artistic labor, gender is always an issue.

Last spring, after *Millennium Approaches* had opened on Broadway, on the day when the Tony nominations were being handed out [May 1993], I left the clamorous room at Sardi's thinking gloomily that here was another source of anxiety, another obstacle to getting back to work rewriting *Perestroika*. In the building's lobby I was introduced to the producer Elizabeth I. McCann, who said to me: "I've been worried about how you were handling all this, till I read that you have an Irish woman in your life. Then I knew you were going to be fine." Ms. McCann was referring to Kimberly T. Flynn; an article in the *New Yorker* last year about *Angels in America* described how certain features of our shared experience dealing with her prolonged health crisis, caused by a serious cab accident several years ago, had a major impact on the plays.

Kimberly and I share Louisiana childhoods (she's from New Orleans, I grew up in Lake Charles); different but equally complicated, powerful religious traditions and an ambivalence towards those traditions; Left politics informed by liberation struggles (she as a feminist, I as a gay man), as well as socialist and psychoanalytic theory; and a belief in the effectiveness of activism and the possibility of progress.

From the beginning Kimberly was my teacher. Though largely self-taught, she was more widely read and she helped me understand both Freud and Marx. She introduced me to the writers of the Frankfurt School and their early attempts at synthesizing psychoanalysis and Marxism; and to the German philosopher and critic Walter Benjamin, whose importance for me rests primarily in his introduction into these "scientific" disciplines a Kabbalist-inflected mysticism and a dark, apocalyptic spirituality.

As both writer and talker Kimberly employs a rich variety of rhetorical strategies and effects, even while expressing deep emotion. She identifies this as an Irish trait; it's evident in O'Neill, Yeats, Beckett. This relationship to language, blended with Jewish and gay versions of the same strategies, is evident in my plays, in the ways my characters speak.

More pessimistic than I, Kimberly is much less afraid to look at the ugliness of the world. She tries to protect herself far less than I do, and consequently she sees more. She feels safest, she says, knowing the worst, while most people I know, myself included, would rather be spared and feel safer encircled by a measure of obliviousness. She's capable of pulling things apart, teasing out fundamental concerns from their camouflage; at the same time she uses her analysis, her learning, her emotions, her lived experience, to make imaginative leaps, to see the deeper connections between ideas and historical developments. Through her example I learned to trust that such leaps can be made; I learned to admire them, in literature, in theory, in the utterances people make in newspapers. And certainly it was in part her example that made the labor of synthesizing disparate, seemingly unconnected things become for me the process of writing a play.

Since the accident Kimberly has struggled with her health, and I have struggled to help her, sometimes succeeding, sometimes failing; and it doesn't take much more than a passing familiarity with *Angels* to see how my life and my plays match up. It's always been easier talking about the way in which I used what we've lived through to write *Angels*, even though I sometimes question the morality of the act (while at the same time considering it unavoidable if I was to write at all), than it has been acknowledging the intellectual debt. People seem to be more interested in the story of the accident and its aftermath than in the intellectual genealogy, the emotional life being privileged over the intellectual life in the business of making plays, and the two being regarded, incorrectly, as separable. A great deal of what I understand about health issues comes from what Kimberly has endured and triumphed over, and the ways she's articulated those experiences. But *Angels* is more the result of our intellectual friendship than it is autobiography. Her contribution was as contributor, teacher, editor, adviser, not muse.

Perhaps other playwrights don't have similar relationships or similar debts; perhaps they have. In a wonderful, recently published collection of essays on creative partnerships, entitled *Significant Others*, edited by Isabelle de Courtivron and Whitney Chadwick, the contributors examine both healthy and deeply unhealthy versions of artistic interdependence in such couples as the Delaunays, Kahlo and Rivera, Hammett and Hellman, and Jasper Johns and Robert Rauschenberg— and in doing so strike forcefully at what the editors call "the myth of solitariness."

We have no words for the people to whom we are indebted. I call Oskar Eustis a dramaturg, sometimes a collaborator; but collaborator implies co-authorship and nobody knows what "dramaturg" implies. *Angels*, I wrote in the published version of *Perestroika*, began in a conversation, real and imaginary, with Oskar Eustis. A romantic-ambivalent love for American history and belief in what one of the play's characters calls "the prospect of some sort of radical democracy spreading outward and growing up" are things Oskar and I share, part of the discussions we had for nearly a year before I started writing *Millennium*. Oskar continues to be for me, intellectually and emotionally, what the developmental psychologists call "a secure base of attachment" (a phrase I learned from Kimberly).

The play is indebted, too, to writers I've never met. It's ironical that Harold Bloom, in his introduction to Olivier Revault d'Allonnes' *Musical Variations on Jewish Thought*, provided me with a translation of the Hebrew word for "blessing"—"more life"—which subsequently became key to the heart of *Perestroika*. Harold Bloom is also the author of *The Anxiety of Influence*, his oedipalization of the history of Western literature, which when I first encountered it years ago made me so anxious my analyst suggested I put it away. Recently I had the chance to meet Professor Bloom and, guilty over my appropriation of "more life," I fled from the encounter as one of Freud's *Totem and Taboo* tribesmen might flee from a meeting with that primal father, the one with the big knife. (I cite Bloom as the source of the idea in the published script.)

Guilt plays a part in this confessional account; and I want the people who helped me make this play to be identified, because their labor was consequential. I have been blessed with remarkable comrades and collaborators: Together we organize the world for ourselves, or at least we organize our understanding of it; we reflect it, refract it, criticize it, grieve over its savagery and help each other to discern, amidst the gathering dark, paths of resistance, pockets of peace and places whence hope may be plausibly expected. Marx was right: The smallest indivisible human unit is two people, not one; one is a fiction. From such nets of souls societies, the social world, human life springs. And also plays.